THE COMPLEX FATE

*It's a complex fate, being an American, and
one of the responsibilities it entails is fighting
against a superstitious valuation of Europe.*

HENRY JAMES

THE
COMPLEX FATE

HAWTHORNE, HENRY JAMES AND
SOME OTHER AMERICAN WRITERS

By

Marius Bewley

*With an Introduction
and two Interpolations by*

F. R. LEAVIS

GORDIAN PRESS, INC.
NEW YORK
1967

810.9
B46C
62731
September, 1968

Originally Published 1952
Reprinted 1967

Published by Gordian Press
by Arrangement with Chatto and Windus

Library of Congress Card Catalog. No. 67-28474

Contents

To
My Mother

Introduction

IAM present in this book (having been honoured by the invitation to be so) as disagreeing with Mr. Bewley over some particular judgments. But my disagreements are minor indeed compared with the major concurrence that makes me welcome his book with a wholly sincere warmth and with great relief. Here is an American critic saying, with the authority of what is unmistakably criticism of a rare intelligence and force, what has long needed saying—or so I have thought. And I am hardly the only English observer who has contemplated with distress and apprehension the lines on which, in America in our time, the conviction that America has, or ought to have, a great literature has developed.

For an Englishman to feel and to express such a concern is no impertinence. What happens to American civilization has clearly the greatest importance for Europe. But, as it is the virtue of Mr. Bewley's book to make so plain, an Englishman has special reasons for taking a poignant interest in the prevailing American ideas about the present and future of American literature. In any case it is wholly proper that he should bear his testimony when a great creative achievement —and this one, belonging to the common language, may be fitly appraised by an Englishman—is slighted.

Mr. Bewley, then, seems to me to be unquestionably right when he says that in the nineteenth century America 'produced a line of novelists'—he names Cooper, Hawthorne, Melville and James—'who represent her greatest achievement in art'. It is a very impressive achievement, and an English critic cannot claim that it has had in this country the attention it deserves. More seriously, it is far from enjoying in America, as Mr. Bewley points out, the honour and the influence that are its due—more seriously, because of the significance of such a default for the prospects of American literature. Of the writers whom he names as

vii

forming a tradition in the American novel Mr. Bewley says:

> They have no considerable successors today, and what they stood for in such varying ways among themselves has been supplanted.

And he intimates, with a directness that an Englishman judging the same might well think proper to leave to an American critic, that something has gone wrong, and that the trouble is a mistaken preoccupation with being American. It is mistaken, because it rejects something profoundly and essentially American that held the promise of a rich future, and rejects it for what is American in an excluding and impoverishing way such as holds no possibility of a great American literature:

> That school of literary appreciation which acclaims American literature simply because it is American has been represented by a strong body of critical opinion in the United States, and it has led to an insidious magnification of the frontier colloquial tradition in American literature. This tradition is one of great importance, but it is not the tradition embodied in America's four major novelists. . . . This frontier tradition has its own high points of achievement, but it represents the extreme isolation of American literature, and it is fragmentary and misleading because it does not provide sufficient scope in itself to treat the largest problem that confronted the American artist in the nineteenth century, and which still occupies him: the nature of his separateness, and the nature of his connection with European, and particularly with English, culture.

And, adducing the 'ancient tendency to regard Henry James as a European rather than an American novelist', Mr. Bewley testifies:

> Yet it is of the essence of James's genius that he was an American in a fuller and finer sense than any of the American-Firsters in criticism who have found his quality beyond their comprehension.

Mr. Bewley puts what seems to me an unanswerable truth with a very timely force that, backed as the statement is by the critical analyses that follow, I should like to believe final.

But such propositions, I know, ask for something far more difficult to obtain than formal assent. It might, for instance, seem paradoxical that his challenge on behalf of James should be needed; for James—together with the James family—has been made into an American institution. But that, of course, is the trouble; it is of the essence of an institutional cult of that kind *not* to find itself at odds with the faith that the true American tradition—the one that ought to prevail in the American literature of the present and the future—is that which looks back to the frontier tradition for its beginnings.

And I should like to make here a point that did not lie in Mr. Bewley's path, intent as he was on the theme indicated by his title. When, as against the tradition discussed by Mr. Bewley, the 'frontier tradition' is made the source of a truly American literature, the idea, I think, derives an illicit respectability from the aura of Mark Twain. I need not presume to discuss what the frontier tradition amounted to, or what was Mark Twain's connection with it. When it is exalted in that way, what we have (it is enough to note) is the spirit of which it may be said that its essential definition of Americanness is given in the collocation of Whitman, Dreiser, Scott Fitzgerald and Hemingway. I am not offering to plot a 'tradition' with those names. But what that is more plausibly a tradition has been anywhere proposed by way of vindicating the narrowly 'American' bent? The writers I have named have all been distinguished with favour as significantly American; and the significance has to be defined in terms of an antipathetic unlikeness to Mr. Bewley's line. The unlikeness, it is true, differs in kind from one to another of them: I picked on them as representative—the prevailing will to go back on the strength and the greatness of the American literary past has unavoidably to be represented in that way if we ask what, positively, it points to instead.

Returning now to Mark Twain: no one, I imagine, disputes that Mark Twain is a truly American writer. Yet if, in accordance with the spirit that asserts itself so formidably, we are to define Americanness by the collocation of Whitman, Dreiser, Scott Fitzgerald and Hemingway, and say that the promise of a truly American literature lies *there*, that is to leave Mark Twain behind, in a too European past, along with Cooper, Hawthorne, Melville and James. For, if we value him for what he is, there can be no question which of the two companies he belongs to.

I am thinking of the great Mark Twain, author of American classics. The English reader of *Huckleberry Finn* doesn't find himself reflecting: 'This is by a fellow-country-man of Whitman.' American as the book is, it is not American in Whitman's way, and conveys no suggestion of a world or an ethos out of which a Whitman might emerge as a characteristic voice. As for Dreiser, it is impossible to think of him as belonging to one tradition with the author of *Huckleberry Finn*, if only because he so clearly belongs to no tradition. He represents the consequences of the later influxes from Europe and the sudden polygot agglomeration of big raw cities, and may with some point be said to belong to the culturally dispossessed. It is possible, of course, to call the state of those who have lost their distinctive heritage, and acquired nothing comparable in its place, distinctively American; but the tendency to treat this state as a positive American tradition out of which a great national literature may be expected to come is depressing. Out of the conditions represented by Dreiser (who writes as if he hasn't a native language) no great literature *could* come; and nothing that can properly be called the beginnings of literature came in his case.

There would seem to be no good reason for believing that literature could any more come out of the conditions represented by Scott Fitzgerald, who shows that a writer, while using English as unquestionably a native inheritance, may yet have inherited little else with it. As the one positive alternative to the actual and very unideal kinds of relation between the sexes ordinary in the milieu he depicts, he never gets beyond the teen-age Romeo-and-Juliet notion of romantic love. Such love is what the hero is baulked of by social snobbery in *The Great Gatsby*. And it is not merely that, in Fitzgerald's world, no vestige, and no suspicion, of any standard of maturity exists. The extremity of the destitution that disqualifies him as a novelist and a creative writer (in spite of the almost classical status that has been conferred on him) is what can be seen in the accounts of his life; those accounts which, offered us so often in apparent unawareness of their implication, have the closest critical bearings on what he wrote. The state of dispossession they illustrate—dispossession of the interests, the awarenesses, the impulsions and the moral perceptions out of which a creative rendering of human life might come—is such that he seems to have had hardly any sense of even the elementary decencies that one had thought of as making civilized intercourse possible (if he was aware of them, it was to show—the relevant episodes are very striking—resentful hostility to any regard for them in others). There is nothing in his writings to contradict what we know of the life.

In Hemingway we have, it may be granted, something positively American. But it is hard to see why, in this, he should be thought to promise well for an American literary future—in saying which one is registering the portentous distance between Hemingway and Mark Twain. The author of *Huckleberry Finn* writes out of a full cultural heritage. The life he depicts is not crude—with the case presented by Hemingway in sight, the critic would be very improvident to use that adjective in connection with *Huckleberry Finn*. Compared with the idiom cultivated by Hemingway, Huck's language, as he speaks it, it is hardly excessive to say, is Shakespearian in its range and subtlety. Mark Twain, of course, has made of the colloquial mode he took such pride in rendering accurately a convention of art and a literary medium. But in doing so he has achieved an inevitable naturalness; the achievement, in fact, is the creation of Huck himself, about whom, I imagine, it has rarely been complained that he is unconvincing. And in Huck, the embodiment of an ungenteel western vernacular, he has made a *persona* for the expression of a mature criticism of life—mature and subtle by the standards of the great European literatures.

I need not enlarge on the relevant significance of this fact. What I will allow myself to emphasize is the maturity and refinement of the criticism. It is not merely that Mark Twain was a generous, compassionate and tender-hearted

xi

man, as well as a shrewd and widely-experienced observer. In the poised humanity, genial but unillusioned, conveyed by the whole work—conveyed in the quality of the life observed and presented, as well as in the attitude towards it—we cannot but recognize the presence of a mature and full heritage of civilization. In the attitude, the radical inclusive attitude of *Huckleberry Finn*, there is nothing of the wisdom of the tough or undeveloped and no bent towards a simplifying reduction of life. There is nothing sentimental or tough about the irony. It is the irony of an unusual adequacy to experience, and an unusual preoccupation with fullness of appraisal, the book having for essential theme the complexity of ethical valuation in any society that has a complex tradition.

In passing from *Huckleberry Finn* to *Pudd'nhead Wilson* one is obviously—one could tell with ease from internal evidence —passing to another work by the same master; and who would not say that the author of *Pudd'nhead Wilson* (that neglected masterpiece which no one, English or American, to whom I have mentioned it has read, so that my rhetorical question hasn't, perhaps, the point it might have had) did not belong rather, and very decidedly, with James than with Whitman or Dreiser or Fitzgerald or Hemingway?

But Mr. Bewley has his focused preoccupation. He defines a tradition in the American novel that has peculiar relevance to the needs of the present, and is (he contends, with what seems to me valid reason) the significantly American tradition in literature. Of the authors he associates (and his account explains why he doesn't include Mark Twain, who isn't significantly American in this way) he says that they

dealt with the American scene, but this is not the basis of their resemblance, which lies rather in their sense of the dangers and deficiencies which they saw encircling the possibilities they believed the country possessed. The tension between their faith and their fears created the best art America has ever produced. They form a tradition, not by virtue of their relation with each other, but because, each in his own fashion, they were *seriously* concerned with the new nation in a way that European novelists are rarely or never concerned with theirs. They felt that the possibilities of creative achievement were intrinsically involved with the new patterns of life which were forming in America, and they feared with all their hearts, though not always consciously, the concomitant losses that inevitably came with the gains.

And Mr. Bewley intimates (see especially pages 73 and 74) that an Englishman may properly feel himself to have a peculiar interest in the vindication and renewal of this tradition. There is, of course, the obvious general sense in which the American literary future will have a special importance for the other peoples speaking the common language; and in the tradition in question lies the possibility of a literature worthy to be called one. But Mr. Bewley has something more pointed to say. Of the 'Hawthorne-James line' he observes that the essential, and far from ineffective preoccupation of these writers was with the possibility for the American ' cut off from his antecedents and embarrassed by the burden of his "commonplace prosperity" ', of developing a 'refined consciousness' of the 'unity that underlies the divisions of the English-speaking world'. He adds:

> It was a tremendously complex problem, and as the world is going, it was and is a problem of such importance that even today one hardly dare plot limits to what it may eventually mean in terms of a future English-speaking civilization.

An Englishman who agrees should make it plain how little he is merely agreeing that a problem faces 'the American'. I myself, then, (let me say) see Mr. Bewley as pointing to a major significance that Henry James has for me, a significance bound up with my sense of his greatness. I am thinking of that drama of critical interplay between different traditions which has so large a part in his *œuvre*. It represents, as I have remarked elsewhere, a comparative inquiry, enacted in dramatic and poetic terms, into the criteria of civilization, and the possibilities. It transcends the vindication of one side against the other, or the mere setting forth of the for and against on both sides in a drama of implicit mutual criticism. The essential spirit of the drama is positive; James is feeling, creatively, towards an ideal possibility that is neither Europe nor America (for 'Europe', as James settled down to his 'complex fate', becoming a good deal of an Englishman while, like Mr. Touchett, remaining an American—and being manifestly more than either—we may read 'England').

This, we know, represents the drama James actually lived; the drama the felt presence of which in his *œuvre* is not confined to those novels and tales which we first think of as answering to the description I have just given. I should like to think that this James figures for us the Anglo-American literary—and so more than literary—future. In such a future, England would be England still, and America America; but the critical-creative interplay relating them, made possible by the difference and the unity, would be such as answered fully to the symbol, justifying and developing its suggestions.

Whatever may be thought of the idea put in this large way, there are two applications of it suggested by Mr. Bewley's book that have a good chance of being recognized at once as acceptable. One is that the line of novelists judged by Mr. Bewley to represent the great American achievement in art provides what should be a study of major importance on this side of the Atlantic. When I say 'of major importance' I am thinking, among other things, of the place such a study might have—should have—in an advanced 'English' course at the university. Think, for instance—if I may illustrate from my local point of view— of the eminent suitability of such a study as a Special Subject for Part II of the English Tripos. It is well-defined, compact and manageable. The major works of the main authors who form the line (Cooper, Hawthorne, Melville and James) are for the Englishman classics of English literature, yet he cannot but recognize them as American. And Mr. Bewley hints pregnantly at ways in which that American line (for the writers forming it are, as he says, in most significant relation and constitute an American literature) offers the Englishman an incomparable approach to the study of a civilization intimately related to his own, and related in ways that make it of peculiar moment that he should understand both the affinities and the differences. As a source of suggestions as

xiv

to the ways in which an intelligent literary-critical approach may develop into a study of that scope, the student now has Mr. Bewley's book (a promise, one trusts, of much to come) to put with the very small group that includes Mr. Yvor Winters' *Maules' Curse*.

The other 'application' I spoke of would be to constate the present urgent need for a lively play of literary criticism between the two major English-speaking countries. Formal agreement, perhaps, comes readily enough on this point. The trouble is that what we have, in practice, in this country, is an undiscriminating readiness in the quarters where our literary fashions are controlled (the literary world, metropolitan and *universitaire*—the system is a comprehensive one) to acclaim American criticism in general for its superior vigour and seriousness. What the specious generosity of recognition expresses and ministers to is the reverse of a concern for vigour and seriousness in English criticism. The tightness of the system in this tight little island remains unimpaired: 'American criticism' becomes a vague ally in the business of making things safe, and putting a face on the suppression of the *mauvais sujet* who won't play the game. What an Englishman concerned for life must count on is a real cross-Atlantic interplay that will make the confident substitution of the unanimities of British 'social' civilization for the standards of criticism more difficult: there is after all a more important society. Meanwhile he has to note with deep discouragement how easily the valuations of London, the British scene being in question, seem to get themselves accepted in New York (though the British Council writ doesn't run there), and in America generally—even when they are represented by visiting families of aristocratic geniuses.

About the ways in which an intelligent interest in the American literary scene on the part of critics here might help the function of criticism in America Mr. Bewley would no doubt have something interesting to say.

I am not (I had better, in closing, be quite explicit) assuming that he agrees with everything—every particular judgement or emphasis—in what I myself have said above.

F. R. LEAVIS

Acknowledgments

A LL of the essays in the present volume were written
during the past three years. 'The Poetry of Wallace
Stevens' was originally published in *Partisan Review*; the
remaining essays first appeared in *Scrutiny*. I am
indebted to the Editors for permission to reprint them
here.

I should like to acknowledge the great kindness and
helpfulness of F. R. and Q. D. Leavis, at whose suggestion many of these essays were first undertaken. I should
particularly like to thank F. R. Leavis for permission
to reprint his 'Disagreement' on *What Maisie knew*.

The opening essays on Hawthorne and Henry James
were written as a kind of exploratory excursion into a
project undertaken while holding a Fellowship from
The American Council of Learned Societies, and I
should like to take this opportunity of expressing my
thanks to the Council.

M. B.

I

Hawthorne and Henry James

I

HAWTHORNE, HENRY JAMES, AND THE AMERICAN NOVEL

DURING the nineteenth century the United States produced a line of novelists who represent her greatest achievement in art. American poetry in the nineteenth century had little to offer, and the drama even less; but in the novel American artists found a form which gave the freest scope to their critical awareness both of the potentialities and the deficiencies of the nation as it was in the process of evolving. The first of these artists, who stands somewhat apart from the others, and who is seriously underestimated at present, is James Fenimore Cooper. And there is Herman Melville, a greater artist, but overestimated today as seriously as Cooper suffers in the opposite direction. The critic who balks at Cooper's dated conventionalities of style, and at the wax-works quality of his heroines, yet seems able to swallow the far worse artificiality of Melville's *Pierre* without gagging. One can, of course, see why the critic is tempted to tolerance in the latter case. Melville's over-ripe prose in that novel is bursting with a consciousness of Jacobean poetry of the Webster-Ford variety (or rather, Shakespeare, for his is the name conventionally invoked), and there are always possibilities of complexity when such considerations enter. Cooper's simpler, more forthright conventionality is of a more datable kind, and therefore more irritating to a certain class of readers. But even at its worst, which can be very bad, it ought not to prove a serious hindrance to the enjoyment of his work, for Cooper's kind of artificiality is not the result of studied effect, but of his being interested in things so radically different from style that, in those passages which do not engage him deeply, he is content to move on in the stilted prose pattern of the day. But when he comes to write of those things which form his central meaning, he is unsurpassed. Joseph Conrad's comment on Cooper is very just:

> He wrote before the great American language was born, and he wrote as well as any novelist of his time. . . . The interest of his tales is convincing and unflagging; and there runs through his work a steady vein of friendliness for the old country which the succeeding generations of his compatriots have replaced by a less definite sentiment.

There is much more to be said for Cooper than that, but that in itself is a great deal.

Melville is more closely related to the last two of the four great novelists who compose the group—Hawthorne and Henry James. There is no evidence that James ever read Melville, but the two have their connection through their common admiration for Hawthorne. With Cooper and Melville I shall not be concerned in the following study, but I wish to present these four novelists together in the beginning, because among themselves they form a tradition in the American novel that has come on hard times in the twentieth century. They have no considerable successors today, and what they stood for in such varying ways among themselves has been supplanted. In *Gleanings in Europe*, Fenimore Cooper wrote, 'There is a morbid feeling in the American public . . . which will even uphold an inferior writer, so long as he aids in illustrating the land and water, which is their birthright.' That was written in 1837, and it has been becoming more true ever since. That school of literary appreciation which acclaims American literature simple because it is American has been represented by a strong body of critical opinion in the United States, and it has led to an insidious magnification of the frontier colloquial tradition in American literature. This tradition is one of great importance, but it is not the tradition embodied in America's four major novelists —although occasionally, as in Melville's case, there may be evidence of an influence from that direction in language or rhythm. This frontier tradition has its own high points of

2

achievement, but it represents the extreme isolationism of American literature, and it is fragmentary and misleading because it does not provide sufficient scope in itself to treat the largest problem that confronted the American artist in the nineteenth century, and which still occupies him: the nature of his separateness, and the nature of his connection with European, and particularly with English, culture. The great merit of the colloquial tradition is the vitality of its speech rhythms and the local colour and raciness of its images —but such a vitality, unsupported by a larger consciousness, is self-consuming, and if it burns brightly it does not burn long. Its effect has always been to support that 'morbid feeling in the American public . . . which will even uphold an inferior writer, so long as he aids in illustrating the land and water, which is their birthright'. It was basically this feeling which gave such support to the second-rate novel of realism which grew up in America at the end of the nineteenth century and the beginning of the twentieth; and it is responsible for an ancient tendency to regard Henry James as a European rather than as an American novelist. Yet it is of the essence of James's genius that he was an American in a fuller and finer sense than any of the American-Firsters in criticism who have found his quality beyond their comprehension.

Cooper, Hawthorne, Melville, and James form a line in American writing based on a finely critical consciousness of the national society. They all dealt with the American scene, but this is not the basis of their resemblance, which lies rather in their sense of the dangers and deficiencies which they saw encircling the possibilites they believed the country possessed. The tensions between their faith and their fears created the best art America has ever produced. They form a tradition, not by virtue of their relation with each other, but because, each in his own fashion, they were seriously concerned with the new nation in a way that European novelists are rarely, or never, concerned with theirs. They felt that the possibilities of creative achievement were intrinsically involved with the new patterns of life which were forming in America, and they feared with all their hearts, though not always consciously, the concomitant losses that inevitably came with the gains.

3

If they had great faith in America, they were also among the greatest critics—and sometimes very bitter ones—America has ever had. Their answers to the problem they explored were various, and they were not always consistent, even with themselves, fluctuating between an occasionally fatuous optimism and cynical disillusion; but they did create the American novel, and it is the finest thing America has to show.

It is generally recognized that Hawthorne was an important factor in James's artistic development, but in the comments on that influence which I have read, critics have been content to let the matter rest in the vaguest and most generous terms of indebtedness. And yet a clear grasp of the nature of this relationship is of the utmost importance in understanding the achievement of the American novel in the nineteenth century; and indeed, its importance for understanding James's own art, considered in itself, can hardly be overestimated. In the following study I wish to examine the way in which Hawthorne's art influenced the novels and stories of Henry James, and to show how they were both concerned in their writing with problems that were essentially American problems.

The question of indebtedness in art, the attempt to trace artistic influences, is quite as likely to lead towards distracting irrelevancies or academic obscurantism as towards any elevation from which one may take a clearer view and form a sounder judgment of the works in question. But some influences distinguish themselves as especially pertinent to any essential critical evaluation, as providing a unique glimpse, from the wire of tenuous connection, of the intentions and motives, the tone and the tradition, of the works stretched out below. I have suggested that the influence of Hawthorne on Henry James is of this pertinent character, and it is now commonly recognized to be so: commonly, but not invariably. Mr. David Garnett, for example, has recently gone on record as regarding Hawthorne's influence, not only as obnoxious to James's work, but as confined to the earliest specimens of his art. 'It was from that sort of nonsense', Mr. Garnett declares, 'that he escaped in the following year

4

when he came to live in Europe. A year in Paris meeting Flaubert, Turgenev, Maupassant, and Zola altered him.' The influence of Hawthorne on James is not only demonstrably far greater than in the case of any of the men here named: it was an influence that persisted to the end, and in certain ways it grew more insistent towards the end. Its importance for James is to be gauged by the fact that Hawthorne was the great American predecessor, the only one through whose art he approached his own native tradition. He showed him the facts of American life used *in art* in a way that James could understand, and James is quite clear on the point. Writing of the earlier novelist James said that Hawthorne had shown

to what a use American matter could be put by an American hand: a consummation involving, it appeared, the happiest moral. For the moral was that an American could be an artist, one of the finest, without going 'outside' about it, as I liked to say; quite, in fact, as if Hawthorne had become one just by being American *enough*, by the felicity of how the artist in him missed nothing, suspected nothing, that the ambient air didn't affect him as containing.

Hawthorne's methods of work, his moral preoccupations, the fundamental problems that confronted him as an artist in America, his attraction to a kind of allegory that was akin to symbolism, even to some extent the actual scenes and materials and types he chose to deal with, made a deep and lasting impression on James's 'fictions'. The idea that James took to precipitate flight in his youth, and breathing a freer air in Europe reduced his art to a series of unamiable comments on America, is one that, for anyone who takes James's work seriously, cannot be tolerated. Great art is not commonly the product of rootlessness, and despite his long life abroad James was able to keep in touch with those values which, for him, and no matter how much he liked or preferred to live in Europe, were the special product of the New World. The prevailing satire—the incessant fun-poking at Americans in Europe, or, for that matter, Americans at home—is, in the end, but the sustained corrective shaking

5

that the vigilant parent must administer to the loved but frequently impossible child. James dealt out the punishment to so many Americans, particularly to so many of his American heroines, that it came to pass off as animus against the nation; but beyond the sense one gets, from the heroines so shaken, of clattering parasols and disarranged bows and ruffles, one recognizes both the design and desire of correcting absurdities and encouraging spiritual fineness. One sees, above all, the ingrained faith that what would ultimately appear when the manners were taught and the garden weeded, would be a benefit to be conferred—a benefit uniquely American and wholly virtuous, and at least as great as anything the Old World had, on her side, to offer in exchange. Today, it seems to be Milly Theale of *The Wings of the Dove*, the heroine who most conspicuously *doesn't* get shaken, who has driven home at last the point of James's benevolent intentions. But what she also goes to prove is that James understood his own genius too well to withhold frequently the disciplinary arm.

It is disconcerting to have to emphasize these points here, for they should be commonly current in Jamesian criticism, and until I read Mr. Garnett's allusions to Hawthorne I had assumed that nowadays they most certainly were. To focus James's art against a background of continental writers is not to focus it at all, and to eliminate Hawthorne from the history of his artistic development is simply to eliminate the best part of James—the part towards which his most serious moral interests gravitated. It is to eliminate from his significant experience the literary tradition in America in which those moral values from which he never withdrew, and to which he seemed to return with greater insistence in his old age, received their peculiarly national celebration. It is a tradition, as I have said, that Hawthorne and James share with Cooper and Melville, but it is not to be confused with the tradition of uncritical acceptance stemming from Whitman, whose influence for American letters is analogous, in its exalted and stultifying afflatus, with the influence of Milton on eighteenth- and nineteenth-century English letters. The tradition of Hawthorne is quite distinct from anything of

6

that kind, and the point, for an English reader, is worth keeping firmly in mind when one insists on the deep American quality in James. Whitman did as much to ruin American poetry and prose as any single influence in America, and in every respect he is the reverse of Hawthorne: for if Hawthorne tried desperately to believe in the Future, it was a hope that the very nature of his moral preoccupations caused constantly to default.[1]

If, for the sake of convenience at this point, one were to attempt a definition of Hawthorne's tradition in a more narrow sense than has so far been undertaken here, one might say that it was rooted in a traditional past, a remote (for America, certainly remote) New England past, in which Europe impinged directly on the New World and Calvinistic theology directly on moral action. By Hawthorne's time both the Old World and the rigours of Calvinism had withdrawn into a hazy distance, but there was a fragrance and a memory that he knew, at least for a time, how to mould into form: how, in the medium of his art, to hold moral and psychological problems in a state of delicate suspension without, as in Whitman's case, precipitating a mud of optimistic conclusions. But the reality of Hawthorne is in his tone—a tone that is largely the evocation of regional intangibles—and it is unwise to generalize about it. James had known Hawthorne's books from his early childhood. He relates in *A Small Boy and Others* the effect of *The Scarlet Letter* and *The House of Seven Gables* on his imagination. Books that exert

[1] James published, at the age of twenty-two, a brilliant review of Whitman's *Drum-Taps*, which ought to be given, but isn't likely to be, a prominent position among his critical writings. It is easily among his best pieces. Mr. Matthiessen reprints the review in *The James Family* with an apology for its 'wrong-headedness'. The evidence that James revised his taste for Whitman's poetry later in life is far from convincing. It is difficult to take James's behaviour at Mrs. Wharton's in 1905 (which she describes in her autobiography) without a grain of salt; and in any event, when James recognized Whitman as America's greatest poet he wasn't at all doing violence to his earlier opinion. The competition for that title was hardly impressive then, and James was probably as right in conferring it on Whitman as he was certainly right in the 1868 review.

their influence in these opening years of life may continue to operate in the sensibility at levels where the consciousness is not habitually active nor attention alerted. They may acquire for the adult memory a picturesque and romantic beauty, but in the restless activity and expansion of a sensibility that is moving on, they may seem at last to rest on the laurels of nearly forgotten achievements, watching like old or early settlers the later stages of developments they no longer understand, but at whose inception they importantly assisted. Much of the influence of Hawthorne on James is of this kind, and it is a matter of extreme tact and delicacy to isolate it. James's first overlapped Hawthorne's last twenty-one years of life, and Henry James, the very young New York City dweller, was not so remote from the New England moral milieu in which Hawthorne, with so much greater detachment than his neighbours, lived, as to leave him an utter outsider. There are passages in the earlier prose of James in which the 'tone' of Hawthorne is so clearly struck that, if we were not told, we should take it without question as the earlier writer's work. But even so, one cannot help sensing that this similarity is due not more to Hawthorne's immediate example than to mutual proclivities of temperament and shades of value that still characterized the American and determinedly local scene on which both James and Hawthorne drew. From one point of view this is an added difficulty in any attempt to trace the specific touches of Hawthorne in James's style and meaning, for they seem to merge in the common atmosphere created by regional effects of climate and colour; but in the end this doesn't minimize—it only increases—the Hawthornian presence. He seems to fade into the New England scene, and it is impossible for James to deal with the one without, whether faintly or urgently, invoking the other. In the end one can say that Hawthorne literally gave James a tradition, for it was through Hawthorne that James found New England artistically accessible. And it was, finally, this sense of rootedness, or more accurately, of fine and enduring relation, that safeguarded him from becoming a kind of Edwardian Maugham. Later, when his novels became a dialectic of nations, the Moderator, instead of a displaced cosmopolitan, was a novelist whose values were centred and whose aims were clearly focused.

Apart from this general contribution of Hawthorne's, and insofar as we can trace them, the *specific* influences seem to have been utilized by James with varying degree of success. It was, of course, Hawthorne's masterpieces, *The Scarlet Letter* and *The House of Seven Gables*, as well as the short stories, which exerted the greatest attraction—but this attraction was, if deepest, of a nature extremely elusive. It was based on similar responses in the two writers to the same problems in the American scene—problems frequently out of sight, and not invariably recognized in their own identities by Hawthorne and James even at the moments they asserted their claims most strongly. What these questions were I shall attempt to describe later in 'The American Problem' and 'Appearance and Reality in Henry James'. I think it will then be seen that Hawthorne's influence on James is not merely a matter of surface similarity, but exists in the very reality with which the novelists deal. But before attempting to analyse this ultimate base of the resemblance, I should like to offer extended considerations of James's debt to the two last completed of Hawthorne's novels, *The Blithedale Romance* and *The Marble Faun*.

The reputation of *The Blithedale Romance* is undeservedly low, and I regret that my discussion of it, being necessarily concerned with the novel as James himself saw it, cannot attempt an evaluation of it on its own merits. But whatever one may think of *Blithedale*, there can be little doubt that *The Marble Faun* is a failure, and sometimes a boring failure at that. Nevertheless, James was directly influenced by both these novels, and it is surprising that the nature and extent of this influence has been so little noticed by critics in the past. It is especially interesting to study the effects of these two novels on James's art in that we can trace the differences between James's early and late modes of assimilating the influence of Hawthorne—can see how relatively clumsily the later James was capable of dealing with it. Yet even in its later phase, and perhaps there most of all, its effect is to underline the essential Americanism of Henry James—an

B

Americanism so fine that, paradoxically, one feels that America would have been its doom—and to reveal the fatuity of insisting, to any considerable extent, on the influences of Flaubert, Turgenev, Maupassant, and Zola.

2

'THE BLITHEDALE ROMANCE'
AND 'THE BOSTONIANS'

THE relation between *The Blithedale Romance* and *The Bostonians* has never, I believe, been commented on, and yet, for the Hawthornian influence on James, it is of the first importance. I wish to trace the outline of that influence in *The Bostonians,* but it is a task one undertakes with diffidence, for the relationship is frequently a hidden one, and its strongest pressures are sometimes felt on more or less concealed areas. At the outset James has placed a distraction in the way. Writing of *The Bostonians* in his *Notebooks* in 1889, when the project was just getting under way, James said:

> Daudet's *Evangéliste* has given me the idea of this thing . . . I wished to write a very *American* tale, a tale very characteristic of our social conditions, and I asked myself what was the most salient and peculiar point in our social life. The answer was: the situation of women, the decline of the sentiment of sex, the agitation on their behalf.

But such a notice as this serves only as a distraction; it presents no real difficulty, for if Daudet's Madame Autheman helped to focus the question, it had been Hawthorne, years before, who had provided the answer before the question had been asked. In his *Hawthorne* (1879), James had already noted that answer, and if he now preferred giving credit to Daudet it is probable that his sensibility had simply 'moved on' to such an extent that he failed to note the rate at which he was taking hints from the Hawthorne novel he had known for so many years.

There is a difficulty in speaking of the 'influence' any novel may have had on another. This difficulty is intrinsic in the nature of the novel itself. The 'influence' is likely to be spread out over a much wider—and mostly unquotable—area than is the case with a poem or play, and it is likely to show itself in

11

a wider variety of ways than is usual in the other instances. And prose rhythm, however personal and distinguished, exhibits an absorbent quality that is in contrast with the revealing intensity with which an 'influence' may be said to vibrate in the more luminous medium of poetry. James had written in his *Hawthorne*:

> There is no strictness in the representation by novelists of persons who have struck them in life, and there can in the nature of things be none. From the moment the imagination takes a hand in the game, the inevitable tendency is to divergence, to following what may be called new scents. The original gives hints, but the writer does what he likes with them, and imports new elements into the picture.

But if this is true in 'the representation by novelists of persons who have struck them in life', it is far more true in their representation of the persons and events and intentions that have struck them in fiction. Such an 'influence', in other words, must be largely a history of 'divergence', and the interest for us in comparing *The Blithedale Romance* with *The Bostonians* is simply that we are able to chart out the course of the 'divergence' with some accuracy. To do so helps illuminate the artistic intentions of both writers; and it helps to deepen the continuity of the American tradition.

The Blithedale Romance was suggestive to James in the first place in having provided a background scene which he wished not so much to emulate as to improve upon. In 1883 James had said that he wanted to write in *The Bostonians* 'a very American tale, a tale very characteristic of our social conditions . . . ' But four years before, his criticism of *The Blithedale Romance* had made the point even more explicitly:

> I should have liked to see the story concern itself more with the little community in which its earlier scenes are laid, and avail itself of so excellent an opportunity for describing unhackneyed specimens of human nature. I have already spoken of the absence of satire in the novel, of its not aiming in the least at satire, and of its offering no grounds for complaint as an invidious picture. Indeed, the Brethren of Brook Farm should

have held themselves slighted rather than misrepresented, and have regretted that the admirable genius who for awhile was numbered among them should have treated their institution mainly as a perch for starting upon an imaginative flight.

But if Hawthorne neglected to fill in the details of the Utopians at Brook Farm, there were enough *positive* hints in other directions that James was willing to utilize—particularly the theme of women's rights that he considered so typical of the American scene. The accent of Mrs. Farrinder or Olive Chancellor or Verena Tarrant, when they are eloquent on that subject, James might have learned directly from experience; and yet it is difficult to think that dialogue like the following was not ringing in James's memory when he came to ask himself 'what was the most salient and peculiar point in our social life':

Since her interview with Westervelt, Zenobia's continued inequalities of temper had been rather difficult for her friends to bear. On the first Sunday after that incident, when Hollingsworth had clambered down from Eliot's pulpit, she declaimed with great earnestness and passion, nothing short of anger, on the injustice which the world did to women, and equally to itself, by not allowing them, in freedom and honor, and with the fullest welcome, their natural utterance in public.

'It shall not always be so!' cried she. 'If I live another year, I will lift up my own voice in behalf of women's wider liberty.'

She perhaps saw me smile.

'What manner of ridicule do you find in this, Miles Coverdale?' exclaimed Zenobia with a flash of anger in her eyes. 'That smile, permit me to say, makes me suspicious of a low tone of feeling and shallow thought. It is my belief—yes, and my prophecy, should I die before it happens—that, when my sex shall achieve its rights, there will be ten eloquent women where there is now one eloquent man. Thus far no woman in the world has ever spoken out her whole heart and her whole mind. The mistrust and disapproval of the vast bulk of society throttles us, as with two gigantic hands at our throats! We mumble a few weak words, it is true, on a limited range of subjects. But the pen is not for woman. Her power is too natural

13

and immediate. It is with the living voice alone that she can compel the world to recognize the light of her intellect and the depth of her heart!'

Verena Tarrant's 'gift' of eloquence may not be directly traceable to Zenobia, whose record in that line is sufficiently remarkable; yet the accent of Zenobia's public manner (and her manner is never more public than when she is most private) is curiously near the idiom of the reformers in *The Bostonians*. This idiom as used by Hawthorne and James, and a little later by W. D. Howells in *The Undiscovered Country*— an unsatisfactory novel that is, at least in its first part, deeply indebted to both its distinguished predecessors—is undoubtedly in touch with the facts as they were, but the line of influence should not, on that account, be underestimated. The tone of Verena Tarrant's little speech at Miss Birdseye's, to take one of a number of possibilities, comes too near the Blithedale precedent for accidental similarity to seem a wholly plausible explanation:

> 'I am only a girl, a simple American girl, and of course I haven't seen much, and there is a great deal of life that I don't know anything about. But there are some things I feel—it seems to me as if I had been born to feel them; they are in my ears in the stillness of the night and before my face in the visions of the darkness. It is what the great sisterhood of women might do if they should all join hands, and lift up their voices above the brutal uproar of the world, in which it is so hard for the plea of mercy or of justice, the moan of weakness and suffering to be heard. We should quench it, we should make it still, and the sound of our lips would become the voice of universal peace! For this we must trust one another, we must be true and gentle and kind. We must remember that the world is ours too, ours— little as we have ever had to say about anything!—and that the question is not yet definitely settled whether it will be a place of injustice or a place of love!'

Verena's style, of course, is her own, and Zenobia's hovers somewhere between Verena's and Mrs. Farrinder's; but in *The Blithedale Romance* Hawthorne had laid down the suffragist vocabulary and the Transcendental speech rhythms authoritatively as far as literature was concerned, and James had the advantage of all Hawthorne had already done—and not done. For although it is difficult to believe, Zenobia's eloquence (despite Miles Coverdale's smile) is presented with a minimum of satirical intention on Hawthorne's part.

James must also have got the idea for Selah Tarrant's mesmeric exhibition, the purpose of which was to 'calm' his daughter before one of her talks, from the somewhat similar performance of Westervelt over the Veiled Lady. Although the surfaces of the suave Westervelt and Selah Tarrant are so opposite, as moral quantities they add up to almost identical portions. But it is part of Hawthorne's failure that Westervelt is endowed with a sinister Gothic quality that is radically misleading in any attempted valuation of what Westervelt stands for. The right note is struck in the matter of teeth.

> In the excess of his delight [Hawthorne writes of Westervelt], he opened his mouth wide, and disclosed a gold band around the upper part of his teeth, thereby making it apparent that every one of his brilliant grinders and incisors was a sham. This discovery affected me very oddly. I felt as if the whole man were a moral and physical humbug . . .

Selah Tarrant, one remembers, had a fatuous habit of unfurling his wrinkles and showing his back teeth in what Olive Chancellor once thought of as his 'terrible smile', a smile that had the effect of illuminating Selah's moral quality, or lack of it.

James complained of 'the absence of satire' in *The Blithedale Romance*, 'of its not aiming in the least at satire, and of its offering no grounds for complaint as an invidious picture'. To read *The Blithedale Romance* in the light of this comment, and to compare its characters, fading away from time to time into unrealized shadows, with the sharply defined and clearly lighted characters in *The Bostonians* is not only to understand why Hawthorne's novel fails, but why it failed in a way that James found useful as a study in writing his own book. Westervelt and Selah, since they are already up for discussion, may serve to point the divergence in method. If

Hawthorne's sense of evil was intense, his grasp of its concrete manifestations could sometimes be relatively relaxed, and his attempt to supply Westervelt with the accoutrements of Gothic Romance simply fail. The false teeth are right, or would be if they did not incongruously contradict all the other notes in the picture—the dark handsomeness, the worldly polish. And Westervelt's mesmeric talent, instead of deepening the mystery Hawthorne so insistently invites to hang over his head, merely heightens the farce. His vaguely glimpsed past offers itself to the imagination as something merely cheap and more vulgar than immoral. Hawthorne didn't know his man—didn't even know his 'evil'; and this must have been one of the chief points against which James reacted. How he reacted we know: for odd as it may seem, Selah is the counterpart of Westervelt in *The Bostonians*. Both are mesmerists who give public performances involving about the same degree and kind of charlatanism, both have highly questionable personal histories; and if Selah is the father of a girl prodigy who literally sells his daughter to Olive Chancellor, Westervelt is the brother-in-law (apparently) of Priscilla (who, under the title of The Veiled Lady is also a girl prodigy in the mesmeric line), and he exploits her in the same way that Selah has exploited Verena. It will be seen that James took over these counters and rearranged them with far greater coherence in his own novel—but the parallelism is unmistakable.

In stripping Selah of every vestige of Gothicism, James showed him up with a cruel explicitness that, while in no way minimizing the 'evil' that Westervelt represented, provided a scathing comment on the nature of that 'evil', and by carrying it over into a realm of social comedy, related it to the whole milieu that had produced it in the first place. *The Bostonians* is one of James's wittiest novels—and one in which the wit, without losing a degree of status, is sometimes played with unusual broadness. To call its comedy 'brilliant' would be to insist on the moral illumination that reveals the dimensions of its meaning rather than on the mere glitter of surfaces that is usually accepted as justification for that adjective when applied to comedy in the social mode. The

16

shifting distinction between comedy and tragedy is, perhaps, finally dependent on a radical ambiguity in the nature of moral experience itself, but whatever the explanation, the comic effects that James brings off on his carefully plotted stage frequently seem to be performed on trap doors opening immediately into subterranean regions of a vastly different character. To illustrate what I mean with a single but typical instance, one might take an excerpt from a description of Selah. He is being considered here from the viewpoint of his long-suffering and not too intelligent wife:

> Her husband always had tickets for lectures; in moments of irritation at the want of a certain sequence in their career, she had remarked to him that it was the only thing he did have. The memory of all the winter nights they had tramped through the slush (the tickets, alas! were not car tickets) to hear Mrs. Ada T. P. Foat discourse on the 'Summer-land', came back to her with bitterness. Selah was quite enthusiastic at one time about Mrs. Foat, and it was his wife's belief that he had been 'associated' with her (that was Selah's expression in referring to such episodes) at Cayuga.

Everything from the superb name, Mrs. Ada T. P. Foat, and the title of her lecture, to that admirably chosen word, 'discourse', is right. The effect is deliciously comic; but when we hear Cayuga mentioned the comedy suddenly assumes a darker kind of life, different from what it was a moment before. We recall that Cayuga has just been mentioned a few pages back. Selah Tarrant had 'been for a while a member of the celebrated Cayuga community, where there were no wives or no husbands, or something of that sort (Mrs. Tarrant could never remember)'.[1] The 'evil' that Selah represents carries the odour of disinfectants about it in that beautifully built up word 'associated', and if he is comic, Selah nevertheless is an actively sordid presence in the book that Wester-

[1] The Cayuga community was undoubtedly suggested to James by the example of the perfectionist community established at Oneida, New York, by John Humphrey Noyes in 1848. Private property and marriage were prohibited, and the community continued to exist until 1880, when the New York legislature finally compelled it to abandon group marriage.

velt could not begin to emulate in *Blithedale*. In connection with this passage, one recalls from a later chapter the occasion of Verena's first visit to Olive Chancellor:

> Verena talked of the marriage-tie as she would have talked of the last novel—as if she had heard it as frequently discussed; and at certain times, listening to the answers she made to her questions, Olive Chancellor closed her eyes in the manner of a person waiting till giddiness passed. Her young friend's revelations gave her a vertigo; they made her perceive everything from which she should have rescued her. Verena was perfectly uncontaminated, and she would never be touched by evil; but though Olive had no views about the marriage-tie except that she should hate it for herself—that particular reform she did not propose to consider—she didn't like the 'atmosphere' of circles in which such institutions were called into question. She had no wish now to enter into an examination of that particular one; nevertheless, to make sure, she would just ask Verena whether she disapproved of it.
>
> 'Well, I must say,' said Miss Tarrant, 'I prefer free unions.'

The effect of Cayuga and Selah's 'associations' has clearly been to confirm Verena's remarkable innocence. Her preference for 'free unions' falls from her lips with charming modesty, as proof against the tortured nerves of Olive Chancellor as it is against the extravagant fraudulency of her father. James's tremendous and precise control over this vocabulary, his ability to impart even a human warmth to its sterilized phrases when they fall from the proper lips, make it possible for him to chisel his characters and values out of a hard rock of reality that gives him the right to challenge *The Blithedale Romance*. He was determined to make *The Bostonians* a satire in a way he almost resentfully recognized *Blithedale* failed, and to bring his full genius to the task of offering in *The Bostonians* 'grounds for complaint as an invidious picture'. It may have been because he felt guilty that he defended himself so earnestly to his brother when the latter charged him with having modelled Miss Birdseye on Hawthorne's aged but still living sister-in-law. At any rate, the defence is not convincing.

18

But if *The Blithedale Romance* was suggestive to James in the respects enumerated above, its chief suggestiveness must surely have resided in the way Hawthorne described the strange domination Zenobia exercised over Priscilla. This theme is ultimately incoherent, and again Hawthorne seems in doubt as to what he is doing. But the theme as he develops it implies on the surface everything that James was to take up so richly in the Chancellor-Tarrant relation. Zenobia, except in her dominating quality, does not equate with Olive Chancellor, but this 'divergence' is something that embodies a good deal of interest in itself, and will have to be examined in some detail later on. Here in the beginning one might offer a quotation or two to indicate the emotional quality of the relationship. Zenobia is not the aggressive element in the way that Olive Chancellor is; Priscilla is so deliberately the victim that it is impossible to feel much sympathy for her, and in the passage below she seems more like Olive Chancellor in Verena's role than like Verena herself. This passage, taken from Chapter IV, describes Priscilla's first meeting with Zenobia. Miles Coverdale, the narrator, has just arrived at Blithedale (the Brook Farm of the story) to begin his experiment in Utopianism. It is the evening of a cold New England April day, and Coverdale and his colleagues (including Zenobia) are sitting around the fire in the farmhouse kitchen after supper, awaiting the arrival of another member of the community, Hollingsworth. Suddenly there is a knock at the door, and Hollingsworth enters with an unexpected guest:

The stranger, or whatever she were, remained standing precisely on that spot of the kitchen floor to which Hollingsworth's kindly hand had impelled her. The cloak falling partly off, she was seen to be a very young woman dressed in a poor but decent gown, made high in the neck, and without any regard to fashion or smartness. Her brown hair fell down from beneath a hood, not in curls but with only a slight wave; her face was of a wan, almost sickly hue, betokening almost habitual seclusion from the sun and free atmosphere, like a flower-shrub that had done its best to blossom in too scanty light. To complete the pitiableness of her aspect, she shivered either with cold, or fear, or nervous excitement, so that you might have beheld her shadow vibrating on the fire-lighted wall. In short, there has seldom been seen so depressed and sad a figure, as this young girl's. . . .

*   *   *   *

As yet the girl had not stirred. She stood near the door, fixing a pair of large brown, melancholy eyes upon Zenobia—only upon Zenobia!—she evidently saw nothing else in the room, save that bright, fair, rosy, beautiful woman. It was the strangest look I ever witnessed; long a mystery to me, and forever a memory. Once she seemed about to move forward and greet her—I know not with what warmth, or with what words—but, finally, instead of doing so, she dropped upon her knees, clasped her hands, and gazed piteously into Zenobia's face. Meeting no kindly reception, her head fell on her bosom.

I never thoroughly forgave Zenobia for her conduct on this occasion. But women are always more cautious in their casual hospitalities than men.

'What does the girl mean?' cried she in a rather sharp tone. 'Is she crazy? Has she no tongue?'

And here Hollingsworth stepped forward.

'No wonder if the poor child's tongue is frozen in her mouth,' said he; and I think he positively frowned at Zenobia. 'The very heart will be frozen in her bosom, unless you women can warm it, among you, with the warmth that ought to be in your own. . . .'

'You do not quite do me justice, Mr. Hollingsworth,' said she, almost humbly. 'I am willing to be kind to the poor girl. Is she a protégé of yours? What can I do for her?'

'Have you anything to ask of this lady?' said Hollingsworth kindly, to the girl. 'I remember you mentioned her name before we left town.'

'Only that she will shelter me,' replied the girl tremulously. 'Only that she will let me be always near her.'

'Well, indeed,' exclaimed Zenobia, recovering herself, and laughing, 'this is an adventure, and well worthy to be the first incident in our life of love and free-heartedness!'

In the end Priscilla, somewhat incredibly, turns out to be Zenobia's half-sister—a fact of which Priscilla, but not Zenobia, has been aware all along; but this fact is not revealed until late in the book, and even when it comes it does little towards offering an acceptable explanation of the psychological nature of the exhibition that has been offered. Hawthorne develops the theme along the lines indicated in the above passage, and finally offers something in the nature of a solution by making both Priscilla and Zenobia fall in love with the same man—Hollingsworth. It is clear that Hawthorne in describing the friendship of Priscilla and Zenobia was not consciously attempting anything like James undertook in *The Bostonians*. James had written in his *Notebooks:* 'The relation of the two girls should be a study of one of those friendships between women which are so common in New England.' Hawthorne had quite accidentally blundered into the psychological aspect of the theme, and having it on his hands, was quite incapable of evaluating it. The passage below reveals Hawthorne at his worst:

It was curious to observe how trustingly, and yet how timidly, our poor Priscilla betook herself into the shadow of Zenobia's protection. She sat beside her on a stool, looking up, every now and then, with an expression of humble delight, at her new friend's beauty. A brilliant woman is often an object of the devoted admiration—it might almost be termed worship, or idolatry—of some young girl, who perhaps beholds the cynosure only at an awful distance, and has as little hope of personal intercourse as of climbing among the stars of heaven. We men are too gross to comprehend it. Even a woman, of mature age, despises or laughs at such a passion. There occurred to me no mode of accounting for Priscilla's behaviour, except by supposing that she had read some of Zenobia's stories (as such literature goes everywhere), or her tracts in defence of the sex, and had come hither with the one purpose of being her slave. There is nothing parallel to this, I believe—nothing so foolishly disinterested, and hardly anything so beautiful—in the masculine nature, at whatever epoch of life; or, if there be, a fine and rare development of character might reasonably be looked for from the youth who should prove himself capable of such self-forgetful affection.

This kind of unintelligence, one can't help thinking, must have been partly due to the Transcendental sweetness of Mrs. Hawthorne that was at last beginning 'to tell' on her husband. This passage is important because it spots a defect of sensibility that was to make it impossible for Hawthorne to effect a successful transition between the manner of his two early romances and the realistic mode he was striving after in *Blithedale*. And yet Hawthorne could, on occasion, deal well enough with manners and society. There are a few effective scenes in *Blithedale* in which the realism is perfectly successful, and one remembers the dozens of wonderful scenes and passages in the *English Notebooks* that prove Hawthorne was not lacking in this kind of talent. What he did lack was a seasoned and maturely focused experience of the world. The deficiency so glaring in the above passage—a deficiency that relates to the fundamental failure in *The Marble Faun*—is, broadly speaking, a deficiency of education—the absence of a tradition of manners that might have formed and refined the essential moral perceptions that come out so strongly in the earlier work. The evaluation or judgment in the passage in question is, at bottom, essentially an evaluation of manners, however deceptively it may pass itself off as one of morals (to momentarily propose a dichotomy between the two). There was a yawning discrepancy in the New England tradition between the two terms, and it was this discrepancy that compelled Hawthorne to favour the 'romance' (as he called it) rather than the novel form.[1] The

[1] Hawthorne seems to have derived a psychological security in thinking of his fictions as 'romances' rather than as novels. One understands more or less vaguely, of course, the nature of the distinction between them; nevertheless, it can be insidiously misleading, and there is no doubt that the term 'romance' puts a much lower value on Hawthorne's works than they deserve. In his essay, 'The Art of Fiction', Henry James has made some observations on these two terms that may profitably be quoted here:

'The novel and the romance, the novel of incident and that of character—these clumsy separations appear to me to have been made by critics and readers for their own convenience, and to help them out

failure of Hawthorne's late work is not a personal failure: it is a failure in his background, something omitted from his tradition and training. But however much we may excuse the unpalatable muddle-headedness of the above passage (or not excuse it, D. H. Lawrence once wrote of this aspect of Hawthorne, '. . . one feels like giving Nathaniel a kick in the seat of his poor little pants'), it remained a blot that could be erased from the American tradition only by the brilliant corrective insights of *The Bostonians*. One now understands fully what James meant when he wrote, 'The portion of the story that strikes me as least felicitous is that which deals with Priscilla, and with her mysterious relation to Zenobia. . . .' Whether there was a conscious recognition of work to be done or not, it must have been when he read that passage that James instinctively took the line of duty that culminated in his greatest American novel.

The Blithedale Romance, then, offers a set of counters that James found ready for re-shifting in *The Bostonians*. We have women's rights, mesmerism, Boston, the suggestion of a neurotic friendship between two women. It also offered a suggestive set of characters. We have already considered how James was able to transform Westervelt into Selah Tarrant. But Hollingsworth, the reformer, has certain affinities with Basil Ransom. Both men 'save' their respective heroines by marrying them at the last minute. Hollingsworth in Chapter XXIII of *Blithedale* turns up at a lyceumhall in a Massachusetts village at which there is to be a mesmeric exhibition involving the Veiled Lady. The New England audience is gathered, and the performance begins. A bearded personage

of some of their occasional queer predicaments, but to have little reality or interest for the producer. . . . One writes the novel, one paints the picture, of one's language and of one's time, and calling it modern English will not, alas! make the difficult task any easier. No more, unfortunately, will calling this or that work of one's fellow artist a romance—unless it be, of course, simply for the pleasantness of the thing, as for instance when Hawthorne gave this heading to his story of *Blithedale*. . . . I can think of no obligation to which the "romancer" would not be held equally with the novelist; the standard of execution is equally high for each.'

23

in Oriental robes makes an address on hypnotism. Hollingsworth recognizes the mesmerist as Westervelt, and a moment later he recognizes Westervelt's 'subject', despite the veil, as Priscilla. Westervelt proceeds to induce a trance in Priscilla, or rather, he fails to induce one:

> Greatly to the Professor's discomposure, however, just as he spoke these words, the Veiled Lady arose. There was a mysterious tremor that shook the magic veil. The spectators, it may be, imagined that she was about to take flight into that invisible sphere, and to the society of those purely spiritual beings with whom they reckoned her so near akin. Hollingsworth, a moment ago, had mounted the platform, and now stood gazing at the figure, with a sad intentness that brought the whole power of his great, stern, yet tender soul into his glance.
>
> 'Come,' said he, waving his hand towards her. 'You are safe!'
>
> She threw off the veil, and stood before that multitude of people pale, tremulous, shrinking, as if only then had she discovered that a thousand eyes were gazing at her. Poor maiden! How strangely had she been betrayed! Blazoned abroad as a wonder of the world, and performing what were adjudged as miracles—in the faith of many, a seeress and a prophetess; in the harsher judgment of others, a mountebank—she had kept, as I religiously believe, her virgin reserve and sanctity of soul throughout it all. Within that encircling veil, though an evil hand had flung it over her, there was as deep a seclusion as if this forsaken girl had, all the while, been sitting under the shadow of Eliot's pulpit, in the Blithedale woods, at the feet of him who now summoned her to the shelter of his arms. And the true heart-throb of a woman's affection was too powerful for the jugglery that had hitherto environed her. She uttered a shriek, and fled to Hollingsworth, like one escaping from her deadliest enemy, and was safe forever.

The manner in which this must have been given hints for the closing chapter of *The Bostonians* should scarcely require emphasizing here. The reader is referred again to that last scene in James's novel in which Basil Ransom carries Verena triumphantly away to marriage from the Boston Music Hall just before her appearance to the impatient audience, on the night that was to have been her greatest triumph. But if the above passage was the hint that James acted on, one can only say again how immeasurably better he did it. Verena's innocence is a positively realized thing in James that does not need the symbolical operation of a mystic veil to protect it from vulgar violation. It beautifully protects itself. We know that if James took the cue, he also took the warning: 'Hawthorne is rather too fond of Sibylline attributes—a taste of the same order as his disposition, to which I have already alluded, to talk about spheres and sympathies.'

The history of Westervelt's and Hollingsworth's influence in shaping the characters of Selah Tarrant and Basil Ransom is one of 'divergence'. But if the 'divergence' is marked in the case of the two men, it is even more curiously so with Zenobia and Priscilla. James's imagination was stimulated by Zenobia, and he showed marked partiality for her. At the cost of repeating a quotation already given in part, I must give James's full tribute to Zenobia here:

> The finest thing in *The Blithedale Romance* is the character of Zenobia, which I have said elsewhere strikes me as the nearest approach that Hawthorne has made to the complete creation of a *person*. She is more concrete than Hester or Miriam, or Hilda or Phoebe; she is a more definite image, produced by a greater multiplicity of touches. It is idle to inquire too closely whether Hawthorne had Margaret Fuller in his mind in constructing the figure of this brilliant specimen of the strong-minded class, and endowing her with the genius of conversation; or, on the assumption that such was the case, to compare the image at all strictly with the model. There is no strictness in the representation by novelists of persons who have struck them in life, and there can in the nature of things be none. From the moment the imagination takes a hand in the game, the inevitable tendency is to divergence, to following what may be called new scents. The original gives hints, but the writer does what he likes with them, and imports new elements into the picture. If there is this amount of reason for referring the wayward heroine of Blithedale to Hawthorne's impression of the most distin-

C

guished woman of her day in Boston; that Margaret Fuller was the only literary lady of eminence whom there is any sign of his having known; that she was proud, passionate, and eloquent; that she was much connected with the little world of Transcendentalism out of which the experiment of Brook Farm sprung; and that she had a miserable end and a watery grave—if these are facts to be noted on the one side, I say; on the other, the beautiful and sumptuous Zenobia, with her rich and picturesque temperament and physical aspects, offers many points of divergence from the plain and strenuous invalid who represented feminine culture in the suburbs of the New England metropolis. This picturesqueness of Zenobia is very happily indicated and maintained; she is a woman in all the force of the term, and there is something very vivid and powerful in her large expression of womanly gifts and weaknesses.

It is no wonder that feeling as he did about Zenobia, James felt that the relationship she was put into with Priscilla represented a kind of inartistic double-dealing on Hawthorne's part. In writing *The Bostonians* James may be said, in one sense, to have avenged Zenobia, and completely exculpated her by showing in Olive Chancellor what, in such a relation, Zenobia would have been. In that description of the first meeting between Priscilla and Zenobia, it is Olive Chancellor with her morbid shyness, her pale pointed features, her nervous manner, and her precipitate flood of emotion during her first private interview with Verena that Priscilla reminds one of. And it is, on the other hand, the highly coloured Verena that Zenobia suggests—Zenobia with the tropical or the jewelled flower in her hair, Verena 'white as women are who have that shade of red hair; they look as if their blood had gone into it'. And both Zenobia and Verena are almost defined in the purity, one might almost say the innocence, of their theatricality. James says of Verena, 'If she had produced a pair of castinets or a tambourine he [Ransom] felt that such accessories would have been quite in keeping.' And Hawthorne, in a similar accent, says of Zenobia: 'It was wronging the rest of mankind to retain her as the spectacle of only a few. The stage would have been her proper sphere.'

When James came to create Verena Tarrant he gave her the role of Priscilla, but he conferred—with a far finer sense of the situation than Hawthorne had displayed—the charm, beauty, and eloquence of Zenobia on her. The motives of Zenobia's victimization of Priscilla remain obscure in Hawthorne. James firmly lodged the motive of Olive Chancellor's victimization of Verena in Olive's own character, and presented a pre-Freudian psychological study of astonishing penetration. On each re-reading the sense of how perfectly James understood the workings of complex hidden tensions comes out freshly, and stronger than before. Gide complained that James always left out 'all the wild darkness', a charge that irritates me increasingly with time, for James is one of the few novelists who do not require a stage blackout to conceal the incapacities of their own psychological, artistic, and moral understandings.

Quantitatively speaking, Olive Chancellor has a greater burden of guilt to carry than any of the characters in *The Blithedale Romance*, or she would have if true self-knowledge formed any part of her character. The evil theme of 'dominance' is parcelled out in *Blithedale*. We have Westervelt's 'dominance' over Zenobia, Zenobia's 'dominance' over Priscilla, and Hollingsworth's 'dominance' over Zenobia. All these 'dominances' are compressed in *The Bostonians* into the single theme of Olive Chancellor's 'dominance' over Verena. And this theme is treated with an understanding and a fullness of development that Hawthorne in any one of his three 'dominances', or in all of them put together, cannot begin to equal. James's understanding of how to relate the characters to each other, how much substance and 'interest' to give them, precisely how to define their respective functions, could not be improved upon. His 'rearrangements' introduce the brightest clarity into the *Blithedale* shadows and confusion.

It remains only to consider Hawthorne's and James's final disposal of their characters. Faced with defeat, both Zenobia and Olive court martyrdom—Zenobia, literally, in a dramatic suicide, and Olive, figuratively, taking upon herself the hideous task of doing what James has made it inescapably clear her whole soul would most recoil from—announcing to the disappointed, shouting audience in the Music Hall that Miss Tarrant would not speak that evening:

> If he [Ransom] had observed her, it might have seemed to him that she hoped to find the fierce expiation she sought for in exposure to the thousands she had disappointed and deceived, in offering herself to be trampled to death and torn to pieces. She might have suggested to him some feminine firebrand of Paris revolutions, erect on a barricade, or even the sacrificial figure of Hypatia, whirled through the furious mob of Alexandria.

The suicide of Zenobia herself James considered nearly the most tragical denouement in all Hawthorne. As for Priscilla and Verena—if they are 'saved' at last, the nature of the salvation in both cases is open to question. Hawthorne is more explicit than James. We have a glimpse of Priscilla years later, taking a walk through the woods with Hollingsworth, who seems to have attained to a remarkably precocious senility, thereby forcing on the willing Priscilla the role of a trained nurse. If, on the other hand, Basil Ransom doesn't have anything to expiate (Hollingsworth's 'dominance' over Zenobia, is, of course, his 'crime', for which, it appears, Priscilla is likely to suffer equally with the culprit) there are some remarkable hardnesses in his character. They are necessary, one feels, if he was to defeat Olive Chancellor. But their presence hardly makes the prospect any better for Verena, and James ends on this note:

> 'Ah, now I am glad!' said Verena, when they reached the street. But though she was glad, he presently discovered that, beneath her hood, she was in tears. It is to be feared that with the union, so far from brilliant, into which she was about to enter, these were not the last she was destined to shed.

The relationship, then, between *The Blithedale Romance* and *The Bostonians* seems to be, point by point, nearer than between any other of Hawthorne's and James's novels. It has seemed worth examining at considerable length at the outset, because it is not a case of simple parallelism or an exhibition of 'influence' only. It would be easy to point out several dozen instances of that sort of thing in James's novels where, in some concrete particular, some turn of plot or twist of character, James had demonstrably borrowed, consciously or unconsciously, from the earlier novelist. Mr. F. O. Matthiessen in *The American Renaissance* has mentioned a number of these parallelisms; but if they are to be useful they should lead beyond themselves, back to deeper similarities and mutual participations. The similarity between these two novels is important, not simply as exhibiting James's indebtedness to Hawthorne, but because both men are seen to be working in a tradition (as well as making it), to be dealing with moral quantities so permanently and recognizably established in the American scene that the success could not, in James's case, be a matter merely of discovery or of aboriginal insight working on untreated material. Part of the success of *The Bostonians* is a matter of subtle creative pressures, of skilled and instructed reticences and boldnesses, of a security of knowledge that could only have occurred where there were the beginnings of a tradition trained (even if imperfectly trained) in handling that particular knowledge. It is an interesting comment on the important function of tradition in the creative act that James's masterpiece among the American novels should have had so conspicuous a precursor in American literature. Those who like to call James an international novelist are usually prompt to supply some European lineage or other; but if the American half of the equation is to be filled out, Hawthorne's is the only name that fits.

The question of whether or not James was conscious of 'using' *The Blithedale Romance* for his own novel is unimportant. The device of the portrait in *The Sense of the Past* unquestionably derived, in its ultimate source, from Colonel Pyncheon's portrait in *The House of Seven Gables*, and yet in the notes for the unfinished novel one can see James working into the idea of its function in his plot with no conscious sense whatever of Hawthorne's precedent. He had known Hawthorne too long and too intimately to be much concerned with him at that level of awareness; but this, so far from minimizing the indebtedness, proclaims its depth and suffusion. The question of how *consciously* James drew on *Blithedale* can, perhaps, be better answered when the nature of the two men's relationship has been more fully explored. But in the meantime it might be well to bear in mind, as decidedly relevant to *The Bostonians*, one of James's many tributes to Hawthorne:

Out of the soil of New England he sprang—in a crevice of that immitigable granite he sprouted and bloomed. Half of the interest that he possesses for an American reader with any turn for analysis must reside in his latent New England savour; and I think it no more than just to say that whatever entertainment he may yield to those who know him at a distance, it is an almost indispensable condition of properly appreciating him to have received a personal impression of the manners, the morals, indeed of the very climate, of the great region of which the remarkable city of Boston is the metropolis.

3

'THE MARBLE FAUN'
AND 'THE WINGS OF THE DOVE'

BOTH *The Blithedale Romance* and *The Bostonians* deal with the theme of the American woman, and principally under her aspect of excessive liberation. But the suffragist movement is only a corner of the whole subject, and there are frequent points at which Hawthorne and James draw near in their treatment of the larger problem, reminding one that both novelists were far from remaining in the particular corner, and that they were capable of bestowing a conspicuousness on their American heroines that had little to do with the sensational effects of organized and militant feminism. The problem is ultimately one for sociological exploration, and one recalls that in *The American Scene* (1907) James offered some pages that, precisely *as* sociological exploration, are probably the best thing we shall ever have in that line. It has become the critical fashion to extol the nobilities and spiritual endowments that James lavished on several of his heroines, and the tendency has been to overlook the fact that in most of his best work the endowments, the way he gets them across to the reader, are intrinsically dependent on his recognition of what, for the final picture, is missing from the background and character of the American maiden. We have already seen his incisive touches rectifying the unsatiric vision of Hawthorne; and we have seen how his very mercilessness could animate the character of Verena Tarrant, exhibiting her virtues with a success forever closed to Hawthorne's more tender conception of Priscilla. Hawthorne's suggestiveness in *Blithedale* had been of the most valuable kind; but years later when James wrote *The Wings of the Dove*, Hawthorne's example operated in a different way. James proved less critical, and although the 'influence' in this case was considerably less extensive, such an imprint as the precedent left on James's art was unfortunate in its effect.

But before discussing this later relation, relatively so much more tenuous than the one already considered, one should envisage James's most persistent attitude to his American girls and women as concretely as possible. The following quotation from *The American Scene*, written so late in James's career, may be taken as a kind of axial statement around which it is possible to group most, if not all, of his American heroines. It tickets their satiric content in a manner cutting enough to be, on occasion, cruel, at the same time allowing dancing room for those emergent virtues which, in the case of, say, Daisy Miller or Pandora Day, are the last things we keep pathetically in view. The importance of the passage will justify the inclusion of a quotation of such length:

She has been, accordingly, about the globe, beyond all doubt, a huge success of curiosity; she has at her best—and far beyond any consciousness and intention of her own, lively as these for the most part usually are—infinitely amused the nations. It has been found among them that, for more reasons than we can now go into, her manner of embodying and representing her sex has fairly made of her a new human convenience, not unlike fifty of the others, of a slightly different order, the ingenious mechanical appliances, stoves, refrigerators, sewing-machines, type-writers, cash-registers, that have done so much, in the household and the place of business, for the American name. By which I am, of course, far from meaning that the revelation has been of her utility as a domestic drudge; it has been much rather in the fact that the advantages attached to her being a woman at all have been so happily combined with the absence of the drawbacks, for persons intimately dealing with her, traditionally suggested by that condition. The corresponding advantages, in the light of almost any old order, have always seemed inevitably paid for by the drawbacks; but here, unmistakably, was a case in which—as at first appeared, certainly—they were to be enjoyed very nearly for nothing. What it came to, evidently, was that she had been grown in an air in which a hundred of the 'European' complications and dangers didn't exist, and in which also she had had to take upon herself a certain training for freedom. It was not that she had had, in the vulgar sense, to 'look out' for herself, inasmuch as it was of the very essence of her position not to be threatened or waylaid; but that she could develop her audacity on the basis of her security, just as she could develop her 'powers' in a medium from which criticism was consistently absent. Thus she arrived, full-blown, on the general scene, the least critized object, in proportion to her importance, that had ever adorned it. It would take long to say why her situation, under this retrospect, may affect the inner fibre of the critic himself as one of the most touching on record; he may merely note his perception that she was to have been after all but the sport of fate. For why need she originally, he wonders, have embraced so confidently, so gleefully, yet so unguardedly, the terms offered her to an end practically so perfidious? Why need she, unless in the interest of her eventual discipline, have turned away with so light a heart after watching the Man, the deep American man, retire into his tent and let down the flap? She had her 'paper' from him, their agreement signed and sealed; but would she not, in some other air and under some other sky, have been visited by a saving instinct? Would she not have said 'No, this is too unnatural; there must be a trap in it somewhere—it's addressed really, in the long run, to making a fool of me?' It is impossible, of course, to tell; and her case, as it stands for us, at any rate, is that she showed no doubts.

It is in the world comprehended within the terms of this quotation that James achieved a classic success with the American female that was beyond Hawthorne's ambition. Hawthorne could exhibit a heavily Dickensian humour at the expense of a matrimonially inclined widow in his short story, *Mrs. Bullfrog*, or show himself genuinely ill-tempered in his crude attacks on the English dowager; but neither the intelligence nor the values that shot through the Jamesian comedy when it dealt with American womanhood was at Hawthorne's disposal. But at another level they had their common ground, for if James, particularly in his late work, can be credited with idealizing the American girl, it was easy enough for him to look back from Milly Theale to a positive apotheosis of New England girlhood that Hawthorne had provided for the general edification many years before. There is a good deal of evidence to suggest that he *did* look back, and receive support from the precedent. Mr. Matthiessen has written in *The American Renaissance*: 'The characters who mark his greatest advance beyond anything in Hawthorne's scope, and who are, indeed, the unique signatures of his sensibility, are his heroines, particularly Isabel Archer and Milly Theale.' As far as Milly Theale goes, exactly the opposite of this proposition seems to me to be true. James was most beyond Hawthorne's scope when he was drawing on that critical and satiric consciousness evidenced in the above quotation, and in *The Bostonians* we have seen how astonishingly far beyond Hawthorne's scope, James, on such a theme, could really be. It is precisely in a character like Milly Theale that he draws especially near to his predecessor, and nearest, one must add, to some of his predecessor's sorriest aspects. Again, the importance of recognizing the relation resides partly in gauging the extent of James's participation in a prevailing American attitude; and especially the recognition should help to qualify the large over-estimation, as relative to the other works, which has overtaken *The Wings of the Dove* in recent years.

The Marble Faun was the last completed and artistically finished novel that Hawthorne wrote. Despite the opinion that accords *The Blithedale Romance* that unenviable distinction, it seems to me unmistakably the worst of the four major novels, although James was deeply impressed by it. He wrote that 'some of the finest pages in Hawthorne are to be found in it', and he thought there was 'a great deal of interest in the simple combination and opposition of the four actors', a remark that makes one think of *The Golden Bowl*. But before taking up the influence of *The Marble Faun* on James's conception of Milly Theale, I wish to glance at its much earlier effect on one of James's stories, *The Last of the Valerii*, which he had written in 1868. Not only will this suggest how the influence of *The Marble Faun*, making its impression thus early, was granted a remarkably long period of gestation in James's artistic consciousness during which its sown seeds might arrive at *any* maturity—it will reveal most of all how

34

critics have tended to attribute to other writers, generally French, an influence which, when distilled to its primal essence, is recognizably, if not blatantly, Hawthorne's. *The Last of the Valerii* is commonly supposed to have resulted from an early translation which James made of Mérimée's story, *La Venus d'Ille*. The two stories have plots that present, in large measure, parallel constructions. In both of them, pagan statues of goddesses are disinterred on estates belonging to persons in the respective stories, and in both cases the goddesses interfere in the marriages of the two heroes—the interference being supernatural in Mérimée's story, psychological in James's. The resemblance ends here, but it is enough to have persuaded most critics that James took the story over from Mérimée, although several have remarked (Matthiessen among them) on a Hawthornian overtone. But it is precisely that Hawthornian element that is the significant thing in the story, and without which *The Last of the Valerii* would be a piece of lifeless clap-trap. Conte Valerio derives from the pagan-Christian Donatello of *The Marble Faun*. Just as Donatello resembles the Faun of Praxiteles, Conte Valerio 'had a head and throat like some of the busts in the Vatican', and: 'I more than once smiled at her [Martha, Valerio's wife's] archæological zeal, declaring that I believed she had married the Count because he was like a statue of the Decadence.' The young heroine Martha, who is characterized by 'dove-like glances', is described, interestingly enough in view of James's later course, as 'a young American girl who had the air and almost the habits of a princess'. There are many points of resemblance between the two stories as far as plot goes (Donatello, it may be remembered, somewhat pointlessly discovers an antique statue of a beautiful goddess in one of the later chapters of *The Marble Faun*), and particularly there is a similarity in the descriptive passages (Hawthorne's and James's scenes in the Pantheon, for example, should be compared); but I do not wish to emphasize this sort of thing. Where the two stories come very close and very significantly together is in the moral tone—the simultaneous love and fear of the past which was so characteristic of both men, and which, in them, is a peculiarly American note.

35

Much later in this study of Hawthorne and James it will be necessary to examine this attitude with some care, but at this point I can only quote a passage from *The Last of the Valerii* which is perfect Hawthorne, and by no means imperfect James. Mérimée's story is a piece of artificial cleverness, but James's story is a subtle—if still rather young—analysis of the conflict between the past and the present when the sense and weight of tradition and history are unworkably heavy. If the reader is inclined to think that James's view seems very simple here, I do not think the meaning of *The Sense of the Past*, written in James's full maturity, will, in its ultimate distilment, reveal anything more complex. This is the passage:

> The poor Count became, to my imagination, a dark efflorescence of the evil germs which history had implanted in his line. No wonder he was foredoomed to be cruel. Was not cruelty a tradition of his race, and crime an example? The unholy passions of his forefathers revived, incurably, in his untaught nature and clamoured dumbly for an issue. What a heavy heritage it seemed to me, as I reckoned it up in my melancholy musings, the Count's interminable ancestry! Back to the profligate revival of arts and vices—back to the bloody medley of mediæval wars—back through the long, fitfully glaring dusk of the early ages to its ponderous origin in the solid Roman state— back through all the darkness of history it stretched itself, losing every claim on my sympathies as it went. Such a record was in itself a curse. . . .

The Last of the Valerii shares its central moral meaning with Hawthorne, and its indebtedness to him is at the very centre of its life. In making the point at such length I have wished primarily to afford relief against any possible shock in my initial assertion that the most forceful influence shaping James's conception of Milly Theale's character and function came from *The Marble Faun*. Demonstrably it had been a profound influence on a characteristic Jamesian story written when he was only twenty-five, and the influence was not of the kind that ended when the story was finished.

The impression it made was deepest in the case of one of the characters, the little New England copyist, Hilda. James is very explicit in his *Hawthorne* as to the extent to which he responded:

The character of Hilda has always struck me as an admirable invention—one of those things that mark the man of genius. It needed a man of genius and of Hawthorne's imaginative delicacy, to feel the propriety of such a figure as Hilda, and to perceive the relief it would both give and borrow. This pure and somewhat rigid New England girl, following the vocation of a copyist of pictures in Rome, unacquainted with evil and untouched by impurity, has been accidentally the witness, unknown and unsuspected, of the dark deed by which her friends, Miriam and Donatello, are knit together. This is her revelation of evil, her loss of perfect innocence. She has done no wrong, and yet wrong-doing has become a part of her experience, and she carries the weight of her detested knowledge upon her heart. She carries it a long time, saddened and oppressed by it, till at last she can bear it no longer. If I have called the whole idea of the presence and effect of Hilda in the story a trait of genius, the purest touch of inspiration is the episode in which the poor girl deposits her burden. She has passed the whole lonely summer in Rome; and one day, at the end of it, finding herself in St. Peter's, she enters a confessional, strenuous daughter of the Puritans as she is, and pours out her dark knowledge into the bosom of the Church—then comes away with her conscience lightened, not a whit less Puritan than before. If the book contained nothing else noteworthy but this admirable scene, and the pages describing the murder committed by Donatello under Miriam's eyes, and the ecstatic wandering, afterwards, of the guilty couple through the 'blood-stained streets of Rome', it would still deserve to rank high among the imaginative productions of our day.

In view of this expressed admiration for Hilda, the close similarity between the symbolism with which James presents Milly and that with which Hawthorne presents Hilda acquires genuine significance inasmuch as this symbolism carries implicit moral values that shed nearly identical lustres over the two girls. It is odd that this similarity has not been remarked, particularly by Mr. Matthiessen; but

37

Milly Theale has no more ardent admirer among contemporary critics than he, whereas he is very justly repelled by Hilda, seeing her as a self-righteous and impossible prig who affords 'an ugly glimpse of American spiritual life, as it was destined increasingly to become in the decades after the Civil War'. It may not be astonishing then that he has failed to note the likeness, for Milly is a far more attractive girl than Hilda. Nevertheless, she is a direct descendant in the moral line, although by the time her generation has been reached the Puritanism has become civilized beyond easy recognition. In his later book, *Henry James: The Major Phase*, Mr. Matthiessen maintained that James, 'did not, like Mallarmé, start with his symbol. He reached it only with the final development of his theme, and then used it essentially in the older tradition of the poetic metaphor, to give concretion, as well as allusive and beautiful extension of his thought.' I do not wish to discuss the nature of James's symbolism here,[1] but the following passage from *The Marble Faun* looks forward so directly towards the central image of *The Wings of the Dove* that one cannot accept the resemblances as wholly coincidental:

[1] Frankly, I doubt if it is a discussable problem in the terms Mr. Matthiessen uses here. There is a good deal of evidence that some of James's symbols had been in his mind for years before he used them, and if this is so there is no reason why such an image may not have planted the little acorn to which James was so fond of referring. F. R. Leavis has pointed, in *The Great Tradition*, to an anticipation of one of James's most important symbols that seems to contradict Mr. Matthiessen's description of his method of composing. In *The Portrait of a Lady* Madame Merle's concern for her rare porcelain coffee cup looks directly ahead to the central symbol in *The Golden Bowl*. Although Mr. Leavis does not quote the passage in his text, it is important enough in the present argument to be reproduced here:

'I think you're very simple.' And Madame Merle kept her eye on her cup. 'I've come to think that with time. I judged you, as I say, of old; but it's only since your marriage that I've understood you. I've seen better what you have been to your wife than I ever saw what you were for me. Please be very careful of that precious object.'

'It already has a wee bit of a tiny crack,' said Osmund dryly as he put it down.

38

Here she dwelt, in her tower, possessing a friend or two in Rome, but no home companion except the flock of doves, whose cote was in a ruinous chamber contiguous to her own. They soon became as familiar with the fair-haired Saxon girl as if she were a born sister of their brood; and her customary white robe bore such an analogy to their snowy plumage that the confraternity of artists called Hilda the Dove, and recognized her aerial apartment as the Dove-cote. And while the other doves flew far and wide in quest of what was good for them, Hilda likewise spread her wings, and sought such ethereal and imaginative sustenance as God ordains for creatures of her kind.

It is even possible that the title of James's novel was suggested by his memory of one of the phrases above. The image of Hilda the Dove is not, it should be said at once, a random image which Hawthorne has applied in one paragraph and dropped. It is the persistent metaphor, the definitive symbol that occurs everywhere Hilda is discussed. It is in terms of this image that those qualities which James isolated in Hilda for particular praise—her purity and 'perfect innocence'—may be said to exist; and I cannot believe, after the hearty congratulation we have seen James offering Hawthorne for Hilda's character, that the metaphor which is the very essence of it should have failed to leave its mark on James's conscious memory. It is extremely difficult to guess from the *Notebooks* and the 'Preface' to *The Wings* just what the real history of the inception of that novel really was.[1]

[1] There is an early anticipation of *The Wings of the Dove* in an unsuccessful short story, *Georgina's Reasons*, which James first published in 1884. It is worth reading because one sees in it a kind of rough, thumbnail sketch of ideas that were to be developed, years later, into the full-blown novel. There is, for example, an angelic invalid in the earlier story, the similarity of whose name, Mildred Theory, to that of Minny Temple and Milly Theale, Mr. Matthiessen has noted. But he does not note a more important and interesting fact—that Georgina herself is an unpleasant, but nearly unmistakable, anticipation of Kate Croy. James gives us a good deal of reason to qualify the harsh judgment which we would ordinarily bring to the actions of Kate Croy. She is warmly alive, and she engages our sympathies and imagination. The ruthless Georgina is clearly meant to be a selfish monster; but even in Georgina's case, James's imagination

Remembering that James had begun his 'Preface' by saying that '*The Wings of the Dove*, published in 1902, represents to my memory a very old—if I shouldn't perhaps rather say a very young—motive . . .', Mr. Matthiessen (among others) has urged that James had his young cousin, Minny Temple, who died of tuberculosis at the age of twenty-four, in mind when he conceived Milly Theale. This is almost certainly true, but the mere desire, persisting over so many years, to commemorate his early friend, was as likely to introduce a note of forcing into the conception of Milly as it was to create, in Matthiessen's words, 'the most resonant symbol for what he had to say about humanity'. Certainly it embarrassed James when he came to apply those satiric touches by which so many of his earlier young women had been endowed with life. And yet if one goes back to the long quotation above in which James offered his critical analysis of the American woman, and if one compares it item by item with what Milly offers, the similarities are striking. For example, it is as a 'new human convenience' that Milly makes her debut at Lord Mark's:

> The lingering eyes looked her over, the lingering eyes were what went, in almost confessed simplicity, with the pointless 'I say, Mark'; and what was really most sensible of all was that, as a pleasant matter of course, if she didn't mind, he seemed to suggest their letting people, poor dear things, have the benefit of her.

And she is no less 'a huge success of curiosity':

> It was so little her fault, this oddity of what had 'gone round' about her, that to accept it without question might be as good a way as another feeling of life. It was inevitable to supply the

is touched off in her closing scene so that he presents her with an endowment of vitality and beauty—makes her, in short, so impressive, so simply *grand*—that the reader admires her in spite of himself. In comparison with Georgina the fade-away Mildred Theory doesn't exist. It is interesting to note thus early this prophecy of James's true (though not professed) bias when he came to write *The Wings*. It is Kate Croy, not Milly, with whom James is successful, and who, along with magnificent Aunt Maud, really holds his interest.

probable description—that of the awfully rich young American who was so queer to behold, but nice, by all accounts, to know; and she had really but one instant of speculation as to fables or fantasies perchance originally launched.

Such passages could be multiplied, and they show that Milly is pre-eminently a legitimate subject for James's usual observations on the American girl—the kind of observation for which his genius was peculiarly suited—but for whatever reason of his own, James withdrew the usual satiric penalties attaching to such insights, and wishing to spare her, he left her instead the victim of his indulgence. In his earlier work these satiric insights had penetrated to the centre and created the substance of his young women, establishing the richness of their reality; but inasmuch as he was commemorating Minny Temple he would not leave the Dove exposed, nor violate the sentimental memory. And yet so ingrained was the habit that he had to take deliberate precautions. There is an uneasy and uncertain note (which the technical concern so elaborately insisted on in the 'Preface' only nominally explains) when he says, speaking in his own voice in the novel itself: 'She worked—and seemingly quite without design— upon the sympathy, the curiosity, the fancy of her associates, and we shall really ourselves scarce otherwise come closer to her than by feeling their impression and sharing, if need be, their confusion.' This uncertainty sometimes reveals itself in a significant unsteadiness of image of which James himself is conscious:

It was her nature, once for all—a nature that reminded Mrs. Stringham of the term always used in the newspapers about the great new steamers, the inordinate number of 'feet of water' they drew; so that if, in your little boat, you had chosen to hover and approach, you had but yourself to thank, when once motion was started, for the way the draught pulled you. Milly drew the feet of water, and odd though it might seem that a lonely girl, who was not robust and who hated sound and show, should stir the stream like a leviathan, her companion floated off with the sense of rocking violently at her side.

James, of course, likes to build Milly's metaphors on a

grand scale ('When Milly smiled it was a public event—when she didn't it was a chapter of history'), but James is quite right about this image: it does seem odd. In *The Portrait of a Lady*, with a far greater sense of proportion and fitness, James had developed the elements of this metaphor just far enough: 'Madame Merle meanwhile, as lady in waiting to a princess circulating *incognita*, panted a little in her rear.' Both Isabel and Madame Merle emerge respectably from this description. But in the above image from *The Wings* it is clear what has happened: tugging at the satiric leash in spite of himself, and with no solid grasp of Milly to hold him back, James has given her a metaphor completely inappropriate to her because he cannot resist the urge to set Susan Stringham, with whom he is more secure, in her proper and ludicrous glory. But it is Milly who looks more ludicrous—as ludicrous, but not nearly as effective, as that 'truly massive young person' Rosanna Gaw in *The Ivory Tower*, who simultaneously resembles a Burmese palanquin and 'a ship held back from speed yet with its own canvas expanded'. If I seem to make a good deal of the point here, it is because James's slip exhibits so woefully the way he *doesn't* have hold of Milly. It is not really a small thing, and it is an error that he could not conceivably have made with Isabel Archer or little Maisie Farrange or Verena Tarrant. Somewhat later in the novel, when he is dealing, not with Milly but with Aunt Maud, he can bring off a somewhat similar metaphor with his customary success: 'Mrs. Lowder, it was true, steering in the other quarter a course in which she called at subjects as if they were islets in an archipelago, continued to allow them their ease. . . .'

And James has a good deal of trouble with Milly's conversation, for none of his heroines are quite as lacking in animation or wit. James seems almost apologetic for having conferred those qualities in greater abundance on Mrs. Lowder, but nevertheless James is never able to make Milly say anything more clever than her 'weak joke' in the following passage: Mrs. Lowder is speaking first:

'God has been good to me—positively; for I couldn't, at my

age, have made a new friend—undertaken, I mean, out of the whole cloth, the real thing. It's like changing one's bankers—after fifty: one doesn't do that. That's why Susie has been kept for me, as you seem to keep people in your wonderful country, in lavender and pink paper—coming back at last as out of a fairy tale and with you as an attendant fairy.' Milly hereupon replied appreciatively that such a description of herself made her feel as if pink paper were her dress and lavender its trimming; but Aunt Maud was not to be deterred by a weak joke from keeping it up.

Milly's witticism sounds a little like Catherine Sloper, but one may, for the measure of distance between the two novels, compare the reality and significant meaning one senses behind Catherine's little patheticisms with the uninteresting, dull inertness of Milly's response.

There is not space here to accumulate instances of the imperfect artistic realization which James brings to Milly, but one's impression of the kind of unsteadiness noted above is enforced, at quite a different level of imagery, by the elaborate 'art' metaphors by which James seeks to define his subtleties. The most important of them is perhaps too long to quote. It is that attempt to describe the relationship between Milly and Kate Croy by placing them, as it were, in a twilight scene from a Maeterlinck play. The passage, which is the most 'purple' one James must ever have written, is in Chapter XXIV, and the reader who wishes to see how near, on occasion, James could draw to Pater and Arthur Symonds, may turn to it there. In the days when James had dealt with his heroines directly, heroines with whom he felt satirically, critically free (having no personal reasons to feel otherwise), this sort of metaphor would hardly have achieved his purposes, for it leaves James in the end very much where he was when he took it up: on the outside. But James instinctively knew that his apotheosized, his 'royal' Milly was, at centre, just another 'exposed maiden', like the others he had written about, and for the sake of maintaining the difference he dared not penetrate deeper into the human substance than such a *fin de siècle* picture allowed.

43

Faced, then, with such difficulties, the hints that he found in *The Marble Faun* on how to canonize an American girl in a novel must surely have been welcome. Once Milly is deprived of her gilding and courtesy titles of royalty the moral quantity she represents in such an unquestioned way begins to merge at once with that represented by Hilda. It is interesting to note that both novelists applied this moral coating quite deliberately from the outside, setting the girls against suggestive backgrounds, and decorating them with symbols of universally acknowledged value. Here is the process going on in Hawthorne. Miriam is on her way to visit Hilda in her tower studio:

> Miriam passed beneath the deep portal of the palace, and turning to the left, began to mount flight after flight of a staircase, which for the loftiness of its aspiration, was worthy to be Jacob's ladder, or, at all events, the staircase of the Tower of Babel. The city bustle, which is heard even in Rome, the rumble of wheels over the uncomfortable paving-stones, the harsh cries reëchoing in the high and narrow streets, grew faint and died away; as the turmoil of the world will always die, if we set our faces to climb heavenward. Higher, and higher still; and now, glancing through the successive windows that threw in their narrow light upon the stairs, her view stretched across the roofs of the city, unimpeded even by the stateliest palaces. Only the domes of the churches ascend into this airy region, and hold up their golden crosses on a level with her eye; except, that, out of the very heart of Rome, the column of Antoninus thrusts itself upward, with St. Paul upon its summit, the sole human form that seems to have kept her company.

Jacob's ladder, the Tower of Babel, heaven-aspiring staircases, church domes and their crosses, and a statue of St. Paul, are all introduced simply for the purpose of shedding their radiance on Hilda. That there can be no mistake about the application, Hawthorne makes Miriam say to Hilda almost immediately after the above paragraph:

> 'You breathe sweet air, above all the evil scents of Rome; and even so, in your maiden elevation, you dwell above our vanities

44

and passions, our moral dust and mud, with the doves and the angels for your nearest neighbors. I should not wonder if the Catholics were to make a saint of you, like your namesake of old. . . .'

Of course the 'elevation' is significant, lifting Hilda above commonness, just as it does Milly in her Venetian palace in the following passage:

The romance for her, yet once more, would be to sit there for ever, through all her time, as in a fortress; and the idea became an image of never going down, of remaining aloft in the divine, dustless air, where she would hear but the plash of water against stone. The great floor on which they moved was at an altitude, and this prompted the rueful fancy. 'Ah, not to go down—never, never to go down!' she strangely sighed to her friend.

'But why shouldn't you,' he asked, 'with that tremendous old staircase in your court? There ought of course always to be people at top and bottom, in Veronese costumes, to watch you do it.'

James's Dove, carrying as she does the title of 'heiress of all the ages', benefits by the reference to the Veronese costumes in the same way that Hawthorne's Dove benefits by the numerous references to religious objects surrounding her studio, and by so many people calling her a Catholic saint. Apart from the central Dove symbol, which becomes a structural device in both novels, and apart from the manner in which the novelists build up their heroines from the outside, there are other fainter echoes of Hawthorne in *The Wings*. In view of James's great admiration for the scene in which Hilda confesses herself in St. Peter's, Milly's speech to Kate Croy on leaving Sir Luke Strett's office after her first interview seems particularly pointed: 'I feel—I can't otherwise describe it—as if I had been, on my knees, to the priest. I've confessed and I've been absolved. It has been lifted off.' A more evasive, but larger and more important resemblance, exists in the situations of the two girls themselves—the similarity of their natures being revealed under the pressure of a

45

moral affliction not their own. Both Hilda and Milly are incorruptibly pure—indeed, positively purifying in their effect on others. (Hilda 'purified the objects of her regard by the mere act of turning such spotless eyes on them'; while Milly, as Kate Croy affirms in the end, has taken both Densher and herself under her wings, and Densher at least is sanctified by that token.) Hilda loses her innocence by proxy, as it were, when she sees her friends commit a crime; and while James is never quite clear as to how much Milly has guessed about the extent of Kate's treachery, the presumption may safely be that she has guessed literally *everything*. At any rate, it kills her, just as Hilda's knowledge of Miriam's guilt induces a psychological crisis of the utmost gravity. Both the Doves are personally stainless, but the guilt of others is unbearable to them; they are both incapable of submitting to the profane touch of the world, or of taking the shock of another's evil. If one now glances back at James's comments on Hilda's character which were quoted earlier it becomes increasingly difficult not to suppose that James's attitude towards Milly must surely have found its reassuring and natively American precedent in *The Marble Faun*: for if Minny Temple is the ultimate source of Milly Theale, Hawthorne's Dove yet seems to have been the only and the perfect artistic model, the fictional prototype.

There are other points of approach as well. The extent to which James took over Hawthorne's device of endowing ancient portraits with extraordinary resemblances to the living has been frequently enough noted by other critics. There are no less than four distinct resemblances of this nature remarked on in *The Marble Faun*, and they are introduced to ends not unlike that which James had in view when Lord Mark shows Milly the Bronzino which her own features resemble. But the only value of items like this is that they understudy the central and important relation that exists between the Doves. To sum up the traits which these two have in common, one would say that the sinlessness of them both is emphasized. They are angels pure and simple. In Milly's case this aspect is minimized, not only because the fashion had changed considerably, but because James wished to show her off as primarily the culminating point of the past, 'the heiress of all the ages'. Whatever else his intention was in doing this, it is obvious that such a conception would reduce the tension in that ambivalent attitude to the past which James shared with Hawthorne. In Milly's gold-filled, American, de-verminizing hands the past might, after all, be soaped and combed into acceptability. Some similar idea must have been gnawing in Hawthorne's thought, for Hilda, the expert little copyist, is an heiress of all the ages in no mean fashion herself:

> If a picture had darkened into an indistinct shadow through time and neglect, or had been injured by cleaning, or retouched by some profane hand, she seemed to possess the faculty of seeing it in its pristine glory. The copy would come from her hands with what the beholder felt must be the light which the old master had left upon the original in bestowing his final and most etherial touch. In some instances even (at least, so those believed who most appreciated Hilda's power and sensibility) she had been enabled to execute what the old master had conceived in his imagination, but had not so perfectly succeeded in putting upon canvas; a result surely not impossible when such depth of sympathy as she possessed was assisted by the delicate skill and accuracy of her slender hand. In such cases the girl was but the finer instrument, a more exquisitely effective piece of mechanism, by the help of which the spirit of some great departed painter now first achieved his ideal, centuries after his own earthly hand, that other tool, had turned to dust.

Obviously both the girls are out to improve the past, but in comparison with Milly's regal ability to buy it up, this mode of recapture seems comparatively subtle. Point by point the notes arrange themselves, and in the end the attributes of the Doves total up to very nearly the same figure. Milly's 'Princess' equates with Hilda's 'Saint', and both girls have a treasure of gilt-edged metaphors deposited in their names enabling them to draw lavishly on dividends that neither one of them has done much to earn in her respective novel. It would seem that James had been 'taken in' by Hilda in a way he hadn't been 'taken in' by Priscilla and Zenobia when he wrote *The Bostonians*, and that the earlier James was capable of profiting in a sharper manner from Hawthorne's art than was the case later on.

I have emphasized the relation between Milly Theale and Minny Temple up to now because it seemed to personalize James's conception of Milly's character in a critically pertinent way. Such commemorative intentions on the part of a writer are frequently inhibiting, and something very similar may have contributed in Hawthorne's case to the failure of Hilda. We know that Hawthorne was in the habit of addressing Mrs. Hawthorne, in his letters to her, as his 'Dove', and the particular kind of moral effulgence that adorns Hilda is the sort of thing against which one must be braced constantly in Mrs. Hawthorne's letters. But Milly has to be viewed in a deeper perspective than this, and I bear in mind the analysis of her character and function that Mr. Quentin Anderson has offered in his extraordinary and valuable essay, 'Henry James and the New Jerusalem'.[1] It will be recalled that Mr. Anderson, examining the relation between the novels of James and his father's psychology and theology, discovered in the son's work, and particularly in the three late novels, a symbolic presentation of the elder James's doctrines—and to such an extent that these novels show in something of the fashion of fictionalized moralities. From the viewpoint of James's intention Mr. Anderson can be extremely convincing, and not least so in his analysis of *The Wings of the Dove* where Milly, the American girl, is shown to be the 'representative of divine love', redeeming mankind in the person of Merton Densher from the constrictive and appropriative love which is an inversion of the Divinity immanent in men. The rescue is effected in terms of the perfect selflessness of Milly's love, as contrasted with the acquisitive instincts on which Kate Croy's love, which is merely the love of phenomenal appearances, is based. Accepting this interpretation as more or less correct insofar as the meaning of *The Wings of the Dove* goes, what I wish to suggest is that the novelist capable of building such a construct would

[1] *The Kenyon Review*, autumn, 1946.

almost inevitably have found a treasure of suggestiveness in *The Marble Faun*. Although it will necessitate something like a recapitulation of points already made, I should like to consider here the relation between Hilda and Milly from the point of view of Mr. Anderson's analysis of *The Wings*. To do so has the double effect, for me at any rate, of adding its own note of persuasion to an already highly convincing case —there was, I conclude, the incipience of something just this outlandish long hanging in the American air—and it helps to reveal a weakness in Milly, an inherited taint, that was something more than a matter of blood or lungs.

The Marble Faun is unmistakably, but a little awkwardly, an allegory on the Fall of Man. Donatello, allegedly the descendant of a faun who, in some antique and guiltless age is said to have fallen in love with a daughter of the Monte Beni family and founded a line, appears to have inherited not only some of the physical characteristics of his remote ancestor, but also the profound Golden Age innocence of the founding faun. He falls in love with Miriam, a member of the Roman art colony, a beautiful girl who bears some secret guilt with her. It is important to note that Miriam is wholly a European product, with high family connections in the Papal government hinted at. The nature of her crime is carefully concealed, but it is clearly part of the texture of the institutionalized and crumbling un-American past that Hawthorne could not help being troubled by. This fact is made unmistakably clear when Miriam's partner in crime is revealed to have been a Capuchin monk. Hawthorne obviously chose the Capuchins because of the famous cemetery of the Cappuccini in Rome where the skeletons of the decomposed friars are on view—a setting that gave him an opportunity to be as explicit as a New Englander could wish about what he thought of the bones of the past. Miriam uses Donatello's love for her to involve him in her own guilt, and from that moment he loses his original innocence and enters a life of endless penance. Now the action and tragedy is centred in these two Europeans, but on the outskirts of that action we have the two Americans, Kenyon the sculptor and Hilda the copyist, keenly aware of the good vibrations from the past, especially as these are transmissible through art objects, but immune to any of those malign influences that have corrupted Miriam and Donatello. Hilda's function is to act as a kind of symbol of absolute good—so absolute, in fact, that she is essentially out of relation with any of the 'fallen' characters except insofar as the very rational Kenyon is able to make an occasional practical application of her highfalutin morality to the lowly estate of the merely human characters in the story. I say 'merely human' with a sense of how more-than-human Hawthorne seems to wish Hilda, for the final and cumulative effect, to appear. She differs from Miriam not so much in not having fallen, but most radically in her practical inability to fall. Kenyon, for example, says of Hilda:

> 'Her womanhood is of the etherial type, and incompatible with any shadow of darkness or evil.'
> 'You are right,' rejoined Miriam; 'there are women of that etherial type as you term it, and Hilda is one of them. She would die of her first wrong-doing—supposing for a moment that she could be capable of doing wrong.'

Read in the full context of the novel, which is literally overgrown with similar lush specimens, such compliments cannot be interpreted as figurative. In the end the intention seems to be that they should literally apply; and though for convention's sake Hilda is content to allow that she is only, even weakly, human, she never seems wholly convinced of the fact. On her first meeting with Miriam after learning of the latter's guilt, she immediately rejects her friendship in these terms:

> 'If I were one of God's angels, with a nature incapable of stain, and garments that never could be spotted, I would keep ever at your side, and try to lead you upward. But I am a poor, lonely girl, whom God has set here in an evil world, and given her only a white robe, and bid her wear it back to Him, as white as when she put it on. Your powerful magnetism would be too much for me. The pure, white atmosphere, in which I try to discern what things are good and true, would be discolored. And, therefore, Miriam, before it is too late, I mean to put faith

50

in this awful heart-quake, which warns me henceforth to avoid you.'

Miriam greedily seizes this occasion for again asserting her belief in Hilda's super-human virtue: 'You have no sin, nor any conception of what it is; and therefore you are so terribly severe! As an angel you are not amiss; but as a human creature, and a woman among earthly men and women, you need a sin to soften you.' Hilda shows her willingness to accept this evaluation of herself, and describes the only kind of universe she would find tolerable:

> 'While there is a single guilty person in the universe, each innocent one must feel his innocence tortured by that guilt. Your deed, Miriam, has darkened the whole sky!'
>
> Poor Hilda turned from her unhappy friend, and, sinking on her knees in a corner of the chamber, could not be prevailed upon to utter another word. And Miriam, with a long regard from the threshold, bade farewell to this doves' nest, this one little nook of pure thoughts and innocent enthusiasms, into which she had brought such trouble. Every crime destroys more Edens than our own.

I have said that the masculine counterpart of Hilda is the American, Kenyon. He participates in the same exalted sentiments, but being 'practical' he can communicate them to the Europeans in a way that is denied to the more exquisite and etherial American Dove. Knowing that Donatello and Miriam are both involved in the same guilt, he suggests a union to them for the sake of mutual encouragement in penance. His manner of speech relates him to Hilda very closely:

> 'Not for earthly bliss, therefore,' said Kenyon, 'but for mutual elevation, and encouragement towards a severe and painful life, you take each other's hands. And if out of toil, sacrifice, prayer, penitence, and earnest effort towards right things, there comes, at length, a sombre and thoughtful happiness, taste it, and thank Heaven!'

But Kenyon is not the incorruptible fountain of grace that

Hilda is. He is capable of asking, 'Did Adam fall that we might ultimately rise to a far loftier paradise than his?' The impeccable Hilda, whose moral theology is unerring, replies:

> 'Oh, hush! . . . This is terrible; and I could weep for you, if you indeed believe it. Do not you perceive what a mockery your creed makes, not only of all religious sentiments, but of moral law? and how it annuls and obliterates whatever precepts of Heaven are written deepest within us? You have shocked me beyond words!'

After this he can only propose marriage, seeing in such a union an unbeatable team:

> '. . . the mind wanders wild and wide; and, so lonely as I live and work, I have neither pole-star above nor light of cottage windows here below, to bring me home. Were you my guide, my counsellor, my inmost friend, with that white wisdom which clothes you as a celestial garment, all would go well. O Hilda, guide me home!'

'Home' to such a pair as this can only mean America, and they postpone their return no longer, for Hawthorne has made it clear all along that their moral tone and achievement has its specific national origin, and can only be permanently sustained in the pure New England air.

I have offered these quotations because they illustrate the extent to which the aura of exaltedness that surrounds Hilda is not meant to be one simply of atmosphere or effect, but is meant to cut out a solid moral reality. Naturally, on such a showing Hilda is a dismal failure artistically. The moral reality that she is supposed to embody, although fuzzily conceived, is clearly enough stated to reveal its radical falseness. It has no counterpart in reality. It is as impossible in the world of imagination as it is in life. By the time Hawthorne got around to creating Hilda he was irrevocably ruined as an artist. And yet we have James's own words describing the intensity of his admiration. It was Hilda that he particularly liked.

Assuming that Mr. Anderson's analysis of *The Wings of the Dove* is essentially correct, it is easy to see what James must have discovered—or thought he discovered—in Hawthorne's novel, even as early as the *Hawthorne* of 1879. The guilt of the past, so largely European, is revealed in all its musty squalor by the contrasting purity of a young girl who, being an American, has no part in that heritage of crime and misery that belongs to the Old World. This girl is a 'saint' (we have everybody's word for it) who purifies by her mere presence. Hawthorne erred, of course, by making her apotheosis so complete that no one except Kenyon, who obviously doesn't need it, can rise to the rarefied levels where her regenerative influence might be effective. But the sanctifying force that is implicit in the Dove image is to be taken just as seriously in Hilda's case as it is in Milly's. She has a mystic sympathy with everything good in the past, particularly when this good is communicable through art objects, but she is so sensitive to evil that the mere presence of a guilty person in the universe is terrible torture to her. The reason of her existence seems to be to set an impossible example in moral perfection unattainable by ordinary and non-American mortals. Everybody defers to Hilda in the same way that everybody defers to Milly, and if James is extremely diffident about approaching Milly except by indirection, we can be grateful to Hawthorne for revealing something of what James might have seen if he had ever got around to giving Milly a straight, hard look. It wasn't, one can't help suspecting, altogether a matter of technical preoccupation that made James deem it wise to cultivate the oblique glance in Milly's direction. Unlike Hilda, Milly is certainly not repulsive, although she takes other people's exaggerated opinions of her worth with irritating complacency. She has, at any rate, a civilized manner. But the girls are sisters under the symbol, and it is a symbol that fails to convince one that its value is valid in either novel. James beautifully refurbished its feathers for a far better showing than it had had in *The Marble Faun* (parts of *The Wings*—those parts that don't deal with Milly—are among James's finest work), but it still remained a little stuffed Dove that 'the restless analyst' had more or less filched from

53

Hawthorne's effects, and it was nothing less than cruel in James to expect a bird like that, instead of a sprig, to carry in its delicate beak the tremendous cedar of meaning that Mr. Anderson has revealed to us.

4
THE AMERICAN PROBLEM

IT might be useful here to recall the two principal points that have already emerged from the foregoing pages. In discussing *The Blithedale Romance* and *The Bostonians* an attempt was made to show how Hawthorne provided James with an artistic precedent for dealing with American attitudes and material. If it is argued that the material was there for the taking, even without Hawthorne, we know that James chose to approach it through the way laid out for him by his compatriot. Later, in discussing *The Marble Faun* and *The Wings of the Dove*, we saw how both men were swayed by a moral bias in favour of America so considerable that their art could no longer perfectly discipline their partiality. The two James novels that have been dealt with here belong to the early and late periods of his career so that Hawthorne's influence is seen to be a constant factor. But the two Hawthorne novels that have been discussed are not his best works, and it would be a mistake to imagine that it was these that made the chief impression on James. In 1870 William James wrote to his brother that he had just been reading *The House of Seven Gables*, and he said:

> I little expected so *great* a work. It's like a great symphony with no touch alterable without injury to the harmony. It made a deep impression on me and I thank Heaven that Hawthorne was an American. It also tickled my national feeling not a little to note the resemblance of Hawthorne's style to yours and Howells's. . . . That you and Howells with all the models in English literature to follow, should needs involuntarily have imitated (as it were) this American, seems to point to the existence of some real American quality.

To which Henry James replied: 'I'm glad you've been liking Hawthorne. But I mean to write as good a novel one of these days (perhaps) as *The House of Seven Gables*.'

William James's remark leads us away from the two late

55

novels that have been discussed here to the two earlier master-pieces, *The Scarlet Letter* and *Seven Gables*, and it leads us into a difficulty. If one senses the greater effect of these novels on James's style—an effect proportionately greater as their genius is greater—one cannot discuss the indebtedness in those relatively tangible terms and propositions that were employed in discussing *Blithedale* and *The Marble Faun*. What one is most aware of is a kind of sympathy between the two men, a sympathy that brings them close together and harmonizes their voices. But 'sympathy' is not quite as vague a word as it sounds. It is possible to mark out its field of operation and to analyse to some extent the reasons for its existence. It exists as an affinity rising out of similar problems faced in similar manners. Once the problem is isolated it may be possible to see how it got out of hand at last, producing such figures as Hilda and Milly. For the failure of these two young women is directly related to an uncertainty in their authors when they deal with the problem in question. The problem is basically the problem of Europe *versus* America, and conjointly with that, the problem of past *versus* present, and both the past and present *versus* the future, the time problem being only another aspect of the geographical one. The conditions under which the two men attempted to solve the problem were different—all the luck was with James from the start, and very little was with Hawthorne—but however disguised, this conflict between their native allegiances and the centrifugal compulsions of temperament lies at the basis of their resemblance.

The problem is easy to come at in James. It was the wholly conscious concern of his art—almost, one might say, his chief incentive to work, and he analysed it with an unprecedented wealth of knowledge. On the other hand, it is doubtful if Hawthorne was ever conscious of the problem in the same way that James was. At best, he was conscious of it by fits and starts, and he was ill-equipped by background to handle it deliberately. It was too hot a subject for his provincial training, which is not to say anything to his discredit. But he suffered intensely from the tensions that the problems set up. These tensions, which he had been able to utilize effectively in his earlier work, became increasingly intractable, and from the time he visited England as American Consul for Liverpool in 1853 they grew unmanageable in his art. There is a sense in which Hawthorne's art undergoes a long and agonizing martyrdom at the hands of the problem—a problem that he never subjected (despite some penetrating insights in *The English Notebooks*) to the fullest illumination of critical inquiry. But it was a martyrdom without which the international novel of James might not have developed so easily.

The most convenient approach to the problem in Hawthorne is by way of a more widely noted but subsidiary problem in his work—his concern with solitude as a 'crime'. This concern is at the centre of his relation with America, and in understanding it one has made a substantial advance on the other problem. Hawthorne's failure to find an American society in which he might function effectively as an artist initiated a habit of withdrawal during the twelve years after he left Bowdoin College in Maine, but this habit was associated in his mind with a mastering sense of guilt that, in the end, led to an over-emphasis on American positives—an over-emphasis without much conviction because it was centred in the fact that the positives were simply American, which came to be accepted as the essential guarantee. We have already seen this happening in *The Marble Faun*, and it is important to bear in mind that the sharpness with which the conflict between the American and European traditions is drawn in that novel is largely the result of Hawthorne's lifelong inability to adjust himself practically to the society that, as an American, he wished to believe in. He wished to express his solidarity with it, and this became a nervous necessity in that degree in which he found it difficult to cast aside his dissatisfactions with it. To state the case succinctly: Hawthorne's compulsive affirmation of American positives, particularly in the political sense, led to a rejection of the idea of solitude; and solitude as an expression of aristocratic withdrawal sided with Europe rather than America when the two traditions stated their respective claims. But unfortunately it also seemed to side with the practice of his art. If one may for a moment be guilty of a heavy-handed

57   E

lining up against each other of elements that were never quite so distinct in Hawthorne's mind, one might say that on one side there was an attraction to solitude, an appreciation of Europe, and a love of the past. This was the side on which Hawthorne's deepest sympathies were engaged, but it was also the side that he distrusted. On the other, there was his democratic and egalitarian denial of solitude, a nervous affirmation of the superiority of America against all comers, and the logically consequential championship of the present and future against the past. Now the tragedy of Hawthorne's case is that his art aligned itself with the side his American conscience could not support, and although Hawthorne conscripted it for the interests he had deliberately chosen, it was always likely to desert at a moment's notice. The pity is that it didn't desert more often. In stating these conclusions in this way before the evidence has been presented, I can only plead the exacerbating tenuity of the issues as they seem to exist in Hawthorne's work. They are as elusive as fog fires, and in threading our way through so much murkiness (even if of a twilight and lovely quality) it is just as well to keep a little map at hand from the first.

The hardships confronting a writer in America before the Civil War were extreme, and Hawthorne encountered almost insuperable difficulties in getting his early work published. There is no need to dwell on these difficulties in detail except to say that they were in some measure the result of conditions accidentally promoted by the political ideals in which Hawthorne believed. His short story, *The Devil in Manuscript*, is entirely autobiographical when he causes Oberon, the author in the piece, to burn his manuscripts (as Hawthorne had burned his own in a fit of discouragement) saying:

'I will burn them! Not a scorched syllable shall escape! Would you have me a damned author?—To undergo sneers, taunts, abuse, and cold neglect, and faint praise, bestowed for pity's sake, against the giver's conscience! A hissing and a laughing stock to my own traitorous thoughts! An outlaw from the protection of the grave—one whose ashes every careless foot might spurn, unhonoured in life, and remembered scornfully in death! Am I to bear all this, when younder fire will insure me from the whole? No! There go the tales! May my hand wither when it would write another!'

In causing the sparks from Oberon's manuscripts to roar up the chimney and set fire to the offending town Hawthorne took a very neat, if somewhat vicarious, revenge on the people who had neglected him, and there is a particular bite in the fact that he arranged the fire for a bitterly cold night when all the pumps were frozen.

The guilt which Hawthorne associated with his predilections for solitude—predilections growing naturally out of a society that could reduce Oberon to such a plight—he described (to choose among a number of possible alternatives) in *Ethan Brand*. This is an indictment of solitude in its largest social sense, but it is a failure because the villain of the piece, Ethan Brand himself, is the only character who has any dignity or seems to have any decency. Twenty years before the night on which the story occurs, Ethan Brand had set out from his native village on a typically Hawthornian quest —to find the Unpardonable Sin. He found it only when he

> . . . had ceased to partake of the universal throb. He had lost his hold of the magnetic chain of humanity. He was no longer a brother-man, opening the chambers or the dungeons of our common nature by the key of holy sympathy, which gave him a right to share in all its secrets; he was now a cold observer, looking on mankind as the subject of his experiment, and, at length, converting man and woman to be his puppets, and pulling the wires that moved them to such degrees of crime as were demanded for his study.

Hawthorne concludes somewhat flatly: 'Thus Ethan Brand became a fiend.' It is noticeable that the description of Ethan Brand's 'crime' sounds suspiciously as if he had become a novelist.[1] At any rate, it seems to point to an irreconcilable

---

[1] Hawthorne drew a self-portrait in the person of Miles Coverdale, the detached and analytic observer of *Blithedale* whom Henry James admired so much, seeming to find in him almost a portrait of himself. But Hol-

conflict in Hawthorne between the demands of his genius and the demands he deemed American society to make on the citizen. He may not have formulated the conflict quite that sharply, but throughout his life it continued to carry on its insidious undermining. In *The Devil in Manuscript* we saw the personal anguish, ending in frustration and social alienation, that Hawthorne experienced from the position of American artists;[1] in *Ethan Brand* we saw how this personal anguish became identified in the citizen's mind with an assertive sense of guilt. A third element enters the picture in a story

grave, the young daguerreotypist in *The House of Seven Gables*, is hardly less a portrait of certain aspects of Hawthorne's character than Miles Coverdale is. Hawthorne causes Holgrave to speak of himself in these terms:

'But you have no conception what a different kind of heart mine is from your own. It is not my impulse, as regards these two individuals, either to help or hinder; but to look on, to analyse, to explain matters to myself, and to comprehend the drama which, for almost two hundred years, has been dragging its slow length over the ground where you and I now tread. If permitted to witness the close, I doubt not to derive a moral satisfaction from it, go matters how they may.'

Obviously young Holgrave was another 'restless analyst' who ought to have been writing novels intead of taking pictures, and it is not fantastic to interpret this as Hawthorne's personal comment on himself as artist. Holgrave is certainly not presented as a villain, but it is difficult to discover much difference between Ethan Brand's 'crime' and Holgrave's description of his own heart. Juxtaposing these passages one sees the seeds of an impossible dilemma in Hawthorne's practice that would eventually mean its ruin.

[1] One should also bear in mind this revealing passage from the Introduction to *The Scarlet Letter*:

'Either of these stern and black-browed Puritans would have thought it quite a sufficient retribution for his sins that after so long a lapse of years the old trunk of the family tree, with so much venerable moss upon it, should have borne, at its topmost bough, an idler like myself. No aim that I have ever cherished would they recognize as laudable; no success of mine, if my life, beyond its domestic scope, had ever been brightened by success, would they deem otherwise than worthless, if not positively disgraceful. "What is he?" murmurs one grey shadow of my forefathers to the other. "A writer of story-books! What kind of a

like *Wakefield*. Wakefield is a man who says goodbye to his wife one day on the pretence of going on a short journey. Instead, for no explicable reason, he takes lodgings in an adjacent street and remains hidden from view for twenty years. He is thought to be dead by his wife and friends, but at the end of that time, again for no explicable reason, he returns one cold and rainy autumn night to the house he had left so many years before. He mounts the stairs and he rejoins his startled widow. The real theme of the story is the question of why Wakefield stayed away for twenty years in solitude. 'He had lost', as Hawthorne says, 'the perception of singularity in his conduct'; but the crux of the matter seems to be that if one has a vigorous will from the first there will be no danger of losing one's active place in society. Not to assert one's will is to 'lose hold of the magnetic chain of humanity', as Ethan Brand had done, and to become a 'fiend'. One can't help observing that Oberon in burning his manuscripts—that is, by a deliberate act of the will—presumably expiated in some degree his offence against society—his separateness, as it were. But Ethan Brand had only one recourse—to burn himself by jumping into the flaming lime kiln. It was probably —one can't resist the conclusion—a deliberate effort of the will that caused Hawthorne to attempt to deal with contemporary life in his late novels. But an exercise of the will is not necessarily an artistic success.

In speaking of these three stories I have not wished to introduce them as first-rate specimens of Hawthorne's art. They are not. But they reveal much about Hawthorne's conception of solitude, and we can trace the elements that have been singled out here functioning successfully in Hawthorne's greatest work, *The Scarlet Letter*. This is not an allegory on the woman taken in adultery, but a subtle exploration of moral isolation in America. The following is a key-passage describ-

> business in life, what manner of glorifying God, or being serviceable to mankind in his day and generation, may that be? Why, the degenerate fellow might as well have been a fiddler!" Such are the compliments bandied between my great grandsires and myself across the gulf of time! And yet, let them scorn me as they will, strong traits of their nature have intertwined themselves with mine.'

ing the ultimate character of the punishment dealt out to Hester Prynne:

> With her native energy of character, and rare capacity, it [the world] could not entirely cast her off, although it had set a mark upon her, more intolerable to a woman's heart than that which branded the brow of Cain. In all her intercourse with society, however, there was nothing that made her feel as if she belonged to it. Every gesture, every word, and even the silence of those with whom she came in contact, implied, and often expressed, that she was banished, and as much alone as if she inhabited another sphere, or communicated with the common nature by other organs and senses than the rest of human kind. She stood apart from moral interests, yet close beside them, like a ghost that revisits the familiar fireside, and can no longer make itself seen or felt; no more smile with the household joy, nor mourn with the kindred sorrow; or, should it succeed in manifesting its forbidden sympathy, awakening only terror and horrible repugnance. These emotions, in fact, and its bitterest scorn besides, seemed to be the sole portion that she retained in the universal heart.

There is a sense in which this is also, like *The Devil in Manuscript*, a commentary on the sanctions directed against the artist, and one feels that the richly embroidered A on Hester's breast might stand for Artist almost as easily as Adultress. To that extent even *The Scarlet Letter* is autobiographical.

Hawthorne's best writing deals with the past, but it is not a past that constitutes a moral retreat from the present, for it was in images of Colonial history that he was able to deal most directly and intelligibly with his own contemporary problems, the things that concerned him most nearly. The reasons for this were the thinness of the American scene—a thinness about which he could be very explicit—and that sense of alienation which was partly the result of the thinness, and which made him ill at ease in dealing with contemporary life. Hawthorne was most contemporary when he was dealing with the American past, and it was there that his critical consciousness was brought most finely into play. One is tempted to say that during his best creative years Hawthorne expatriated himself in time no less than Henry James was to do geographically a few years later. For both men the immediate pressure of the American scene was the reverse of stimulating, and yet it was irrevocably their subject. But it was a subject that had to be seen at an angle and from a proper distance. In this American past—a past in which, incidentally, he acquired an extensive erudition—Hawthorne was able to make discriminations that would be impossible for him later on. In *The Marble Faun* we saw how unhappily Hawthorne could handle the conflict between the American and European traditions, but on the ground of Colonial history he was capable of no such crudeness. He understood perfectly the separate strands that went into the making of American culture, and he was able, with a fine historical sense, to distinguish and evaluate them with unobtrusive tact. It was only when his exigent conscience harried him into the present that his touch became unsteady. For an example of Hawthorne at his best, here is a description of Governor Bellingham's garden from Chapter VII of *The Scarlet Letter*:

> Pearl, accordingly, ran to the bow-window, at the farther end of the hall, and looked along the vista of the garden walk, carpeted with closely shaven grass, and bordered with some rude and immature attempt at shrubbery. But the proprietor appeared already to have relinquished, as hopeless, the effort to perpetuate on this side of the Atlantic, in a hard soil and amid the close struggle for subsistence, the native English taste for ornamental gardening. Cabbages grew in plain sight; and a pumpkin-vine, rooted at some distance, had run across the intervening space, and deposited one of its gigantic products directly beneath the hall window; as if to warn the Governor that this great lump of vegetable gold was as rich an ornament as New England would offer him. There were a few rose-bushes, however, and a number of apple trees, probably the descendants of those planted by the Reverend Mr. Blackstone, the first settler of the peninsula; that half-mythological personage, who rides through our early annals seated on the back of a bull.

The contrast between the English tradition and the American modification being imposed on it is so subtly introduced here that it almost passes without notice. But Hawthorne has achieved a delicate weighing of the two components in which a critical assessment is implicit. The easy, blatant triumph of the pumpkin-vine in the Governor's garden relates itself effectively to the emergence of those attitudes and qualities from which American culture would have to grow, and with a just decorum it is not the rose bushes but the pumpkin-vine and its great lump of vegetable gold that Hawthorne offers as the chief visual attraction in the garden—a decoration entirely appropriate and functional. Immediately after the above paragraph Governor Bellingham, with a group of friends, is seen approaching the house down one of the garden avenues:

> Governor Bellingham, in a loose gown and easy cap—such as elderly gentlemen loved to endue themselves with, in their domestic privacy—walked foremost, and appeared to be showing off his estate, and expatiating on his projected improvements. The wide circumference of an elaborate ruff, beneath his grey beard, in the antiquated fashion of King James's reign, caused his head to look not a little like that of John the Baptist on a charger. The impression made by his aspect, so rigid and severe, and frost-bitten with more than autumnal age, was hardly in keeping with the appliances of worldly enjoyment wherewith he had evidently done his utmost to surround himself.

The passage continues, describing in similar detail the companions of Governor Bellingham. This group of black-gowned men, officials and divines, who carry such a weight of European history on their shoulders, who announce it in their very dress and the cut of their beards, following, as they do, hard on the reference to the Reverend Mr. Blackstone seated on the back of a bull, point in a highly dramatic way to that strange blend of ingredients that was producing America. The theme of the English-America contrast is nowhere stated here. It grows out of the details of the picture as naturally as a tree might grow in Governor Bellingham's garden. The control and relevance is so subordinated to the evolving dramatic situation that one may easily overlook its

64

presence. The two fragments that have been quoted are only snippets that lose a great deal out of context, but even in such a piecemeal state it is apparent that Hawthorne could invoke this cultural contrast with a high degree of success. In *The Scarlet Letter* he was able to resolve the contrast artistically; but as he came to focus his attention on the nearer scene, the cleavage between the cultures deepened, and for Hawthorne at least the tension became unmanageable. I have already spoken of Governor Bellingham's pumpkin-vine, and it may be taken as a minor instance of how this resolution was effected. The rude but democratic pumpkin, obtruding itself with peasant manners almost into the Governor's reception hall, both identifies the short-comings of the country and embellishes its virtues. Hawthorne's hand is very sure: the lovely trellising vine, the echo of Milton's Edenic 'vegetable gold', its friendly familiarity— all this tempers one's regrets that the ornamental gardening was unsuccessful. It is easy to understand how many such images operating with equal effectiveness and subtlety in the same direction can resolve the antagonism that Hawthorne failed to keep under control in *The Marble Faun*. But more important still is the fact that the conflict presented itself under different colours in Colonial history. It was not self-conscious in the way it became after the Revolution; it was not even a conflict as much as it was the sense of something new evolving—a positive character in the process of formation, offering the possibility of critical examination rather than of choice between alternatives. As long as Hawthorne worked in this particular past he was comparatively at ease, for the atmosphere had much of the density that Hawthorne, like James, missed in the America of that day. In a passage from the Preface to *The Marble Faun*, closely resembling a more famous passage from James,[1] Hawthorne wrote:

No author, without a trial, can conceive of the difficulty of writing a romance about a country where there is no shadow,

[1] This is the passage from James, or at least part of it: 'No State, in the European sense of the word, and indeed barely a specific national name. No sovereign, no court, no personal loyalty, no aristocracy, no church, no

no antiquity, no mystery, no picturesque and gloomy wrong, nor anything but a commonplace prosperity, in broad and simple daylight, as is happily the case with my dear native land. It will be very long, I trust, before romance writers may find congenial and easily handled themes, either in the annals of our stalwart republic, or in any characteristic and probable events of our individual lives. Romance and poetry, ivy, lichens, and wall flowers, need ruins to make them grow.

That was written in 1859, from Leamington Spa, after Hawthorne had been in Europe for six years, and it shows symptoms of unmistakable strain. One senses an animus behind the double-edged compliments to his 'dear native land', but at the same time he is unable to praise Europe for anything but its ruins. The fineness of perception that we glanced at in *The Scarlet Letter* has gone, and we know what a fiasco he made of *The Marble Faun*. When Hawthorne deserted Colonial history for the contemporary scene he lost, somewhat paradoxically, his grasp of contemporary problems. If it is objected that *The House of Seven Gables* is a contemporary novel, its success still resides in that sense of the past that suffuses its pages, and which Hawthorne, characteristically, is bent on condemning. He did not have the knowledge or the personal security to deal with cultural antagonisms as such that James took as his special province, and when he allowed them to emerge as the dominant theme in his work he became confused, biased, and ineffectual. He had made his real settlement with Colonial history. But we have seen how his fear of solitude combined with a fear of the past, and led him

clergy, no army, no diplomatic service, no country gentlemen, no palaces, no castles, nor manors, nor old country-houses, nor parsonages, nor thatched cottages, nor ivied ruins; no cathedrals, nor abbeys, nor little Norman churches; no great Universities nor public schools—no Oxford, nor Eton, nor Harrow; no literature, no novels, no museums, no pictures, no political society, no sporting class—no Epsom nor Ascot!'

James's enumeration is the more affecting when we realize that he is listing the things of which Hawthorne was deprived as an American, and which might be taken as an explanation of some of the human thinness in his work.

to invade the modern scene.[1] And the American-European conflict in his late work was further intensified by his trip to Europe at the age of forty-nine as American Consul at Liverpool. He was too old to enjoy any of the advantages that flowed in on young Henry James, and apart from some Lord Mayor's banquets and some dull literary dinners in London, he seems to have been exposed to very little good English society.[2] He was thoroughly unsettled by his seven years abroad, and never again recovered the fineness of his association with the American Colonial past. Mr. Randall Stewart has written in his essay 'Hawthorne in England', which appears in his edition of *The English Notebooks*: 'The accumulated result (as exhibited in the journals and letters, in *Our Old Home* and the posthumous novels) is a comparative weighing of the English and the American civilizations,

[1] Hawthorne's own feelings about his 'expatriation' in the past may very well have come to resemble Ralph Pendrel's in *The Sense of the Past*. We remember that Ralph's return to the present 'saves' him. He is

'. . . saved from all the horror of the growing fear of *not* being saved, of being lost, of being *in* the past to stay, heartbreakingly to stay and never know his own original precious Present again; that horror which his conception of his adventure had never reckoned with . . .'

There is an unkind irony in the fact that the very success of Hawthorne's dealings with the American past were based on, and further developed, a kind of awareness that was bound to betray itself. The contemporaneity that he seemed so much in control of there inevitably sent him back to the Present, where the contemporaneity was lost.

[2] The description he gives in *The English Notebooks* of the consulate office in Liverpool in which he had to spend so much of his time underlines the difference between Hawthorne's and James's years in Europe:

'My apartment (about twelve feet by fifteen, and of a good height) is hung with a map of the United States, and another of Europe; there is a hideous coloured lithograph of General Taylor, life size, and one or two smaller engraved portraits; also three representations of American naval victories; a lithograph of the Tennessee State-house, and another of the Steamer Empire State. The mantle-piece is adorned with the American Eagle, painted on the wood; and on shelves there are a number of volumes, bound in sheepskin, of the laws of the United States and the Statutes at large. Thus the consular office is a little patch of America, with English life encompassing it on all sides.'

which can scarcely be equalled elsewhere for its painstaking detail.'

If we confine ourselves to the *Notebooks* and disregard *Our Old Home*, which is a dull rewriting of them, the insights occasionally seem extraordinary, but the weighing goes on indefinitely until it becomes clear that Hawthorne is no longer capable of anything more than a series of separate choices which he arranges as counters in some chosen design. He has succeeded in uprooting his sensibility without meaning to do so, and the conditions do not exist in which it might be possible for him to strike new roots in English soil. From this time his work became unsatisfactory in a way one can imagine James's would have done had he returned to America in middle life and remained there. The conditions under which Hawthorne had achieved a poised reconciliation of the diverse elements in his character could not, once abandoned, be re-assumed merely for the asking, and after his return to America his attempt to write a novel dealing with Colonial and Revolutionary times, *Septimius Felton*, is an embarrassing and heavy-handed failure.

It has been argued in this paper that the question of America *versus* Europe is intrinsically involved in Hawthorne's case with the opposition of past and present, and it will be necessary here to examine that aspect of the problem a little more closely. For the American, Europe *is* the past in a symbolic way that it can never quite be for the European himself; and in glancing here at the ambivalence in both James's and Hawthorne's dealings with it the conclusion forces itself that the two men would have had to resemble each other in spite of themselves. They distrusted the past, but they reached out towards it instinctively as towards a totality of experience, and the inadequacy of the American present without a sense of European tradition persisted in tormenting their consciousness. Hawthorne wrote in *The English Notebooks*:

> My ancestor left England in 1635. I return in 1853. I sometimes feel as if I myself had been absent these two hundred and eighteen years—leaving England just emerging from the feudal

system, and finding it on the verge of Republicanism. It brings
the two far separated points very closely together. . . .

This was to become a recurrent and tormenting subject in
Hawthorne's later work, and it is one which he takes up
again and again in the posthumously published fragments.
A young American returns to England and attempts to establish his legal claim to ancient family estates. Hawthorne gets
so far, but he never gets further than that, breaking off each
time in a confusion of floundering symbols and a despair of
finishing. Hawthorne's incoherence on this theme may be
partly due to an innate difficulty in the symbolism of the
returned American itself—a difficulty of which he was not
sufficiently conscious to deal with it successfully. The image
works directly away from the possibility of such a resolution
as we examined in the passage devoted to Governor Belling
ham's garden. Its tendency is to fuse the two cultures in a
single figure, rather than to achieve a skilled counterpointing
of their separate characters, allowing each to retain its full
identity and integrity, but mutually balancing and supporting each other.[1] In the international novel, as he developed
and refined it, James had been able to acquire the necessary
skill in counterpoint, and it is with reluctance that one

[1] The preliminary studies for *Dr. Grimshaw's Secret* (written 1860–1)
which Mr. Edward Hutchins Davidson has recently published for the
first time in his valuable study, *Hawthorne's Last Phase*, are of particular
interest here. Hawthorne was not, of course, trying to present a new type
of Europeanized American. He kept the contrast between the nations
firmly fixed in his mind. But he saw the resolution in what would ultimately be an intolerable fusion:

'It must be shown, I think, throughout that there is an essential
difference between English and American character, and the former
must assimilate itself to the latter, if there is to be any union.'

But Hawthorne offers, to qualify this, pre-Jamesian hints of the possibilities of the international marriage as a more workable solution. Of the
English aristocrat in his story, he says:

'I think he should be drawn with a natural generosity and nobleness,
doing credit to the best influences of his position; but some misfortune
must unavoidably grow out of his position, and ruin him, through the

declines the occasion offered here to insert, with appropriate analysis, a Jamesian passage to balance the Bellingham passage of Hawthorne's offered earlier. But such passages are so frequent in James that no one can miss them. They form the very texture of his writing, and James showed us in Gilbert Osmund what the 'fused' American was like. And one should remember that in at least two works, an early story called *A Passionate Pilgrim*, 1872, and *The Sense of the Past*, James attempted to present a character that would not be an American merely exposed to and enlarged by the European experience, but one who returned to Europe as to his proper home. James's knowledge and tact got him through the ordeal pretty well, but it is significant that *The Sense of the Past* was never finished, while *A Passionate Pilgrim* has a tragic ending—Searle, the American who returns to claim his share of the ancestral estates, discovering before his premature death, not that he is both American and English, but that he is neither in any significant way.[1]

means of the American, who must make amends to the reader's feelings by marrying an Englishwoman, with every prospect of happiness.'

It is very revealing to read these preliminary studies together with the Notes for *The Sense of the Past*. Nothing shows up more strikingly the similarity between the preoccupations of the two men. On the basis of these studies alone, one might say that Hawthorne's interests had shifted on to grounds from which only James's art could provide the saving issue. Hawthorne had raised problems that were technically beyond his solution, but they lead American literature directly into the work of Henry James.

[1] Hamlin Garland in a book of reminiscences called *Roadside Meetings* recounts a visit he made to James at Rye during which James made remarks that recall *A Passionate Pilgrim* vividly to mind. It is impossible to judge James's tone—certainly one would hesitate to accept Garland's interpretation on such a delicate matter—but the following paragraph has a great deal of interest, no matter how one interprets it :

'He became very much in earnest at last and said something which surprised and gratified me. "If I were to live my life over again," he said in a low voice, and fixing upon me a somber glance, "I would be an American. I would steep myself in America, I would know no other land. I would study its beautiful side. The mixture of Europe and

A Passionate Pilgrim, however, is important here only because it reveals how a concern with similar problems caused Hawthorne and James to organize their conceptions quite naturally around similar images. But *The Sense of the Past* is a different matter. Although it seems that James, had he finished the novel, would have offered important modifications to break the symmetry, the nature of the double identity belonging to Ralph Pendrel belongs equally to the present and the past, to America and to Europe. It is nothing less than a symbol into which the whole American problem under the two aspects that have been considered here is compressed. But the compression, or 'fusion', is essentially anathema to the nature of the problem itself, so that the central conceit of James's novel was working against rather than for his meaning. Ralph Pendrel's portrait, or rather the portrait of his ancestor that hangs in No. 9 Mansfield Square, is the integrating point in James's story—the symbol in which the past and the present, Europe and America, become one. But they are not one, and the increasingly attenuated qualifications (when James speaks of *The Sense of the Past* his style is always rarefied, even for the late period) with which he found himself obliged to accommodate his story to that fact threatened to destroy the whole structure, so that we are tempted to say that in Hawthorne's symbol James encountered Hawthorne's failure. This is the essential point, which it has seemed just as well to make at once. But *The Sense of the Past* is important enough in the Hawthorne-James relation to justify a closer look at James involved in working out his difficulties—if floundering in them (rather gracefully of course) wouldn't, indeed, be the better phrase. When he took up once more the unfinished fragment of *The Sense of the Past* fourteen years after he had abandoned it, he wrote a preliminary statement out for reference during the actual com-

America which you see in me has proved disastrous. It has made of me a man who is neither American nor European. I have lost touch with my own people, and live here alone. My neighbours are friendly, but they are not of my blood, except remotely. As a man grows old he feels these conditions more than when he is young. I shall never return to the United States, but I wish I could." '

71

position. Mr. Mathiessen prints it with *The Notebooks*, and it is worth quoting at some length here:

My idea of course—and that's what seems to me really so fine—that of the exchange of identity between my young American of to-day and his relative of upwards of a hundred years ago, or whatever, on the ground of the latter's reviving for the former under the prodigy of the actual man's so intense and so invoked and so fostered historic faculty, clumsily so to dub it, or in other words his sense of the past, the thing he has always wanted to have still more than historic records can give it, the thing forming the title, as the early part of the Introduction gives it, of the remarkable Essay or Study that he has published, a distinguished and striking little effort, and which we have learnt about to begin with. Yes, it glimmers back to me that at sight of the picture in the London house—all his comings back to see which, to come in for which, have also from the first been dealt with—he has had the extraordinary emotion of recognizing himself, his very self in the person of an ancestor, as if nothing but his clothes had been altered, to the dress of the time, and it is himself who looks out recognizingly *at* himself, just as the so interestingly painted image looks out recognizingly at *him*. My fantastic idea deals then with the phenomenon of the conscious and understood fusion, or exchange, that takes place between them. . . . Well, the sublime idea thrown out to me by the passage in the London house comes back to me as *this*: that there, face to face with my tremendously engaged and interested hero is this alter ego of a past generation of his 'race', the inward passion of whose also yearning mind and imagination was the sense of the future—he having so nursed and cherished that, wanted so to project himself into it, that it makes him the very counterpart of his eventual descendant. . . . What is involved in my prodigy, and makes the real drama, story or situation of it, is that one or the other of the young men in consequence of what so supernaturally passes between them, steps back or steps forward into the life of the other exactly as that life is at that moment constituted, at that moment going on and being enacted, representing each the other for the persons, the society about him, concerned but with the double consciousness the representation of which makes the thrill and the curiosity of the affair, the consciousness of being the other and yet himself also. What appealed to me as of an intensely effective note of the supernatural and sinister kind was this secret within his breast, that is within the hero's breast (for the two, in the 'situation', are reduced to one) of his abnormal nature and of the effect on the others that a dim, vague, attached and yet rather dreadful and distressful sense of it produces on them.

The saving grace of the conceit—the touch that might have prevented a basic distortion of the reality so symbolized if the novel had been completed—is Ralph Pendrel's consciousness of his abnormal nature. One can't guess quite what James would have done with it, but he gives little indication in the novel and the Notes of working it out with that sureness or perception that characterized his best international novels. We know of course that the Midmores were designed to show up the greater fineness of their American relative,[1] but the symbol of the exchanged identity was, by its very nature, absorbent of the differences. Nevertheless, *The Sense of the Past* is important in any consideration of the Hawthorne-James line, for in it we can see them very plainly working shoulder to shoulder. The effect of their industry comes simply to this: despite their frequent or infrequent lapses and failures they established a strategy by which the American, cut off from his antecedents and embarrassed by the burden of his 'commonplace prosperity', might develop a refined consciousness of that cultural and racial unity that underlies the divisions of the English-speaking world. It was a tremendously complex problem, and as the world is going, it was

[1] James was aware that he had used the central conceit of the double or divided identity in his earlier story, *The Jolly Corner*. It is curious to compare this story with *The Sense of the Past*, for while it seems that Ralph Pendrel was to have been presented as a more sensitive and intelligent person than his English friends, this is a reversal of the balance in *The Jolly Corner*, which is anti-American with a vengeance. James seems to have been unaware, however, that he had used the device of the returned American's resemblance to an ancestral portrait in *A Passionate Pilgrim*, a fact which illustrates how ancient was his concern with the themes and symbols of *The Sense of the Past*.

73   F

and is a problem of such importance that even today one hardly dare plot limits to what it may eventually mean in terms of a future English-speaking civilization. The symbolism of *The Sense of the Past* may have belonged to an earlier strategy than James was entitled to employ. It can be argued that a symbolism of identification is basically the result of insecurity and embarrassment—but James was neither insecure nor embarrassed; and if he at last thought it expedient to abandon his unfinished novel, there is yet a propriety in his having taken up so late in life these symbols and themes that were so deeply immersed in the Hawthornian tone.

Mr. T. S. Eliot in his brief essay on James entitled *The Hawthorne Aspect*, an essay so filled with illuminating observations, has remarked that James showed for Hawthorne 'the tenderness of a man who had escaped too early from an environment to be warped or thwarted by it, who had escaped so effectually that he could afford the gift of affection'. While one might wish to discuss and qualify Mr. Eliot's precise meaning in that verb 'escape', the statement pretty nearly sums up the quality and the significance of the relation. If I have preferred the word 'sympathy' here, it is because its meaning seems to point with steadier intention towards those common problems and afflictions that came down on the two Americans when they endeavoured to practice their art. If James felt 'tenderness' for Hawthorne, it was the tenderness of a battle-comrade for a fatally wounded friend, and it would not have been the best kind of tenderness if James (as that insidious 'escape' implies) had deserted the field, and left the problems triumphant. In the foregoing discussion I have tried to define what those problems—or rather, that Problem, was. It exists under various disguises in the work of both men, and especially in Hawthorne's case the disguises are difficult to penetrate. But if, in the end, it was too much for Hawthorne, his precedent and example helped to focus James's attention, and to give him confidence by assuring him that at least one good American had been in that valley before. We have already considered in some detail Hawthorne's influence on two of James's novels. It will always be better to consider his influence as specifically as possible, for it is extremely elusive of generalizations. That is the good and vital thing about it. But there is still a rather frightening question one is tempted to ask. To what extent did Hawthorne actually modify the development of James's art? Wouldn't James, after all, have been very much himself had Hawthorne never lived and written? Such a question can't really be answered, of course, but it does underline the direction of Hawthorne's influence, and it offers an occasion to advance criticisms of James's art that today are too frequently forgotten in a spirit of general acclaim. Intricately woven into the fabric of James's work, side by side with the moral preoccupations, there is another strand of a very different character. I can imagine some hypothetical Devil's Advocate advancing a case like the following against James:

This Devil's Advocate might begin by quoting this extraordinary sentence from James's 1870 essay on Newport: 'For my own part, I prefer to imagine nothing but the graceful and the pure; and with the help of such imaginings you may construct a very pretty sentimental undercurrent to the superficial movement of society.' And then he would pass on to quote from the much later chapter in *The American Scene* entitled 'The Sense of Newport'. This chapter is consecrated to nostalgia, to the evocation of the past in terms of a small group of Americans who in the 'sixties and 'seventies made their home in Newport,

> a collection of the detached, the slightly disenchanted and casually disqualified, and of the resigned and contented, of the socially orthodox: a handful of mild, oh delightfully mild, cosmopolites, united by three common circumstances, that of their having for the most part more or less lived in Europe, that of their sacrificing openly to the ivory idol whose name is leisure, and that, not least, of a formed critical habit.

This group is frequently the dramatis personæ of James's books, and he has a habit of making life disconcertingly easy for them. He is emotionally concerned to give them the climate in which they can most perfectly live, or most graciously suffer. In many of his books—in *The Ambassadors*, for instance—the characters remind one a little of Proust's.

75

But unlike Proust, he wipes the shadows of damnation from under their eyes, and for their sakes he averts his gaze at embarrassing moments. Little Bilham cries out for the Faubourg St. Germain as Proust presented it; but he is safer with James, because James will never bring age and ruins toppling on his head. James's interest is in creating a sophisticated and liveable moment, and in maintaining it from moment to moment. The terrorist explosions towards which his tremendous insights would, in any other writer, move, he must at all events avoid, for the fine high windows of the Jamesian villa are no less breakable than they are valuable. He knows that the material conditions for his values are too deeply embedded in the lives of their opposites to destroy the one without endangering the other. Unlike Proust, he will not play Samson and pull the temple down on our guilty heads. In the end he is a kind of Edwardian Atlas holding up the old cracked heavens.

This at any rate is the argument I conceive the hypothetical Devil's Advocate might build up against James, and perhaps there is enough truth in it to make his admirers a little nervous. But in the end such a conception of James is seen to be mostly false. It has just enough basis in fact to emphasize the extent to which he overcame the temptation: and in fact a good deal of the energy in his work arises from his steady and clear-sighted opposition to such an attitude.[1] What I

---

[1] James was fully conscious of this tendency in himself, and he usually (but not always) set it in its proper light. It was precisely *as* a temptation that he gave it a classic formulation in his interesting but uneven story, *Crapy Cornelia*. His description of Mrs. Worthingham's opulently graceful but spiritually indelicate settlement with life is personally felt in a way that is significant:

'Her outlook took form to him suddenly as a great square sunny window that hung in assured fashion over the immensity of life. There rose toward it as from a vast swarming *plaza* a high tide of motion and sound; yet it was at the same time as if even while he looked her light gemmed hand, flashing on him in addition to those other things the perfect polish of the prettiest pink finger-nails in the world, had touched a spring, the most ingenious of recent devices for instant ease, which dropped half across the scene a soft-coloured mechanical blind,

wish to insist on here is simply this: it was against *that* attitude, *that* line of possible development in James, that Hawthorne's example steadily and consistently operated. He kept before the later novelist the constant reminder that an American artist must be peculiarly concerned, at a serious moral level, with certain national and social problems, and this shared concern unfolded, in the writings of both men, into still deeper problems and resemblances that became, in their turn, the very texture and meaning of their art. It was Hawthorne, then, who helped make James into an American novelist, and who prevented him from becoming a 'slightly disenchanted and casually disqualified' cosmopolite. The nature of the indebtedness makes it difficult to measure with much precision, but we may be sure that it was largely there, and it is greatly to James's credit that all his life he paid his generous tribute without stint. For those critics who maintain a 'romancer' like Hawthorne could only have a limited interest, in contrast to the continental writers, for a

a fluttered fringed awning of charmingly toned silk, such as would make a bath of cool shade for the favoured friend leaning with her there—that is for the happy couple itself—on the balcony. The great view would be the prospect and privilege of the very state he coveted— since didn't he covet it?—the state of being so securely at her side; while the wash of privacy, as one might count it, the broad fine brush dipped into clear umber and passed, full and wet, straight across the strong scheme of colour, would represent the security itself, all the uplifted inner elegance, the condition, so ideal, of being shut out from nothing and yet of having, so gaily and breezily aloft, none of the burden or worry of anything.'

To state the problem correctly, of course, is not the same as answering it, but it may move a long way in that direction. The weakness of *Crapy Cornelia* lies in the fact that James, when he came to answer the problems implicit in the above quotation, interpreted them to a scale that rendered them too easily tractable, and one cannot be sure that his forty-eight-year-old hero, White-Mason, doesn't overcome the grandiose temptation of luxurious irresponsibility in the present by submitting to an equally pernicious sentimentalization of the past. Nevertheless, the kind of intense awareness exhibited above gives the lie direct to those hostile critics who suppose James to have been gifted with a facility for dismissing those terrors and distresses that lacerate the breasts of the socially minded.

novelist like James, he has himself supplied the appropriate answer:

> I have alluded to the absence in Hawthorne of that quality of realism which is now so much the fashion, an absence in regard to which there will, of course, be more to say; and yet I think I am not fanciful in saying that he testifies to the sentiments of the society in which he flourished almost as pertinently (proportions observed) as Balzac and some of his descendants—Mm. Flaubert and Zola—testify to the manners and morals of the French people. He was not a man with a literary theory; he was guiltless of a system, and I am not sure that he had ever heard of Realism, this remarkable compound having (although it was invented some time earlier) come into general use only since his death. . . . Nevertheless he virtually offers the most vivid reflection of New England life that has found its way into literature. . . . Hawthorne's work savours thoroughly of the local soil—it is redolent of the social system in which he had his being.

5

APPEARANCE AND REALITY
IN HENRY JAMES

(i)

IN any tradition sustained as largely as the American one has been by a given set of ideals ('the American dream', as critics sometimes say), the collision between the practical and the visionary may cause a shock whose repercussions will become a characteristic in the art and literature that the tradition produces. Perhaps all art represents a conflict between appearance and reality, but American literature is inclined to register the shock with peculiar earnestness and simplicity. Sometimes the result of the struggle is that both the writer and the reader seem to emerge with a great uncertainty as to what is appearance and what is reality, or how to distinguish between truth and falsehood, or how to bring evil to a particular focus, or how to celebrate goodness. These problems took hold of Henry James, and they came at last to occupy a central position in his work. The reader is not always aware of their presence because it is probable that James himself did not really know how insidiously these considerations were in control. But it is impossible not to feel their effects operating throughout his work. These effects are frequently of great impressiveness, and in some of his greater stories and novels they betray his recurrent preoccupations: in some of his greater, but not his greatest, for the uncertainties seem to get the upper hand, and they are not uncertainties that enlarge, but rather they seem to diminish human nature. I believe it has sometimes been said by critics that James's long residence abroad relaxed his moral judgment so that he was incapable of distinguishing between a gentleman and a cad. If James sometimes appears inept in these matters, it is simply because the confusion is of a profounder sort than the critics imagine. Cads and gentlemen are made such by the social perspective in which they exist, and in viewing any

79

given context of appearance and reality James developed an astigmatism that was essentially American. The fault that the critics deplore is not due to the fact that James stayed abroad too long, but that he didn't get out of America soon enough.

This concern with the relation between appearance and reality is at the basis of Hawthorne's art, but for Hawthorne the strain between the two terms is not as great as it was to become for James. Hawthorne spoke of 'a haunting perception of unreality', but he was still able to reconcile appearance and reality within the framework of a social and political orthodoxy, even if the cost of doing so was high. Hawthorne and James are seen to be involved with the same problem in a passage like the following from Hawthorne's *The New Adam and Eve*:

> We who are born into the world's artificial system can never adequately know how little in our present state and circumstance is natural, and how much is merely the interpolation of the perverted heart and mind of man. Art has become a second and stronger nature; she is a stepmother, whose crafty tenderness has taught us to despise the bountiful and wholesome ministrations of our true parent. It is only through the medium of the imagination that we can lessen those iron fetters, which we call truth and reality, and make ourselves even partially sensible of what prisoners we are.

From one point of view *The Scarlet Letter* is an exploration of the relation between appearance and reality. We have the visible embroidered letter that Hester Prynne wears on her breast, and the hidden letter, burned into the living flesh, that Arthur Dimmesdale wears beneath his tunic. And related to this problem we are faced, as later in James, with the difficulty of bringing evil to a particular focus. Is it centred in the adulterous couple, in the wronged husband, or in the horrors of puritan society? Hawthorne's achievement is that he is able to keep his terms so clear, the problem so precise, without at the same time sacrificing anything of its frightening complexity. This conflict between appearance and reality, and the consequent difficulty of knowing evil, is poetically explored in one of Hawthorne's greatest masterpieces, his short story, *Young Goodman Brown*, and in the even greater short story, *My Kinsman, Major Molineux*.[1] I haven't the space to examine these stories here as a preliminary step towards discussing the conflict in James, but the recurrence of this problem in American literature should be borne in mind, for it helps to define the quality of James's sensibility. But Hawthorne was able to make this conflict the subject of a great deal of his work without being victimized by it in the way James came to be. Perhaps I can make my point by referring to one of Hawthorne's most recurrent images—the looking glass. Several years ago Mr. Malcolm Cowley discussed this image at considerable length, and he noted that it expressed Hawthorne's concern with the distinction between appearance and reality. The image is important because it functions as a stabilizing metaphor which, if it demonstrates the distinction between the two terms, simultaneously demonstrates their intrinsic relation. In such a metaphor the two terms cannot be wrenched apart in any destructive way. In a story like *Dr. Heidegger's Experiment* the mirror image leads us back into a profounder sense of reality itself.

(ii)

There is a typical motive in most of James's short stories which is reworked in a great variety of ways, and with great technical skill. Sometimes the technique is almost too skilful, too pat. What the technique amounts to is an exploitation of the ambiguities of experience for the purpose of revealing, of showing up, 'the world's artificial system'. In other words, the stories are designed to call into radical question the validity of the relation between appearances and the reality

[1] *My Kinsman, Major Molineux* is especially interesting in any study of Hawthorne. The problems that were discussed in a preceding article as being typical of both Hawthorne and James, the conflict between America and Europe, and the conflict between the past and the present, as well as the appearance-reality conflict, are gathered into a single poetic treatment in this story, which is one of the greatest masterpieces in American literature, and which deals with the creation of 'the first American' in the person of its hero, Robin.

they profess to represent. I wish to consider two representative stories of this type here, and suggest how they illuminate certain puzzling questions that confront us in *The Golden Bowl*.

The first of these short stories, *The Path of Duty* (1885), is the less interesting. In it we see James treating the whole problem to a comparatively straightforward development. The plot deals with the love affair and engagement of Sir Ambrose Tester. Infatuated with a married woman, Lady Vandeleur, whose husband appears to be in the prime of health, Sir Ambrose allows himself to be badgered into marriage by his father, who wishes to see an heir to the title before he dies. Sir Ambrose becomes engaged to a charming English girl, Joscelind Bernardstone, who falls deeply in love with him, but for whom he only feigns, in the interests of decorum, a lover's affection. The engagement is confirmed in the interested eyes of London society by the couple appearing together frequently in public. Everything appears to be in order when, unseasonably, Lady Vandeleur's husband dies, leaving the beautiful widow free to marry Sir Ambrose, which she is clearly eager to do. But he in his turn is not now free, although the marital bars have not yet been decisively lowered. The question therefore arises whether or not he is justified in breaking his engagement with Joscelind, who is unaware of the relation existing between Lady Vandeleur and himself. The situation is complicated by the fact that the American woman who relates the story as a personal acquaintance of the characters involved is convinced that Joscelind would not survive the shock of a break, a conviction she communicates both to Sir Ambrose and Lady Vandeleur. In the end Sir Ambrose and Lady Vandeleur make an honourable sacrifice of each other's persons. In short, they take the path of duty, and Sir Ambrose marries Joscelind. The story ends on this note:

> Lady Vandeleur, as you know, has never married again; she is still the most beautiful widow in England. She enjoys the esteem of everyone, as well as the approbation of her conscience, for everyone knows the sacrifice she made, knows that

she was even more in love with Sir Ambrose than he was with
her. She goes out again, of course, as of old, and she constantly
meets the baronet and his wife. She is supposed to be even 'very
nice' to Lady Tester, and she certainly treats her with exceeding
civility. But you know (or perhaps you don't know) all the
deadly things that, in London, may lie beneath that method.
I don't in the least mean that Lady Vandeleur has any deadly
intentions; she is a very good woman, and I am sure that in her
heart she thinks she lets poor Joscelind off very easily. But the
result of the whole situation is that Joscelind is in dreadful fear
of her, for how can she help seeing that she has a very peculiar
power over her husband? There couldn't have been a better
occasion for observing the three together (if together it may be
called, when Lady Tester is so completely outside) than those
two days of ours at Doubleton. That's a house where they have
met more than once before; I think she and Sir Ambrose like it.
By 'she' I mean, as he used to mean, Lady Vandeleur. You saw
how Lady Tester was absolutely white with uneasiness. What
can she do when she meets everywhere the implication that if
two people in our time have distinguished themselves for their
virtue, it is her husband and Lady Vandeleur? It is my impression that this pair are exceedingly happy. His marriage *has*
made a difference, and I see him much less frequently and less
intimately. But when I meet him I notice in him a kind of
emanation of quiet bliss. Yes, they are certainly in felicity, they
have trod the clouds together, they have soared into the blue,
and they wear in their faces the glory of those altitudes. They
encourage, they cheer, inspire, sustain each other; remind each
other they have chosen the better part. Of course they have to
meet for this purpose, and their interviews are filled, I am sure,
with its sanctity. He holds up his head, as a man who on a very
critical occasion behaved like a perfect gentleman. It is only
poor Joscelind that droops. Haven't I explained to you now
why she doesn't understand?

The Path of Duty is an undistinguished story, but it presents
in its simplest guise that basic pattern to which so many of
James's stories were to conform. Both the irony in the title
and in the pun contained in the name of the country house

where the infatuated pair meet, Doubleton, point to that conflict between appearance and reality we are discussing. The path of duty as it exists in 'the world's artificial system' is a matter of appearance only, although it is an appearance that claims spuriously to be related to reality. Yet the relation, if it exists at all, is so perverse that Sir Ambrose and Lady Vandeleur have sinned by being virtuous, and lied by adhering to their conception of the truth. This reversal of values for the purpose of revealing a deeper truth in a given situation can be effectively utilized in a given instance, but it tends to detach the writer at last from those values that normally constitute human life, and we shall be able to trace one unfortunate effect of the habit when we consider *The Golden Bowl*.

James published the second story which I wish to consider here, *The Liar*, in 1889. In this plot the interaction of truth and falsehood, of appearance and reality, is far more complicated. It is easy to ask after reading the first story: Where or what is the path of duty? But it is equally easy to read the second story without its occurring to anyone that the essential question is: Who is the liar? Because this ambiguity is so intricately embedded in the narrative it will be necessary to deal with the plot here in somewhat greater detail than the other story called for. *The Liar* opens when Oliver Lyon, a successful young portrait painter, arrives as a house guest at Staves, Arthur Ashmore's house in Hertfordshire, commissioned to do a portrait of old Sir David Ashmore. A house party is in progress, and as Lyon settles down to work on the picture during the ensuing days, he renews, among the guests, an early friendship with a young woman he had known years before when he was an art student at Munich, and whom he had asked, in those days, to marry him. He has since lost sight of her until this occasion, when to his great pleasure he observes her sitting near him at dinner on the first evening. She in her turn is delighted to meet again her admirer of some years before, and she introduces him to her husband, Colonel Clement Capadose, who is also a guest in the house. Before having actually spoken to her, Lyon has obliquely observed at dinner that her eyes frequently direct themselves to a handsome man across the dinner table with looks that Lyon accepts as proof of her love for the gentleman so singled out. He later proves to be her husband, and Lyon, who still greatly admires his former friend, begins to feel the stings of envy. Nevertheless, Colonel Capadose, who is not only a handsome but an amiable man, greatly interests him, and Lyon begins to draw him out, a procedure that is easy because Colonel Capadose obviously enjoys talking. As the friendship warms it becomes obvious that the Colonel is a good deal given to exaggeration, or even to deliberate romancing. This weakness is easily accepted by Colonel Capadose's friends, who understand how harmless it is, and are content to overlook it. At first even Lyon sees the truth in this attitude:

> The observation of these three days showed him [Lyon] that if Capadose was an abundant he was not a malignant liar and that his fine faculty exercised itself mainly on subjects of small direct importance. 'He is the liar platonic,' he said to himself; 'He is disinterested, he doesn't operate with a hope of gain or with a desire to injure. It is art for art's sake and he is prompted by the love of beauty. He has an inner vision of what might have been, of what ought to be, and he helps on the good cause by the simple substitution of a *nuance*.'

It soon becomes Lyon's chief interest to observe Mrs. Capadose, to study her face in the hope of seeing some spasm of revulsion at her husband's vulgarity pass across it.

> Lyon had no nefarious plan, no conscious wish to practise upon her shame or loyalty; but he did say to himself that he should like to bring her round to feel that there would have been more dignity in a union with a certain other person. He even dreamed of the hour when, with a burning face, she would ask *him* not to take it up. Then he should be almost consoled— he would be magnanimous.

After the dispersal of the house party, Lyon does not lose sight of the Capadoses in London. He assiduously cultivates their acquaintance. He paints, as a gift for them, their little daughter, and allows this to form the prelude towards his

85

asking, as a special favour, that Colonel Capadose should also sit for his portrait—the object merely being that Lyon, as he tells them, wishes to render the Colonel's interesting face as a subject pre-eminently suitable to his art. James puts it in these terms:

> The desire grew in him to paint the Colonel also—an operation from which he promised himself a rich private satisfaction. He would draw him out, he would set him in that totality about which he had talked with Sir David, and none but the initiated would know. They, however, would rank the picture high, and it would be indeed six rows deep—a masterpiece of subtle characterization, of legitimate treachery.

The Colonel, out of amiability, consents to sit, and as the portrait grows under Lyon's hand, the 'legitimate treachery' of Lyon's original intention also grows:

> The only point that troubled him was the idea that when he should send his picture to the Academy he should not be able to give the title, for the catalogue, simply as 'The Liar'. However, it little mattered, for he had now determined that his character should be perceptible even to the meanest intelligence—as overtopping as it had become to his own sense of the living man.

Two things are worth noting here. First: that reference to the quality of the future audience is significant. It supplies a clue to what is happening in Lyon's consciousness. He no longer looks for fineness of appreciation, but has grown eager for the most vulgar public applause, whereas a few pages earlier he had wished to appeal only to the initiated few. Now, to secure this applause, he is willing to betray his friendship with Mrs. Capadose, and simulate a friendship with the husband that is entirely a lie. Second: his static conception of Colonel Capadose as a liar has blotted out any finer sense of the Colonel as a human being. It has become completely 'overtopping . . . to his own sense of the living man'. Oliver Lyon is on the point of committing that crime which for both Hawthorne and James was the worst possible: of violating the integrity of another man's personality, of seeking to take possession of it through false images and conventional laws.

86

But Lyon's treachery is deeper yet. He hopes, by exposing the husband to public scorn, to enter into an emotional union with the wife—a kind of adulterous liaison of the spirit in which the two lovers of earlier years will find a deeper communion than ever yet in the sense of the wife's revulsion from the vulgarity of her lying husband. Having earlier failed to marry her, Lyon's triumph will be the final one. They will be happy together in knowing how much better a husband the portrait painter would have made. The situation that will have been arrived at then will be very much the same situation that James presented in the closing paragraph of *The Path of Duty*, which was quoted above. But in actual fact things do not work out as Lyon wishes. The Colonel and his wife secretly destroy the calumniating portrait, and when Colonel Capadose denies the act of vandalism his wife supports her husband in the lie—supports him whole-heartedly, beautifully, competently.[1] She is thus presented to the reader through Lyon's eyes as a contaminated nature, and a shudder is invited. But in actual fact it is only Mrs. Capadose who has known how to discriminate between appearance and reality in this story, who knows that it is not her husband but Lyon who is the liar.

So far from being a contaminated character in James's eyes, as critics have consistently maintained, Mrs. Capadose is an early forerunner of Maggie Verver in *The Golden Bowl*. *The Golden Bowl* is a gigantic parable in which we see how truth is fabricated out of lies. The theme is so subtly developed that one is hardly aware of what is actually taking place, but once the process is isolated it is hard and glittering enough to convince anybody. The theme itself as it appears in *The Golden Bowl* does magnificent credit to James's technical skill,

[1] Something might be made of the fact that Colonel Capadose places the blame for the vandalism on a nameless, drunken artist's model who has earlier wandered into Lyon's studio while the Colonel was sitting. But the model has nothing whatever to lose from Capadose's allegation, and everyone, including Colonel Capadose, knows that she will never be seen or heard of again, whereas it was no anonymous figure, but Colonel Capadose, his wife and child, that Lyon was eager to pillory in the eyes of all London society.

but it also points to a deep, a downright fantastic perversity of temperament that is positively American. Like Hawthorne, James wanted to escape from 'the world's artificial system', but it is doubtful if 'those iron fetters, which we call truth and reality' can really be lessened in the way James thought.

The plot of *The Golden Bowl* is well known. Maggie Verver, the charming and devoted daughter of the fabulously wealthy, art-collecting American, Adam Verver, marries an impressively descended but impoverished young Italian nobleman, Prince Amerigo. Maggie's conscience bothers her because she feels she has disrupted the happy relationship with her father, and she thinks that if he were to marry again—someone very suitable, of course—the old delightful intimacy might be re-established. An old acquaintance of the Ververs, Fanny Assingham, at this point invites a girlhood friend of Maggie's to stay with her. It occurs to Maggie, as a result of this renewed proximity, that Charlotte Stant might make an excellent wife for her father. The marriage occurs in due course, and for a time things seem to be happening almost as Maggie had wished. But at last Maggie discovers that Fanny Assingham had neglected to tell her that the Prince and Charlotte had been in love long before their present marriages, but that their common poverty had compelled them to relinquish each other. It has become evident to Maggie at the same time that their recent marriages—the Prince's to Maggie and Charlotte's to Mr. Verver—stand good to take the tooth out of their earlier sacrifice. The danger that now confronts Maggie seems to have more positively physical aspects than that which confronted poor Joscelind Bernardstone in *The Path of Duty*, but in other respects the situations are very similar. Maggie is simply threatened with exclusion. But unlike Joscelind, Maggie *does* understand. She has the fineness of intuition to know that if she makes a scene (apart from the effects of this on her carefully guarded relation with her father) the intimacy of the guilty couple will be confirmed. They will take open arms against Maggie, or worse, draw spiritually closer in the sense of their shared guilt. Therefore, Maggie must prove herself a very Iago for the sake of preserving her marriage—for the sake of making something valid out of it; and she ends up by lying as valiantly as Mrs. Capadose. She lies to keep both the Prince and Charlotte at first, and then only Charlotte, whom she sees as the real danger, in ignorance of her own knowledge of their misconduct—her theory being that this will give her time to get the two separated, or somehow reclaimed, without that crisis which she knows would defeat her.

> She was learning almost from minute to minute to be a mistress of shades—since always when there were possibilities of intimacy there were also, by that fact, in intercourse, possibilities of irridescence; but she was working against an adversary who was a master of shades too and on whom if she didn't look out she would presently have imposed a consciousness of the nature of their struggle. To feel him in fact, to think of his feeling himself, her adversary in things of this fineness—to see him at all in short brave a name that would represent him as in opposition—was already to be nearly reduced to a visible smothering of her cry of alarm. Should he guess they were having in their so occult manner a *high* fight, and that it was she, all the while, in her supposed stupidity, who had made it high and was keeping it high—in the event of his doing this before they could leave town she should verily be lost.

This course that Maggie embarks on clearly involves all the deception that a 'mistress of shades' can draw on, and it is James's task to justify it. He attempts this on a grand scale in the scene in which, in the darkness of a summer night, the two young women confront each other on the terrace at Fawns, Adam Verver's magnificent great house, for the purpose of mutual betrayal. This is the scene, I think, rather than the one that gives us Mrs. Assingham breaking the chalice, in which all the power of James's gift for symbolism is concentrated. On this occasion Maggie lies—not casually or spontaneously, but with the deepest thought and purpose —lies, indeed, as for something dear and sacred, and she continues to act on her lie, building it into the structure of her final happiness. The thing to insist on here is that the lie is not merely a lie of convenience: James deliberately invests it with a certain sanctity. It seems to be offered, not only as

89   G

the expression of a beautiful consciousness, but as a kind of philosophic comment on the nature of reality. This scene occurs in Chapter II of the Fifth Book, and this chapter, excerpted from the novel itself, may be taken as one of the most astonishing things James ever wrote. The very words on the page seem paralysed in an apprehension of disaster, and an atmosphere of dread is evoked from circumstances which, innocent in themselves, loom through the summer darkness in sinister outline. The action, the movements of Charlotte and Maggie, occur with ritualistic slowness and economy, and the confrontation scene has a density of symbolism that presents the conflict between Maggie and Charlotte as a showing forth of those deeper conflicts between appearance and reality, truth and falsehood, that always lie at the heart of James's deepest meaning.

The chapter opens while Adam Verver, Charlotte, Amerigo, and Fanny Assingham are playing cards in the smoking room at Fawns. Maggie has withdrawn to a sofa in a far part of the great luxurious room, and pretending to read a French Review, she stealthily watches, over its top, the four people intent at their game, yet all the while, as Maggie knows, playing on each other more than they play at bridge. James uses the card game to draw out incisively the lines of relationship between the characters of his drama, and by it he evokes the idea of 'play', of trained skill and canny prevision, that becomes an implicit theme in all that follows. This, together with images of the theatre (particularly when Maggie leaves the house and sees the same scene framed through the lighted window, as on a stage) has the effect of dehumanizing—of puppetizing, as it were—the persons so revealed. What this opening has really done has been to establish symbolically the possibility of Maggie's control over events and persons—to show her suggestively as a kind of puppeteer. But Charlotte is a threat to this control, and later in the chapter when Charlotte, taking Maggie by the arm, shows her the same scene through the same window, she is presenting herself as a rival puppeteer intent on manipulating appearances in a different way. This theme of the *doubleness* of control over appearances that is possible in the situation is developed to an unrivalled pitch of subtlety in the chapter as a whole, but to follow that particular thread of analysis through to the end would unduly prolong the present paper. But we are made to understand that the relation between appearance and reality is instable and uncertain, and that 'the world's artificial system' can be tampered with, or reduced to obedience—reduced, that is to say, to a game of cards or a staged effect, where there is always the possibility of an alternative play or a new illusion. This is a highly tractable version of reality, subject to alteration, and therefore amenable to the lie that Maggie presently throws into the middle of it. It ultimately degrades the dignity of the people acted on, but it invests the ones who act with a sinister interest and power.

But to return to our account of the action in this chapter: missing Maggie from her post on the sofa where she has been reading the French Review, Charlotte relinquishes her seat at the card table to Colonel Assingham who has been, for this purpose, kept in the background, and seeks out Maggie on the terrace. Charlotte is not aware how much Maggie knows about her illicit relation with Amerigo, or how much she doesn't. But it is characteristic of Charlotte that she is not, to Maggie's degree, a player on appearances. She is capable of a clandestine love affair—of keeping up a comparatively vulgar and straightforward sham—but she is not a virtuoso on the finer hypocrisies. She has not, therefore, been able to bear the uncertainty of her position, and she plans, for once in the novel, to put a straight question to Maggie and wait for an answer which, whether true or false, she will insist on being straight also. 'Have you any ground of complaint against me?' Charlotte asks. 'Is there any wrong you consider I've done you?' In asking the question Charlotte foresees only two possible answers. If Maggie accuses her of misconduct with Amerigo, Charlotte, although not desiring this answer, counts on her own ability to bring the contest off successfully when it is moved to this level of open defiance. A 'scene' is something her comparatively unattenuated femininity can cope with. On the other hand, if Maggie lies, Charlotte counts (mistakenly, as it proves) on Maggie's being helplessly confined in a false position, leaving Charlotte a freer hand than ever with Amerigo. But Charlotte has only the moderately rich and rather complacent deceitfulness of a woman infatuated with one man while comfortably married to another. In contrast to her, Maggie's ability to lie has all the grandeur of scope, all the philosophic internal consistency, that belongs to the masculine nature. Despite the appearances of things, Charlotte has no more of a chance against Maggie than Charles the Bold had against Louis XI. And it is as a kind of female Charles the Bold that Charlotte, with her overwhelming question, seeks out the seemingly abject Maggie, who is hiding on a far corner of the terrace. Maggie sees her coming through the shafts of light that cut out patches of visibility from the encircling darkness, and this patterning of light and darkness in which their game is played is itself a symbol of the mottled surface of truth and falsehood that the two are plotting out between them, just as, similarly, the wonderfully realized sense of distance down which Maggie sees Charlotte approaching becomes a symbol of the reach of Maggie's penetration. She aims her lie for the future with unerring vision, and by pretending to be the hunted she brings down her quarry at last. At this point James resorts to the imagery he had recently used in *The Beast in the Jungle*. Charlotte is a 'creature who had escaped by force from her cage'. The quality of a beast of prey is insisted on: '. . . there was in her whole motion assuredly, even as so dimly discerned, a kind of portentous intelligent stillness'. The terrace scene is charged with the greatest impressiveness—a kind of unforgettable theatricality—and as Maggie looks down from her station, no less than John Marcher in the earlier story, she seems to see the Jungle of her life, and the lurking beast, ready to spring. The radical flaw, on any deeper scrutiny, is simply that Charlotte isn't, after all, an abstract Beast in the Jungle, and James pays a high price for that reference to her having broken out of her cage. This reference to Charlotte's cage (but this is by the way) relates very significantly to Maggie's later impression of her husband, after she has won him back, as 'caged': 'a man who couldn't now without an instant effect on her sensibility give an instinctive push to the

92

door she hadn't completely closed behind her'. James is aware of the implications (as the quotation pursued to the end would show), but his attempt to explain them away is unsatisfactory enough to leave Maggie a pretty poor version of a charming, harmless heroine.

Confronted, finally, with Charlotte's question—the question that has already been quoted—Maggie chooses to put herself in a false position. It would be tedious to analyse here the whole of her reasoning, but the sum of it seems to be that she sees how, by debasing herself in front of Charlotte, by literally wallowing in her abjectness, she will have the effect of caricaturing, as it were, Charlotte's sense of her own security that may arise from her (Maggie's) lie. She will, in short, persecute Charlotte by the extreme stylization of the way a wronged wife can submit to injury. It will then be Charlotte herself whom Maggie's lie will have the effect of placing in a false position, even to the extent of making her position so untenable that she will take to flight. In James's fantastic description of Maggie's central treachery that comes at the close of this chapter, we can trace the devoutly interlocked fingers of falsehood and truth:

> . . . Charlotte, though rising there radiantly before her, was really off in some darkness of space that would keep her in solitude and harass her with care. The heart of the Princess swelled accordingly even in her abasement; she had kept in tune with the right, and something certainly, something that might resemble a rare flower snatched from an impossible ledge, would, and possibly soon, come of it for her. The right, the right—yes, it took this extraordinary form of humbugging, as she had called it, to the end. It was only a question of not, by a hair's breadth, deflecting into the truth. So supremely was she braced. 'You must take it from me that your anxiety rests on a misconception. You must take it from me that I've never at any moment fancied I could suffer by you. You must take it from me that I've never thought of you but as beautiful, wonderful and good. Which is all, I think, that you can possibly ask.'

It is impossible to quote with much effectiveness from a scene so tightly and poetically organized, but if one re-reads the chapter with these remarks in mind, it may be granted that a large part of the sinister quality, that air of pervasive unlocalized evil that is so characteristic of James, is due to an inversion of ordinary human values, and even of appearance and reality itself. It is as if the old traditional moral vessels that had long held our sense of evil had been cracked, and evil itself seeped through on to the whole fabric. One is almost shocked by James's unrivalled ability to elevate this inversion to a level of sublimity. At the close of this chapter, just after Maggie has pronounced the tremendous lie quoted above, Charlotte embraces and kisses her. The act is unmistakably meant to suggest the betrayal in the garden, but although we can follow James's intention, the betrayal itself remains a little ambiguous.

This scene in which Charlotte confronts Maggie is balanced by a second scene later on in which Maggie confronts Charlotte, and this scene has to be studied with the one just examined in order to see Maggie's plan working out to the full. The conflicting characters that James wishes to establish for the two girls are no doubt suggested by the fact that Charlotte confronts Maggie in darkness, and Maggie confronts Charlotte in sunlight, but after the first scene, the second, good as it is, comes off rather weakly. Maggie comes to Charlotte, as the latter immediately recognizes, 'to grovel'. Maggie here plays out to the hilt her chosen plan of being 'abject', and it drives Charlotte in desperation, in this scene, to commit herself to the decision of returning to America with her husband.

When Maggie at the close of the book gathers her reward, the pot of gold at the foot of her arch of lies, it appears that in his own profound and Jamesian way Amerigo has also been lying to Charlotte, and he has proved his fidelity to Maggie by virtue of that lying. This is established very clearly:

> But Maggie at last broke it. 'If Charlotte doesn't understand me it's because I've prevented her. I've chosen to deceive her and lie to her.'
>
> The Prince kept his eyes on her. 'I know what you've chosen to do. But I've chosen to do the same.'

94

There is no need to elaborate here on the Prince's lie. Its nature has, of course, been rarefied. But it provides a promising basis for communion between the spiritually reunited husband and wife, and they draw near to each other in their sense of it, just as, in *The Path of Duty*, we have watched Sir Ambrose and Lady Vandeleur achieving a highly *questionable* union on the basis, not of their lie, but of their 'duty'. The reversal of values could hardly be more complete.

Up to a point this reversal has the effect of social criticism. But the world of a novelist depends also on the permanence and validity of certain social surfaces and appearances, and on the assumption that they somehow represent reality. It is doubtless a good thing for an artist to call into question 'the world's artificial system', but there would seem to be limits beyond which he could not, for the sake of his art, profitably pursue his questioning. In some of his late work I think James was on the point of crossing this boundary, and of writing novels which, in spite of their realistic pretensions, give us a world of instable and displaced values: for in the world as we live in it, values are known through appearances, and it is impossible to question the one without casting suspicion on the other. I am not concerned here with why James seemed to insist on this reversal of values beyond the point of safety. Mr. Quentin Anderson in his distinguished essay, *Henry James and the New Jerusalem*, has given us a sketch of the late novels in relation to the philosophy of Henry James's father which might prove enlightening in this respect. All I am interested in here is the evidence of James's distrust of appearance as that evidence exists in his art, and the unfortunate effect it had on his art. For I think it can be shown without resorting to evidence *outside* the novels themselves that James wrenched appearance and reality apart, at least in some of his work, far beyond any requirement of social criticism. The novels in which this discerption is accomplished, or at least threatened, are not, I think, his very best work, although, a little paradoxically, *The Golden Bowl* comes near to being included in that category. On the other hand, those novels in which appearance is successfully and intelligibly correlated with reality are, as a group, more distinguished than those in which the correlation is notably imperfect; and two of these novels, *The Portrait of a Lady* and *What Maisie Knew* are, I think, James's two great masterpieces. I would insist on the latter novel especially at this point, for occurring as it does in the late period, or just on the eve of it, it has been overshadowed by the three long novels of the so-called 'Major Phase', and it has been disgracefully neglected.

I wish to discuss *What Maisie Knew*, a novel in which appearance and reality co-exist without violence to each other, and *The Turn of the Screw*, its companion piece in many ways, but also its exact contrary in others; for *The Turn of the Screw* is little more than a hide-and-seek game between the two terms. If any of James's fictions could be called a metaphysic demonstrating the enmity of appearance and reality, it is this one. The comparison I hope will clarify certain issues that are important in evaluating James as a novelist.

(iii)

In the career of a poet or novelist, particularly in the case of a writer as fertile as James, it should be expected that a given impetus or arc of interest would not be exhausted in a single work, and that corners of the given problem that remain obscure in the one work might be illuminated from the point of view adopted in another if that second work seems to be significantly related. There seems to be such a relation between *What Maisie Knew* and *The Turn of the Screw*. I haven't the space here to make a complete comparison between the two novels, and in any event I am not sure that would be profitable. The similarity between them is highly suggestive, but it cannot in the nature of the case be conclusive. What, finally, is of the greatest interest is the light the comparison throws on the contrasting relations between appearance and reality in the two books. For the success of *Maisie* arises partly from the stability of that relation as it exists there, whereas the instability of the relation in *The Turn of the Screw*, if it generates an effective atmosphere in the novel, nevertheless limits the possibilities of achievement. For the sake of conciseness it will be necessary here to assume a familiarity with the novels on the part of the reader, and press on immediately to the important concluding chapter of *What Maisie Knew*. We find the little girl here the centre of a struggle among parties who wish to claim her for themselves. And these parties arrange themselves in the same identical relationships with each other that exist in *The Turn of the Screw* between the governess on the one hand, and Peter Quint and Miss Jessel on the other, for the possession of Miles and Flora,—the chief difference being that in *Maisie*, Mrs. Beale (Maisie's former governess, but now her stepmother) and Sir Claude (her stepfather) are not ghosts. But the step-parents in *Maisie* and the servants in *The Turn of the Screw* correspond in deeper ways than any suggested by superficial arrangements with the other characters. Maisie, in her innocence, has been used as a convenience for keeping assignations in the illicit liaison that has grown up between her stepmother and stepfather, and to a disturbing degree she has been taken into the confidence of her elders. It is her proud pitiful little boast that she brought them together, and her reward is in the happiness which she imagines they have in being together. But Maisie's innocence remains uncontaminated throughout. She speaks as if with precocious knowledge, but what the reader knows is that her precocity exists in a sensitive response to human feelings and relationships around her, but as yet a response unsupported by adult knowledge. Now if one examines the passages in which Miles's and Flora's former relation with Peter Quint and Miss Jessel are expatiated on in Chapter VIII of *The Turn of the Screw*— those passages which particularly seem to suggest that the children have been morally corrupted—we find that the essence of Miles's offence consists in his having lied to Mrs. Grose, the housekeeper at Bly, concerning his familiarity with Peter Quint. And it is obvious that his reason for doing so is to shield Quint's and Miss Jessel's assignations from the prying curiosity of the other servants. This fact, when the governess learns of it from Mrs. Grose, is interpreted by her in the blackest possible colours for little Miles. But we must remember that this 'sin' is precisely the one of which Maisie has been guilty. Surrounded by adulterous lovers, Maisie has never failed to lie for them when necessary—to lie valiantly, scrupulously, innocently. Her lies do not disturb us on these occasions as Maggie Verver's do just because we understand how innocent and good Maisie really is. Her innocence is not contaminated by the lies; it purifies them. The difference between Miles and Maisie is simply that in the latter case we know at last what Maisie knew, and in Miles's case we only know what his governess imagines he knew. And about the governess there will be more to say.

The equation between the step-parents and the servants cannot be a perfect one of course, for we do not know enough about the servants. Despite his crippling weaknesses of character, Sir Claude is an attractive person, and his regard for Maisie has been genuine. On the other hand, Peter Quint is a somewhat mysterious figure (in the flesh, I mean) to whom, with sinister implications, 'vices more than suspected' are attributed. But Maisie's nefarious mother, Ida, speaking to Maisie of Sir Claude, can say:

> 'You're old enough at any rate to know there are a lot of things I don't say that I easily might; though it would do me good, I assure you, to have spoken my mind for once in my life. I don't speak of your father's infamous wife [Mrs. Beale]: that may give you a notion of the way I'm letting you off. When I say "you" I mean your precious friends and backers. If you don't do justice to my forbearing, out of delicacy, to mention, just as a last word, about your stepfather, a little fact or two of a kind that really I should only *have* to mention to shine myself in comparison, and after every calumny, like pure gold: if you don't do me *that* justice you'll never do me justice at all.'

The atmosphere of *Maisie* doesn't make the most of these hints and charges against Sir Claude, but they add up to as much of the same thing in terms of tangible evidence as Mrs. Grose's charges against Quint. We haven't, actually, any more reason for supposing Peter Quint to have been a monster of iniquity than we have for believing Sir Claude to be. I am speaking of course of Peter Quint as a man, and not as a ghost. There is a great difference between the two, and it isn't absurd to insist on the point, for all the critics who have accepted the validity of the apparitions have also postulated the identity between Peter Quint the man and Peter Quint the ghost. But we have James's word for it that 'Peter Quint and Miss Jessel are not "ghosts" at all, as we know the ghost, but goblins, elves, imps, demons as loosely constructed as those of the old trials for witchcraft'. It is perhaps of the essence of the confusion imposed by *The Turn of the Screw* that the question of the true nature of the ghosts (one conceding their supernatural character) should remain obscure; but in view of James's words it is surprising that the critics who have commented on this novel have never for a moment entertained any of those salutary doubts that occurred to Hamlet on the platform before Elsinore. My point is that it is unjustifiable to carry our moral judgment on Peter Quint the ghost back to Peter Quint the man, for we do not know the way in which the ghost represents the man in this particular instance. Mrs. Grose's remarks about Quint, so blackening in all they *could* mean, are insufficient to warrant the establishment of an identity between them. In making our final judgment on the nature of the relation between the children and the servants it will be necessary, then, to make it in terms of the living servants, and not of the apparitions. Of these latter, one of the few definite things we know of them (from the *Preface*) is that they are 'evoked', a term used of evil spirits, but not usually, I think, of human spirits. At any rate, the word posits a real relation between the demons and someone living at Bly; and it will be seen, I think, that the person is the governess and not the children.

Struggling with Sir Claude and Mrs. Beale for possession of Maisie in the last chapter of the earlier novel we have Maisie's governess, Mrs. Wix. Mrs. Wix represents, clearly, a norm of respectability in the book, and her desire to rescue Maisie from the irregular influences to which she is exposed with her step-parents *seems* to be both passionate and disinterested. However there are some very enigmatic aspects about Mrs. Wix that ought to be noted. There is some danger of disproportionately magnifying these aspects but previous critics seem to have ignored them entirely. The atmosphere of 'horror' in *Maisie* is one of its solid achievements, more substantial and enduring than the 'horror' of *The Turn of the Screw*, and these touches in Mrs. Wix, however they are to be interpreted in other respects, add their own contribution to that atmosphere. Elderly, ugly, fantastic as she is, Mrs. Wix falls in love with Sir Claude. The fact isn't insisted on, and it might even be possible to interpret in non-erotic terms her passionate avowal to Maisie that she 'adores' Sir Claude, although I doubt it. The revealing glimpse we are given into the real situation—so shocking to our nerves just because it is so sudden and only a glimpse—occurs in Chapter XXIV. Although the allusions are veiled, Mrs. Wix's behaviour and speeches are such as to be understandable only in terms of an utter infatuation for the young man, and there are moments when our belief in her disinterestedness wears thin. Her desire to keep Sir Claude and Mrs. Beale separated, if it arises primarily from her concern for Maisie, seems at some points not to be untouched by sexual jealousy. And the ugly possibility arises in the reader's mind that Mrs. Wix's attachment to Maisie may match Mrs. Beale's in this: that for them both, and however much they may like Maisie for herself, the little girl provides a means of closing in on Sir Claude. In what seems to me a misreading of the text, Mr. Joseph Warren Beach has said in *The Method of Henry James*: '. . . Mrs. Wix and Sir Claude are actually "taken in" by what seems to be her eventual development of a "moral sense" like their own'. The more one re-reads the passages in which Mrs. Wix endeavours to inculcate a 'moral sense' in Maisie, the more uneasy one becomes. Mrs. Wix's assumptions about Maisie's knowledge in these passages, and her tone of offensive reproach, constitute as much of a violation of Maisie's innocence as anything in the course of Maisie's short career. And one cannot rid oneself of the feeling that it is precisely that 'moral sense' which Mrs. Wix seeks to give Maisie that will deliver the child into the governess's hands, and as a consequence of that, will ultimately draw Sir Claude into her orbit as well. Mrs. Wix's 'moral sense' at these points is nothing more than allegiance to 'the world's artificial system', and it is not to be identified with anything in Sir Claude. In the last chapter, accusing Maisie of having lost her newly developed 'moral sense', Mrs. Wix accuses Sir Claude of culpability:

'You've nipped it in the bud. You've killed it when it had begun to live.'

She was a newer Mrs. Wix than ever, a Mrs. Wix high and great; but Sir Claude was not after all to be treated as a little boy with a missed lesson. 'I've not killed anything,' he said; 'on the contrary I think I've produced life. I don't know what to call it—I haven't even known how decently to deal with it, to approach it; but, whatever it is, it's the most beautiful thing I've ever met—it's exquisite, it's sacred.'

The differentiation between Mrs. Wix's 'moral sense' and Sir Claude's moral sensibility could not be more complete. But there is a good deal more to Mrs. Wix than these unpleasant distortions. Her 'moral sense' is capable of being educated into fineness, and it is this potentiality that both Sir Claude and Maisie recognize in their different ways. It is in the light of this recognition that Maisie goes off with Mrs. Wix at last. It is Maisie's mission in life (James is very clear about it) to educate her elders, but of the three people struggling for possession of Maisie in the concluding chapter, only poor old Mrs. Wix remains amenable to education. Sir Claude already knows as much as Maisie, but he is hopelessly trapped by circumstances which his weakness is unwilling to surmount; and for Mrs. Beale there has never been a question of education at all. If Maisie's wonderful little character is to continue to have a field for operation, if it is to grow into a maturity as fine as its childhood has been, Mrs. Wix is the only possible choice for Maisie in the end.

In these remarks I have presented most of the evidence for drawing the comparison between *What Maisie Knew* and the ghost story of the following year. It will be seen that the earlier novel throws a great deal of illumination on facts that are imperfectly presented in *The Turn of the Screw*. Beyond the emotional distortions provided by the governess's presentation of the facts about Peter Quint and Miles, we have no more factual evidence for supposing Miles to have been morally corrupted than we have for supposing Maisie to be vicious. Yet on the same evidence we convict the children at Bly, but we let Maisie off because we have to. The governess at Bly, we say, is so persuasive. A detailed examination of the governess's technique of persuasion will provide an insight into a full-scale operation by James of that habit, the ravaging symptoms of which we have looked at in *The Golden Bowl*, of tearing appearance and reality apart.

Miles and Flora are presented to us entirely through the governess's words, and she is 'a mistress of shades'. The reader and the housekeeper at Bly are equally helpless in her hands. The dialogue in *The Turn of the Screw* is written with an economy remarkable for James at any period, for in building up her case against the children the governess must make every word count. One can study her method at its absolutely representative level in Chapter II, in which she receives the letter from Miles's headmaster saying the boy is dismissed from his school. Neither the governess nor ourselves ever know the facts of the case, and there is no reason for magnifying the incident into an incriminating episode. Mr. Edmund Wilson has rightly remarked in his essay, *The Ambiguity of Henry James*, that the governess 'colours' the dismissal 'on no evidence at all, with a significance somehow sinister'. But it is this process of 'colouring' that calls for attention here. The governess, with the opened letter from the headmaster in her hand (a letter which, as we know, merely announces the fact of the dismissal), is talking to Mrs. Grose, the estimable but illiterate housekeeper. At this time the governess has never seen Miles, and knows nothing about him; but she feels free to ask:

'. . . Is he really *bad*?'
The tears were still in her eyes. 'Do the gentlemen say so?'
'They go into no particulars. They simply express their regret that it should be impossible to keep him. That can have but one meaning.' Mrs. Grose listened with dumb emotion; she forebore to ask me what this meaning might be; so that, presently, to put the thing with some coherence and with the mere aid of her presence to my own mind, I went on: 'That he's an injury to the others.'

At this, with one of the quick turns of simple folk, she suddenly flamed up. 'Master Miles!—*him* an injury?'

There was such a flood of good faith in it that, though I had not yet seen the child, my very fears made me jump to the absurdity of the idea. I found myself, to meet my friend the better, offering it, on the spot, sarcastically. 'To his poor little innocent mates.'

Towards the evening of the same day the governess renews her questioning of poor Mrs. Grose:

'I take what you said to me at noon as a declaration that *you've* never known him to be bad.'

She threw back her head; she had clearly by this time, and very honestly, adopted an attitude. 'Oh never known him—I don't pretend *that*.'

I was upset again. 'Then you *have* known him——?'

'Yes, indeed, Miss, thank God.'

'You mean that a boy who never is—— ? '

'Is no boy for *me*.'

I held her tigther. 'You like them with the spirit to be naughty?' Then, keeping pace with her answer, 'So do I.' I eagerly brought out. 'But not to the degree to contaminate——'

'To contaminate?'—my big word left her at a loss.

I explained it. 'To corrupt.'

This is the first time we see the governess's system in operation. With no evidence to go on except an extremely ambiguous letter, and with a great deal to contradict her, the governess is yet able in an incredibly short space to present Miles as, in all probability, vicious; herself as virtuous in supposing that he is so; and to bully the poor housekeeper into a state of partial assent. Her technique is nearly perfect. She begins by asking if Miles is really '*bad*', and the printed italics hide an undefined wealth of meaning in the term. She then says what is certainly *not* true, but what would certainly be believed by Mrs. Grose on the governess's word—that Miles's dismissal 'can have but one meaning', and 'that he's an injury to others'. These are gratuitous contributions of her own that have an insidious look of plausibility about them.

When the housekeeper protests, the governess ascribes it to her simplicity. However, in order not to proceed too quickly for persuasion she seems to meet Mrs. Grose half way, and turns the last statement into an ironic comment; but it is clear that the irony exists at the expense of Miles's 'poor little innocent mates'. The governess, if ever so softly at this point, is implying that the friends Miles might have made at school would not have been the 'innocent' ones who could have been easily injured. It should be noticed that the vague suggestiveness in the italicized '*bad*' begins to be narrowed at this point by opposing 'innocent' to it as its contrary. The quality of the viciousness that is to be attributed to Miles and Flora is already progressing towards definition. In the second part of the quotation above, the italicized '*you've*' is significant. It will suggest to Mrs. Grose and to the reader easily enough that although Mrs. Grose has never known Miles to be bad, there are those who have. Mrs. Grose, however, being a good woman with sane ideas about how boys should behave, in spite of the earlier drilling she has suffered from the governess, still interprets 'bad' quite innocently. But this very sanity or normality on the housekeeper's part is attributed by the governess to an 'attitude'. Mrs. Grose, the governess would say, has fallen into a protective stance in regard to Miles. It is obviously Mrs. Grose who maintains an impartial and judicial attitude towards the evidence (or rather, the lack of it), but these very virtues are turned against her by the governess. Mrs. Grose says that she *has* known Miles to be bad (using the word in its innocent sense), and she thinks this is only proper for a boy. But the governess, with a tingle of nerves, interprets Mrs. Grose's 'bad' in the sinister sense, and she proceeds to persuade Mrs. Grose that it was in this sense that she has used the word. The two following questions that the governess asks Mrs. Grose end with significant dashes, allowing Mrs. Grose and the reader to fill in the blanks with any of the unspeakable words that the governess's concluding remarks will shortly suggest. The reader should also notice that obscene tightening of the governess's grip on Mrs. Grose's arm as the governess closes in on that *usually* innocent word, 'naughty'. It operates with coy and almost sickening force here, and the governess quickly consolidates her gains by running the full declension that began with '*bad*': 'contaminate', and 'corrupt'.

All of the governess's speeches submit to this kind of analysis, but I want to clinch the matter with one final example that is particularly pertinent. The governess is by this time on her way to uncovering the fact that Miles was aware of the relationship between Peter Quint and Miss Jessel, and that he tried to conceal the fact of the relation for the sake of his friends. Now we know that Maisie Farrange has done the same thing for her friends in all innocence, but the governess of Bly is able to interpret it as something fiendish. She has Mrs. Grose cornered again and is questioning her with sadistic delight. She has just asked her if Miles never mentioned Quint in relation with Miss Jessel:

She saw, visibly flushing, where I was coming out. 'Well, he didn't show anything. He denied,' she repeated; 'he denied.'

Lord how I pressed her now! 'So that you could see he knew what was between the two wretches?'

'I don't know—I don't know!' the poor woman wailed.

'You do know, you dear thing,' I replied; 'only you haven't my dreadful boldness of mind, and you keep back, out of timidity and modesty and delicacy, even the impression that in the past when you had, without my aid, to flounder about in silence, most of all made you miserable. But I shall get it out of you yet! There was something in the boy that suggested to you,' I continued, 'his covering and concealing their relation.'

'Oh he couldn't prevent——'

'Your learning the truth? I daresay! But heavens!' I fell, with vehemence, a-thinking, 'what it shows that they must, to that extent, have succeeded in making of him!'

'Ah nothing that's not nice *now*!' Mrs. Grose lugubriously pleaded.

'I don't wonder you looked queer!' I persisted, 'when I mentioned to you the letter from his school.'

The manner in which the governess deflects the course of Mrs. Grose's thoughts from their original channel is particularly clear here. Obviously Mrs. Grose has been on the point of remarking that Miles could not have prevented Quint and Miss Jessel from meeting, but the governess characteristically interrupts for the purpose of making Mrs. Grose say something else—something more incriminating for Miles. And then with a skilful sideswoop she applies the effect of *that* towards building up the black suggestiveness of the headmaster's letter. It has been recently observed that the governess is a great symbolic religious figure offering herself as an expiatory victim for the children, but she seems more like a fit subject for euthanasia to me. In his preface James said of the governess, 'We have surely as much of her own nature as we can swallow in watching it reflect her anxieties and inductions', and the words are exactly right. James's choice of the word 'inductions' seems especially pointed, for the governess never has any facts about Miles or Flora to deduce a case from. What she offers is a tissue of surmises built upon the slenderest possible quantity of evidence.

During the past several years it has become usual for American critics to dismiss Mr. Edmund Wilson's analysis of *The Turn of the Screw* as inept,[1] but it remains, in spite of an unfortunate emphasis on the question of the reality of the ghosts, the best thing we have on James's story. Mr. Wilson's Freudian interpretation of the actions of the governess is probably as good as any explanation is likely to be if we insist on a realistic one, even if one isn't partial to Freudian terms in literary criticism; and it is easy to see how those several difficult elements we noticed in Mrs. Wix's character—her erotic infatuation with Sir Claude and a questionable quality in her 'moral sense'—might easily have proved the seeds from which the governess of the following year developed. However that may be, the governess is intent on possessing the children in a way which, for both Hawthorne and James represented a violation of human personality. Westervelt, Chillingworth, Olive Chancellor, Gilbert Osmund, are all guilty of this crime in one way or another. It is the distinguishing mark of *The Turn of the Screw* (which it shares

[1] For example, the American critic, Mr. Stanley Edgar Hyman, always a little chagrined when Mr. Wilson's name is mentioned, has referred to 'Edmund Wilson's cockeyed reading of *The Turn of the Screw*'.

with *Ethan Brand* in Hawthorne's canon) that it attempts to abstract the crime from its individuating particularities in life, and present it in its horrible purity. The children are presented as charming types of innocence. Mr. Richard Chase (who nevertheless sees the children as corrupted) has remarked on the significance of their names. Miles is a little soldier, as his name indicates, while Flora's name suggests all the promise and loveliness of spring. (The withered fern, discussed below, makes its point more tellingly because of Flora's name.) On the other hand, the governess has no name. She is as anonymous as the persuasions and pressures of 'the world's artificial system', whose doctrines, as a teacher of innocence, she endeavours to inculcate in the children. There is nothing more pathetic in James's works than the way the children make a valiant but foredoomed attempt to escape from her tyranny. This is especially true of Miles, but particularly touching is Flora's little attempt to escape the suffocating surveillance of her teacher. Taking advantage of a moment of freedom (to which, incidentally, the chivalrous Miles may have helped her) the child has obeyed an instinctive impulse to go off by herself, and she has wandered down to the little lake at Bly. But her respite is a short one, for no Fury was ever more vigilant than the governess, who, dragging the long-suffering Mrs. Grose with her, presently tracks her down. The child sees them coming:

> Flora, a short way off, stood before us on the grass and smiled as if her performance had now become complete. The next thing she did, however, was to stoop down and pluck—quite as if it were all she was there for—a big ugly spray of withered fern.

For a moment we have the image of a little martyr, even to the blessed palm. But this palm is ugly and withered, for it celebrates the hideous martyrdom of innocence. Flora is not to leave her childhood by the gradual maturing of knowledge as we have watched Maisie's powers of judgment and choice unfold into an exquisitely poised moral intuition. She is to become an 'old, old woman' at a stroke—to have forcibly imposed on her mind all the guilty knowledge of a distorted maturity. For the governess's determination that Flora and Miles shall confess to *seeing* the demons that haunt her own vision is, in effect, a determination to shape their innocence to her guilt. For what are the demons but objective symbols of the governess's distorted 'moral sense'? *The Turn of the Screw* enacts for us the long siege of innocence, of the natural state of childhood, that is undertaken by the malign representatives of 'the world's artificial system'. After the governess has failed to make the little girl see the haggard damned ghost of Miss Jessel at the lake's edge, she quotes Flora as crying: 'I don't know what you mean. I see nobody. I see nothing. I never *have*. I think you're cruel.' It gives us some idea—that 'I never *have*', with its use of the past tense—of all the children must have been through at the governess's hands, pressures, suggestions, and tyrannies that we aren't informed of, and it tells us how they must, with natural delicacy of perception, have sensed something of what, all this time, has been going on in the governess's mind.

The 'horrors' that the little girl speaks to Mrs. Grose a few pages later are authentic 'horrors' well enough. It is precisely those 'horrors' that the withered fern celebrated in anticipation. The governess has at last succeeded in giving Flora her own understanding of the world the children moved in with Peter Quint and Miss Jessel. And in doing so she has corrupted Flora far beyond anything within the power of the servants, whose memory has been so abused. Flora speaks 'horrors'; but what 'horrors', we are inclined to ask, might Maisie not have produced, if properly instructed, from the rich background provided by her familiar knowledge of her mother's lovers (Mr. Perriam, Lord Eric, the Captain, Mr. Tischbein); or from her weird meeting with Mrs. Cuddon, the hideous wealthy American mulatto who pays Maisie's father to be her lover; or from her association with her adulterous step-parents? But Maisie never speaks any 'horrors'. Her wonderful creative innocence is able to move through all her afflictions unscathed, and she finally achieves a fineness of moral knowledge far beyond anything within the range of Mrs. Wix's highly imperfect 'moral sense', which is based on a negative appreciation of guilt, itself partaking of the guilt it judges. Maisie's final triumph consists in the fact that she is able to resist this aspect of Mrs. Wix as successfully as she resists the contamination of Mrs. Beale; and when Maisie and Mrs. Wix go off together at the end of the novel one knows that it is Mrs. Wix who will do all the learning in the future.

Before dropping this matter, I wish to say something more about the question of the ghosts that has so tormented critics. I have already quoted from James's *Preface*: '. . . Peter Quint and Miss Jessel are not "ghosts" at all, as we now know the ghost, but goblins, elves, imps, demons as loosely constructed as those of the old trials for witchcraft . . .' In other words, James's ghosts here are to be taken on the same level that we accept Hawthorne's ghosts: as supernatural agents having an accredited place in the story and promoting a moral meaning, but not raising the problem of belief or disbelief as such. I doubt if it would be profitable to discuss whether or not Judge Pyncheon in *The House of Seven Gables* was acting under the influence of that other classic piece of witchcraft supernaturalism, Maule's Curse. At any rate, one is quite willing to evaluate his action on its own merit without becoming involved in such questions as distract us from the real problems in *The Turn of the Screw*. What Peter Quint and Miss Jessel actually contribute to the action of the story, they contributed long before the arrival of our gruesome governess at Bly, when they walked the earth in flesh and used Miles and Flora as conveniences for their assignations. Mr. Wilson's essay indisputably establishes, I think, that no one except the governess sees the demons—but whether these demons that the governess 'evokes' are related, in anything but external appearance, to the dead persons they represent, *ought to be* highly problematical. The fact that Mr. Wilson has based his interpretation on a Freudian analysis of the governess may be a little irritating at first, but an extension of Mr. Wilson's theory actually provides the best logical explanation possible.[1]

[1] There is evidence to support Mr. Wilson's theory in addition to those instances of Freudian imagery which he cites. Returning from church on that fatal Sunday when Miles has asked her to get in touch with his uncle for the purpose of sending him again to school, the governess symbolically

The governess's own repressions, projecting themselves externally in certain images, are actually endowed with the sanctions of objective supernatural evil. The governess 'evokes' by a kind of sympathetic magic demons that correspond to her own hidden evil. It is, then, the governess who is possessed, and her own possession becomes a type of the possession with which she threatens the children. But the demons threaten the children only indirectly, only insofar as they act through the governess. The governess's action is elevated in this way above the mere level of neurosis, but when the demons have performed this function of validating the governess's evil, they cease to matter in themselves.

This ambiguity amounts to trickery, of course—trickery of a kind that seems to me to be below the level of an artist of James's stature. And yet it is also more than trickery. It is the most tortuous exemplification in James's work of that tension between appearance and reality—or, in this case, a wanton wrenching apart of the two terms. There are a number of essential questions that simply cannot be answered without bringing to *The Turn of the Screw* that kind of attention which a work of art ought not to require. And yet the questions are not idle ones if one assumes that a work of art has a moral value. The whole meaning of *The Turn of the Screw* revolves around the question of whether the children are innocent or have been corrupted. But without resorting to evidence from another novel, *What Maisie Knew*, the question seems to me unanswerable. Appearance and reality have been separated in *The Turn of the Screw* to just this appalling extent. It is

establishes her identity with Miss Jessel by 'sinking down at the foot of the staircase—suddenly collapsing there on the lowest step and then with a revulsion recalling that it was exactly where, more than a month before, and just so bowed with evil things, I had seen the spectre of the most horrible of women'. Mounting then to her own room, the identity so established continues to pursue the governess. She discovers the 'ghost' of Miss Jessel, seated at her own desk, like 'some housemaid' who is about to apply herself 'to the considerable effort of a letter to her sweetheart'. This *should* establish, if anything can, the nature of the repressed infatuation of the governess for her employer, and it shows how it lies at the centre of all her dealings with the children.

almost impossible to bring the problem of evil in the novel to a particular or significant focus because of this separation, and we are left with a story on our hands that, practically speaking, most readers will accept at the level of *The Lady or the Tiger*. And yet James seems to have been presenting for us here a parable that illustrates his profoundest meaning—a meaning, or a metaphysic, that would morally justify Maggie Verver's apotheosis of falsehood, as we analysed it in the earlier part of this paper. What James has, in effect, accomplished, is an undermining of the laws of evidence, and a destructive foray into the grounds for moral judgment. It will be profitable, I think, to conclude this study with a summary comparison between the moral worlds James offers us in the two novels that have been discussed here.

In *What Maisie Knew* Sir Claude and Mrs. Beale are living, morally responsible people who may be held accountable for their own acts, and the novel is the most magnificent portrayal in the language of the unfolding discretionary powers of a human being. *What Maisie Knew* presents us with a world of horror, but the essence of that horror consists in the way we are able to isolate the *grotesqueness* of moral evil as it caricatures and distorts human action and motive—to isolate it through the innocent eyes of a little girl whose vision is not sufficiently dulled by conventional experience to absorb the singularity of the irregular world in which she lives. *What Maisie Knew* seems to me by far the greatest novel of the later James—and second only, I think, to *The Portrait of a Lady* in the entire canon of James's work. In *Maisie* we have one of the most fully lighted moral worlds that James ever offered for our inspection. There is a steady and irreproachable correspondence between appearance and reality in this novel, but the relationship is not felt as static. It is realized with a complex density. There are no 'set' characters circulating dully around moral fixities, and yet their actions, and the judgments we are invited to pass on those actions, do suggest an intelligible moral framework for experience that corresponds to our own knowledge of the world.

In *The Turn of the Screw* this clarity is lost. Sir Claude and Mrs. Beale are killed off, and reappear as 'ghosts', whose past action we have no way of evaluating unless we are willing to accept the conventional criticisms of Mrs. Grose, or the black insinuations of the horrible governess. We have entered a world of complete unreality in this novel in which, if we could grasp anything as solid even as ghost-flesh we should feel comparatively reassured. *The Turn of the Screw* is, of course, another attack on 'the world's artificial system', but the attack goes so deep that when the artificial system has been destroyed, it is doubtful if anything is left. Rather than the quotation from Hawthorne's *The New Adam and Eve* with which I opened this article, a different quotation from his story, *The Christmas Banquet*, would seem to apply to this novel. Hawthorne has caused one of his characters in this story, Gervayse Hastings, to describe the affliction which has placed him among the most unfortunate of men:

> It is a chillness—a want of earnestness—a feeling as if what should be my heart were a thing of vapor—a haunting perception of unreality! Thus seeming to possess all that other men have—all that men aim at—I have really possessed nothing, neither joy nor griefs. All things, all persons . . . have been like shadows flickering on the wall. It was so with my wife and children—with those who seemed my friends: it is so with yourselves, whom I see now before me. Neither have I myself any real existence, but am a shadow like the rest.

In *The Turn of the Screw* we almost seem to have entered Gervayse Hastings' world. Nothing is real, and we are sure of nothing. If Miles and Flora are innocent (and they undoubtedly are) their very innocence is a tragedy, for it is utterly incomprehensible to 'the world's artificial system', and their martyrdom is meaningless. 'It is only through the medium of the imagination', Hawthorne wrote, 'that we can lessen those iron fetters, which we call truth and reality, and make ourselves even partially sensible of what prisoners we are.' The trouble with *The Turn of the Screw* is simply that the fetters are lessened to such an extent that moral action seems to lose any intelligible form. We are confronted with a kind of chaos that appears to be controlled only by the artificial props of the story.

It would no doubt be possible to discuss the matter of this paper in another terminology than the one chosen here. But the terms, appearance and reality, point to the profoundly American character of the problem, and they illuminate still further the nature of the similarity between Hawthorne and Henry James. The conflict between appearance and reality obviously relates to what, in an earlier essay, I called the American Problem: that is, the conflict between America and Europe, and between the past and present. It is at the very heart of James's work, and analysis would show that the conflict, in one way or another, is the seed of most of James's stories. But it is those stories in which the conflict is kept within reasonable limits that are James's true masterpieces.

6

'WHAT MAISIE KNEW'

A DISAGREEMENT BY F. R. LEAVIS [1]

I AGREE with Mr. Bewley in setting a very high value on
What Maisie Knew, the work, of those he discusses, in which
I am most interested. Nevertheless I find myself protesting
vehemently against his treatment of it. In fact the *What
Maisie Knew* he offers us is not the *What Maisie Knew* I admire,
and I am convinced that it is not James's. The parallel that
Mr. Bewley proposes with *The Turn of the Screw* seems to me
wholly invalid, and in the course of making it out he falsifies,
I think, both his terms.

I am not myself much interested in the famous thriller, and
such attention as I now give it is wholly incidental to the
defence of *What Maisie Knew*. Not that I don't think *The Turn
of the Screw* a success in its way. It achieves perfectly what
James aimed at. It is a triumph, conceived in a spirit that
Poe might have applauded, of calculating contrivance, and
I cannot see why so much heavy weather should have been
made of interpreting it as notoriously has been—even if
James hadn't told us so plainly in the Preface the nature of
the aim and the calculation.

For Mr. Bewley, of the two tales, *The Turn of the Screw*
might almost seem to be the major concern. It is in the
interest of his version of that story that he makes out the
version of *What Maisie Knew* against which I protest.

> The whole meaning of *The Turn of the Screw* revolves around
> the question of whether the children are innocent or have been
> corrupted. But without resorting to evidence from another
> novel, *What Maisie Knew*, the question seems to me unanswer-
> able. Appearance and reality have been separated in *The Turn
> of the Screw* to just this appalling extent. It is almost impossible

[1] Mr. Bewley has invited me to elaborate certain dissentient remarks
of mine on his essay.—F. R. L.

to bring the problem of evil to a particular or significant focus because of this separation.

Unless at the level of the play on the nerves of a Christmas ghost-story, I find nothing appalling about *The Turn of the Screw*, though on the other hand, I can't doubt that James means us to believe the children corrupted. The 'ambiguity' that Mr. Bewley examines as 'a destructive foray into the grounds for moral judgment'—as demanding 'that kind of attention which a work of art ought not to require'—is created, it seems to me, by Mr. Bewley himself, and I find the ingenuity of the creating, the way in which he arrives at his 'evoked' demons, with the odd elusive status he attributes to them, astonishingly perverse. The actual inferiority of *The Turn of the Screw* is a less interesting affair than that which we are asked to contemplate.

If it is 'impossible to bring the problem of evil to a particular or significant focus' in *The Turn of the Screw*, that is because, in that story, 'evil' had no particular significance for James. When he tells us, in the *Preface*, that Peter Quint and Miss Jessel are not 'ghosts' at all, that is not by way of making it possible for us to believe (which is Mr. Bewley's suggestion) that the bodily valet and governess might very well have been quite unsinister. He has already told us that 'this perfectly . . . irresponsible little fiction is a piece of ingenuity pure and simple, of cold artistic calculation, an *amusette* to catch those not easily caught', and he is explaining how his *ad hoc* inventions, Peter Quint and Miss Jessel, have the function of producing a given kind of effect:

> They would be agents, in fact: there would be laid on them the dire duty of causing the situation to reek with the air of Evil.

The nature of his interest here in Evil he makes perfectly plain:

> Portentous evil—how was I to save that, as an intention on the part of my demon-spirits, from the drop, the comparative vulgarity, inevitably attending throughout the whole range of possible brief illustration, the offered example, the imputed

vice, the cited act, the limited deplorable presentable instance? To bring the bad dead back to life for a second round of badness is to warrant them as indeed prodigious, and to become hence as shy of specifications as of a waiting anti-climax.

Peter Quint, then, and Miss Jessel are the consistently bad ghosts of bad persons—James is explicit about it (if that were necessary). Again:

> What, in the last analysis, had I to give the sense of? Of their being, the haunting pair, capable, as the phrase is, of everything—that is, of exerting, in respect to the children, the very worst action small victims so conditioned might be conceived as subject to.

But though James would seem to leave us in no doubt as to the status he intends for the 'haunting pair' as actors in the drama, and agents of portentous evil, he nevertheless doesn't care what we conceive the evil to be, so long as we feel the situation to 'reek with the air' of it. He has no particular vision or felt significance pressing for definition. His idea is to trick us into generating for ourselves the dire 'significance' that—where these things are in question—we find most congenial:

> Only make the reader's general vision of evil intense enough, I said to myself—and that already is a charming job—and his own imagination, his own sympathy (with the children) and horror (of their false friends) will supply him quite sufficiently with all the particulars. Make him *think* the evil, make him think it for himself, and you are released from weak specifications.

Mr. Bewley, with so many other readers, justifies James's reckoning. And yet James, I am sure, would have been surprised at the perversity that focuses the evil, not in the 'haunting pair', but in the governess. And Mr. Bewley, we know, has not been alone in doing that. For this perversity (may I say?) I see no real excuse; but for an explanation why it should have been possible we can invoke, I think, the quality that makes *The Turn of the Screw* so limited in interest

—the story has no ponderable significance; it is a mere thriller: 'my values', says James, 'are positively all blanks save so far as an excited horror, a promoted pity, a created expertness . . . proceed to read into them more or less fantastic figures'. A non-significant thriller, done, nevertheless, with the subtlety of the great master, will naturally tend to escape recognition for what it is, and to get its subtlety accepted by some admirers of James as being of another order —the servant, that is, of some intended significance: hence ingenuities of interpretation and the discovery of radical ambiguities.

All the same I am very much surprised that Mr. Bewley should be still able to think Mr. Edmund Wilson's interpretation worth invoking in support. For when the 'unfortunate emphasis on the reality of the ghosts' has been dealt with, what is left? Since, as critics have pointed out—e.g. A. J. A. Waldock and (see *Partisan Review* for February, 1949) Oliver Evans—Mrs. Grose, the housekeeper, recognizes the dead valet in the highly specific description of the sinister intruder given by the governess, who had never before heard of Peter Quint, it is hard to see why Mr. Bewley should go on explaining the apparitions as somehow 'evoked' by the governess in consequence of her alleged infatuation with her master. Or rather, one can see that his 'evoked', and the corresponding odd status attributed to the 'demons', represents Mr. Bewley's attempt to accept, at the same time, both Edmund Wilson's theory and the conclusive criticism of it. But I have to insist that Mr. Bewley himself has invented that equivocal status, and the kind of ambiguity or trickery with which he credits James.

From Edmund Wilson he takes over too that remarkable misrepresentation of the 'authority' that James, in the Preface, tells us he has given the governess. It hadn't occurred to James that he might be taken to be encouraging a view of the governess that credits her with a capacity for mesmeric moral bullying. All he means (as Oliver Evans points out) is that he has invested her with authority for the reader, who will know that he is to trust her implicitly.

But the refutation of Mr. Bewley's reading of *The Turn of*

the Screw doesn't depend on anything that James *tells* us. We need only, without distorting preconceptions, read the story itself. Mr. Bewley will not mind my saying that his *parti pris* finds major support in an ignorance of English possibilities that he shares with Mr. Wilson. Elaborating his case against the governess he says:

> One can study his method at its absolutely representative level in Chapter II, in which she receives the letter from Miles's headmaster, saying that the boy is dismissed from his school. Neither the governess nor ourselves ever know the facts of the case, and there is no reason for magnifying the incident into an incriminating episode. Mr. Edmund Wilson has rightly remarked in his essay, *The Ambiguity of Henry James*, that the governess 'colours' the dismissal 'on no evidence at all, with a significance somehow sinister'.

But James, by the time he wrote the story, was Englishman enough to know that no English headmaster would have dared to expel a boy—and a boy belonging to a family of a distinguished 'County' standing—without being prepared to substantiate against him as grave a charge as the governess divines from the letter.

> With no evidence to go on except an extremely ambiguous letter, and with a great deal to contradict her, the governess is yet able in an incredibly short space to present Miles as, in all probability, vicious. . . .

The evidence of the letter, for an English reader, must tell very heavily indeed; and as for the 'great deal that contradicts' it, there we have James's theme under the aspect that answers to Mr. Bewley's general formula: the conflict between appearance and reality. The children look so angelically good, but their very 'innocence', in its sustained imperturbability, is a measure of their corruption. That is the peculiar horror (the thrill focused in the brave governess's agonized sense of isolation and helplessness) that James intends as the note of *The Turn of the Screw*.

We have the note sharply enough defined in the scene in

which Miles deliberately—it is unmistakable—turns on his 'innocence' with special intensity and holds the governess entranced while he performs on the piano, with the result that she forgets to keep watch on Flora, who is thus enabled to slip away and keep an assignation with the female 'demon', Miss Jessel. The 'innocent' charm of the boy is really poised and sinister calculation, the antithesis of child-like: that is what unquestionably (it seems to me) we are meant to feel. As for Flora's depravity, the housekeeper (will Mr. Bewley argue that she is bullied into it?) bears fully explicit testimony to that in her talk with the governess after the scene by the lake.

The attempt to establish a parallel doesn't, then, generate light: I hope I have said enough about *The Turn of the Screw* to enforce that judgment. But it is the consequences, or concomitants, of that attempt for *What Maisie Knew* that I care about. That Mr. Bewley should stultify (as I see it) James's intention by preserving the innocence of Miles and Flora doesn't trouble me much, so little being at stake; but when he projects Evil into *What Maisie Knew* I brace myself for a stern repelling action. For with 'portentous evil' (to use James's own phrase) James is not at all concerned in that masterpiece. With squalor, yes; but that is another matter. The tone and mode of *What Maisie Knew*—this is what one has to insist on—are those of an extraordinarily high-spirited comedy. The comedy doesn't exclude pathos, that is true; but the pathos bears no relation to that of *The Turn of the Screw*. It is no more the pathos of innocence assailed or surrounded by *evil* than the distinctive pathos of the early part of *David Copperfield* is that.

This comparison has point, for the idea, the treatment— and how do we distinguish from theme here?—of *What Maisie Knew* would pretty obviously not have been conceived by James if he hadn't read *David Copperfield*. It was in Dickens that he found the tip that taught him how he might deal, in this kind of comedy, with his moral and emotional intensities —those to which he was moved by his glimpses of late Victorian Society. It is not too much to say that he had at times been horrified by these glimpses: there is a letter of the 'eighties in which, shocked by a peculiarly repellent scandal of the day, he prophesies for Great Britain an equivalent (it would appear) of the French Revolution. The note of moral horror is to be found in *A London Life* (1888), where the horror is registered in the innocent consciousness of Laura, the nubile American girl who has to watch the career of her married sister, the Society beauty, in the fastest London *beau monde*, a career resembling Maisie's mamma's. But over against Laura is her friend, old Lady Davenant, who, far from registering moral horror, takes a Regency attitude towards the scandals. James's own attitude has enough of her in it to produce the witty and satirical treatment in which *A London Life* relates closely to *What Maisie Knew*. He suggests, however, in the story, a third attitude besides Laura's and Lady Davenant's. We have it when Laura asks herself:

> Was she wrong after all—was she cruel by being too rigid? . . . It was not the first time the just measure seemed to slip from her hands as she became conscious of possible, or rather of very actual differences of standard and usage. On this occasion Geordie and Ferdie asserted themselves, by the mere force of lying asleep upstairs in their little cribs, as on the whole the just measure.

This hint is developed in *What Maisie Knew*; the hint that the criterion of judgment must be the consequences for the children. Instead of developing it in *A London Life* he takes the opportunity for satiric humour offered by the pair of hearty and insensitive cubs, who are obviously going, not to suffer, but to belong happily and whole-heartedly to their class and kind.

The next story to consider when we are inquiring into the genesis of *What Maisie Knew* is *The Pupil* (1891), which James reprinted for the Collected Edition in the same volume as *Maisie* and with which he associated it in the Preface in an account that bears out my case. There is a clear relation between Laura's role of critical innocence in a world of moral squalor and the joint roles of the pupil, Morgan Moreen, and his unfortunate exploited tutor, Pemberton. Moreover Morgan, the precociously intelligent and incorruptibly nice child, develops a potentiality of pathos that one perhaps hardly registers as such in the brace of hearty, healthy young cubs in *A London Life*. But in *The Pupil* we no longer have the note of horror; the squalor the story deals in is not of a kind to evoke any sense of 'portentous evil', and it is not sexual. Except for not paying their bills the Moreens are intensely respectable. In fact—it should be plain once the suggestion has been made—they are the Micawbers translated higher in the social scale and given a cosmopolitan setting; seen, also, too fully for what they are to be presented with a warmly sympathetic humour. James has unmistakably found his inspiration in Dickens.

When we come to *What Maisie Knew* we see that the hint now has been taken from David himself; David—'only Brooks of Sheffield'—puzzling over the banter of Mr. Murdstone's friends, and David the Micawbers' lodger, the small child deprived of parents and committed to a paradoxical kind of adulthood among adults—small child and man-of-the-world:

> I never can understand whether my precocious self-dependence confused Mrs. Micawber in reference to my age, or whether she was so full of the subject that she would have talked about it to the very twins if there had been no one else to communicate with. . . .

So prompted, James achieves a remarkable economy, which brings at the same time a rich gain in positive values. In Maisie we may say we have Laura, the innocent girl of *A London Life*, but this time bringing to the part the innocence of actual childhood. Morgan, the 'pupil', with his precociously developed moral perception and his sensitive integrity, has come in between, contributing obvious elements to the conception of Maisie, in whom, moreover, we have once again the pathos. And James, looking back on *The Pupil* in the light of his new conception, has seen that he doesn't need Pemberton, the tutor, or any equivalent adult observer and commentator.

The whole is presented through Maisie   through her developing awareness and understanding. The thing might seem to be impossibly difficult, and it is done with almost incredible perfection.

It was to be the fate of this patient little girl to see much more than she at first understood, but also even at first to understand much more than any little girl however patient, had perhaps ever understood before. . . . She was taken into the confidence of passions on which she fixed just the stare she might have had for images bounding across the wall in the slide of a magic-lantern. Her little world was phantasmagoric—strange shadows dancing on a sheet. It was as if the whole performance had been given for her—a mite of a half-scared infant in a great dim theatre.

The performance as apprehended by the child, with her growing powers, in her phantasmagoric little world, and fitted more and more with meanings, is evoked with astonishing vividness and economy:

By the time she had grown sharper, as the gentlemen who had criticized her calves used to say, she found in her mind a collection of images and echoes to which meanings were attachable—images and echoes kept for her in the childish dusk, the dim closet, the high drawers, like games she wasn't yet big enough to play. The great strain meanwhile was that of carrying by the right end the things her father said about her mother —things mostly, indeed, that Moddle, on a glimpse of them, as if they had been complicated toys or difficult books, took out of her hands and put away in the closet. A wonderful assortment of objects of this kind she was to discover there later, all tumbled up too with the things, shuffled into the same receptacle, that her mother had said about her father.

The things that Maisie hears and sees are much of the order of those which horrified Laura in *A London Life*, but *What Maisie Knew*, in tone, is even more removed from that earliest of the three stories than *The Pupil* is. Inspired by the hint from Dickens, this un-Dickensian genius has found a way of treating without the note of horror matter from which it might seem to be inseparable so long as there was to be no sacrifice of moral intensity. And that *What Maisie Knew* is a happy example of marked moral intensity no admirer will question. But to suggest as Mr. Bewley does in making his comparison that *What Maisie Knew* like *The Turn of the Screw* deals with evil is to convey an utterly false impression. It deals with moral squalor; with ugly conduct that from some approaches might very well be brought under 'depravity'; but this last term suggests a vibration that is absent from *What Maisie Knew*. Though sexual misconduct, adultery, figures so centrally, it has clearly evoked as such no noticeable moral thrill in James—no marked interest for itself, in fact; though a creative writer's moral preoccupation could hardly be more intent and penetrating than James's is here. What we are given is comedy; where adulterous relations are concerned, the comedy of 'history repeating itself':

> . . . an upright scarlet plume, as to the ownership of which Maisie was instantly eager. 'Who is she?—who is she?'
> But Mrs. Beale for a moment only looked after them. 'The liar—the liar!'
> Maisie considered. 'Because he's not—where one thought?' That was also, a month ago in Kensington Gardens, where her mother had not been. 'Perhaps he has come back,' she said.
> 'He never went—the hound!'
> That, according to Sir Claude, had been also what her mother had not done, and Maisie could only have a sense of something that in a maturer mind would be called the way history repeats itself.
> 'Who *is* she?' she asked again.

In its central aspect it is the comedy of a child's innocence; a comedy that, while being so high-spirited, is at the same time, and essentially, a rendering of the pathos of Maisie's situation:

> She therefore recognized the hour that in troubled glimpses she had long foreseen, the hour when—the phrase for it came back to her from Mrs. Beale—with two fathers, two mothers and two homes, six protections in all, she shouldn't know 'wherever' to go.

There is no tendency to the sentimental in this pathos. Perhaps the distinctive quality of it as, in its astringent purity and strength, the extraordinary subtle methods of James's comedy disengage it from the given situation, is better suggested by the following passage, which, with its 'bread and butter', has an obvious symbolic force:

> The next moment, however, he laughed gaily enough. 'My dear lady, you exaggerate tremendously *my* poor needs.' Mrs. Wix had once mentioned to her young friend that when Sir Claude called her his dear lady he could do anything with her; and Maisie felt a certain anxiety to see what he would do now. Well, he only addressed her a remark of which the child herself was aware of feeling the force. 'Your plan appeals to me immensely; but of course—don't you see?—I shall have to consider the position I put myself in by leaving my wife.'
>
> 'You'll also have to remember,' Mrs. Wix replied, 'that if you don't look out your wife won't give you time to consider. Her ladyship will leave *you*.'
>
> 'Ah my good friend, I do look out!' the young man returned while Maisie helped herself afresh to bread and butter. 'Of course if that happens I shall have somehow to turn round; but I hope with all my heart it won't. I beg your pardon,' he continued to his stepdaughter, 'for appearing to discuss that sort of possibility under your sharp little nose. But the fact is I *forget* half the time that Ida's your sainted mother.'
>
> 'So do I!' said Maisie, her mouth full of bread and butter and to put him in the right.
>
> Her protectress, at this, was upon her again. 'The little desolate precious pet!'

The strength of the pathos, as of the comedy in which it finds its felicitous definition, is the strength of the affirmation of positive values that it conveys. We have it here, the affirmation; the normative concern with a concept of an essential human goodness: ' "So do I!" said Maisie, her mouth full of bread and butter and to put him more in the right.'— The comedy of that 'So do I!' is a far subtler thing than the isolated passage might suggest. Our response, as we read the passage in its context, is neither her 'protectress's' (Mrs. Wix), nor the antithesis, which would be a snigger, but something more complex.

Maisie is good. She represents a positive concept of goodness, though we have no difficulty in taking her as an actual individual little girl. Mr. Bewley, of course, is far from wishing to dispute this proposition. Nevertheless I have to protest against the misrepresentation involved in his attempt at assimilating Maisie to the children of *The Turn of the Screw*: it is to me a more striking illustration of the power of a wrong-headed preconception to distort than his presentment (utterly baseless, I think) of the governess as a neurotically cunning moral bully who insinuates ideas into the mind of the unsuspecting housekeeper. He writes:

> . . . we find that the essence of Miles's offence consists in his having lied to Mrs. Grose, the housekeeper at Bly, concerning his familiarity with Peter Quint. And it is obvious that his reason for doing so is to shield Quint's and Miss Jessel's assignations from the prying curiosity of the other servants. This fact, when the governess learns of it from Mrs. Grose, is interpreted by her in the blackest possible colours for little Miles. But we must remember that this 'sin' is precisely the one of which Maisie has been guilty. Surrounded by adulterous lovers, Maisie has never failed to lie for them when necessary—to lie valiantly, scrupulously, innocently.

But on what evidence does Mr. Bewley assert so roundly that Maisie lies, and lies 'for' the 'adulterous lovers'? That we are to think of Miles and Flora as practising deliberate cunning, deceit, and doing so in collusion with the depraved haunting couple, I do not see how we can doubt, if we take without *parti pris* what James gives us. But it seems to me that on the evidence of the text Maisie wholly deserves the tribute that Sir Claude pays her: 'I know when people lie—and that's what I've loved in you, that you never do.' And this is the worst that she can bring against herself: 'There had been times when she had had to make the best of the impression that she was deceitful; yet she had never concealed anything bigger than a thought.' 'For Maisie moreover,' we have been told, 'concealment had never necessarily seemed deception; she had grown up among things as to which her foremost knowledge was that she was never to ask about them.'

Maisie doesn't lie. And that Mr. Bewley can suggest that the 'pacific art of stupidity' she does practise amounts to lying, and that she practises it in the interest of adulterous lovers, merely shows how disastrously infelicitous are the generalizing preoccupations that can attempt to parallel *What Maisie Knew* with *The Turn of the Screw* as dealing in evil, horror and sexual depravity. This sufficiently explicit key passage occurs early in *What Maisie Knew* (it opens the second paragraph of Chapter II):

> The theory of her stupidity, eventually embraced by her parents, corresponded with a great deal in her small still life: the complete vision, private but final, of the strange office she filled. It was literally a moral revolution accomplished in the depths of her nature. The stiff dolls on the dusky shelves began to move their legs and arms; old forms and phases began to have a sense that frightened her. She had a new feeling, the feeling of danger, on which a new remedy rose to meet it, the idea of an inner self or, in other words, concealment. She puzzled out with imperfect signs, but with a prodigious spirit, that she had been a centre of hatred and a messenger of insult, and that everything was bad because she had been employed to make it so. Her parted lips locked themselves with the determination to be employed no longer.

She acts with more and more subtlety on 'her little instinct of keeping the peace'. We have the comedy and also 'the small strange pathos on the child's part of an innocence so saturated with knowledge and so directed to diplomacy'. But the 'little instinct of keeping the peace' is more than that; it is the agent of a positive judgment that develops as we watch it more and more discrimination. Hatred, malice, desire to wound or humiliate or make uncomfortable—these are what Maisie resolves she will not lend herself to. And we see this kind of discrimination, as it becomes more experienced, becoming a surer and surer judgment of personality. There are poignant conflicts when judgment cannot square with established loyalties and pieties, but, though these conflicts promote the growth that brings greater subtlety, judgment never loses: that is Maisie's moral genius, which it is an extraordinary proof of James's genius to make us accept so unhesitatingly.

She exercises her 'art of stupidity' against her beloved Sir Claude, after the encounter with Ida and the Captain in Kensington Gardens. She does so, partly because 'His conversation with her mother had clearly drawn blood, and the child's old horror came back to her, begetting the instant moral contraction of the days when her parents had looked to her to feed their love of battle'; but also because she had seen the Captain to be a kind, loyal and innocent soul (whatever conventional morality might have to say about him).

These judgments, personal and real as they are, represent the only morality she can conceive, as comes out in the comedy, with its characteristic pathos, of her parting exchange with the Captain:

> 'Goodbye.' Maisie kept his hand long enough to add, 'I like you too.' And then supremely: 'You *do* love her?'
> 'My dear child—!' The Captain wanted words.
> 'Then don't do it only for just a little.'
> 'A little?'
> 'Like all the others.'
> 'All the others?'—he stood staring.
> She pulled away her hand. 'Do it always!'

This particular effect gets its completion in the farewell scene with Ida at Folkestone, when Maisie is moved to 'horror', 'the first flare of anger that had ever yet lighted her face for a foe', by her mother's reception of a reference to the Captain (' "I thought you liked him." '—' "Him!—the biggest cad in London!" ').

The education we see Maisie undergoing is exemplified in the change of her attitude towards her old governess—that one who marries her father. In nothing does James's art, on reflection, astonish us more than in his power of giving us in so short a space (*What Maisie Knew* is only a *nouvelle*) Maisie growing up from little more than an infant to almost an adult. Miss Overmore's beauty and elegance had charmed her little pupil. Maisie continues to be under the spell, but we watch her, as she develops, becoming more and more critical, and more and more conscious of being critical, of the personality behind the beauty and the elegance. Finally, in the close of the book, the erstwhile governess being now Mrs. Beale and Sir Claude's mistress, Maisie pronounces definitively against her—at the moment when Mrs. Beale lays herself out to play a fully maternal role.

Mrs. Wix has neither beauty nor elegance; in fact, in a Dickensian way (she fairly obviously derives from Dickensian inspiration) she is positively ugly. She represents good nature, affectionateness and maternal feeling, these virtues being altogether unrecommended by external advantages. On first acquaintance Maisie suffers a revulsion, and the significance of its being so quickly and finally overcome is emphasized by the episode of Mrs. Cuddon. Maisie sees that Mrs. Cuddon is kind; she divines an essential, if obscure, resemblance to the Captain. But the poor lady's ugliness is too much for the child, who repels her advances, and shudders away with a wounding obviousness.

The virtues, then, that Mrs. Wix represents are solid and strongly self-recommendatory, and she represents too (unlike Mrs. Cuddon, who is keeping Maisie's papa) respectability —as Mr. Bewley notes. He notes it, but nevertheless he makes an attack on her respectability that is perhaps the oddest of the perversities (so they seem to me) of his treatment of *What Maisie Knew*.

> Elderly, ugly, fantastic as she is, Mrs. Wix falls in love with Sir Claude. The fact isn't insisted on, and it might even be possible to interpret in non-erotic terms her passionate avowal to Maisie that she 'adores' Sir Claude, although I doubt it.

And Mr. Bewley talks of Mrs. Wix's 'erotic infatuation'. But I venture that he finds no difficulty about interpreting in non-erotic terms Maisie's passionate avowal that she 'adores' Sir Claude—as she clearly does. It should surely be plain enough (even if we hadn't James's note to that effect) that Mrs. Wix's and Maisie's 'adorations' are of the same order. Girl and woman, it is true, are both females, and Sir Claude is an attractive man, and 'erotic' in these days is a term of extensive and uncertain application. But it is surely a very odd term to apply to poor Mrs. Wix's state, and the context given it by Mr. Bewley adds to the emphasis with which it must be rejected.

> The atmosphere of 'horror' in Maisie is one of its solid achievements, more substantial and enduring than the 'horror' of *The Turn of the Screw*, and these touches in Mrs. Wix, however they are to be interpreted in other respects, add their own contribution to that atmosphere.

I, as I have said, detect no atmosphere of 'horror' in *What Maisie Knew* and I see Mrs. Wix's adoration of Sir Claude sufficiently defined in such a passage as this:

> He laughed back at Mrs. Beale; he looked at such moments quite as Mrs. Wix, in the long stories she told her pupil, always described the lovers of her distressed beauties—'the perfect gentleman and strikingly handsome'.

Sir Claude, in short, is the *beau idéal* of her romantic day-dreams, and her feeling about him is as much, and as little, 'erotic' as Maisie's, if more positively a matter of comedy—since, after all, a childish 'adoration' in her is less in place than in a child. I concede to Mr. Bewley, without embarrassment, that perhaps Maisie as well as Mrs. Wix is jealous of Mrs. Beale.

An element of jealousy may contribute to Maisie's decision to go back to England with Mrs. Wix. But I have to insist that sex, in this story, is only marginal to James's preoccupation; he shows, here, no moral feeling at all that is directed upon sex as such. The absence of such feeling is an essential condition of the kind of poignant comedy in which, in this story, his genius manifests itself. Think, for instance, of the way in which, in the closing act at Boulogne, it is conveyed to us that Sir Claude has spent the night with Mrs. Beale. Preparing, in the morning, to go out for breakfast with Maisie, Sir Claude looks for his stick.

> 'A moment—my stick.'
> But there appeared to be no stick. 'No matter, I left it—oh!' He remembered with an odd drop and came out.

'You left it in London?' she asked as they went downstairs. 'Yes—in London: fancy!'

It is in Mrs. Beale's room. There is no hint here of any moral intensity directed upon sexual misconduct (the context makes that plain), or of enough interest in it as such to lead to moral judgment about it at all. The moral sense that James defines and conveys in this story is that focused in Maisie, of whom, Mr. Bewley will agree, it is not paradoxical to say that, though her attitude towards Sir Claude is feminine right enough, she remains to the end uninterested in, and uncognizant of, sex. Her discriminations and judgments regard the qualities of personality and the capacities for sensitive personal relations revealed by her adults as they perform the evolutions that are so largely set off by the spring of which she remains unaware. The 'moral sense' that Maisie can't produce for Mrs. Wix's satisfaction is the one that, in the world of *What Maisie Knew*, doesn't matter. The satire that plays upon it appeals for its positives to the sense defined in Maisie herself.

To come back to the drama at Boulogne: Maisie sees that Sir Claude is lying and that he is ashamed of his relations with Mrs. Beale. Though she may not put it to herself so, she has divined that for Mrs. Beale she figures as a mere convenience. And at this point I may remark that Mr. Bewley's account of *What Maisie Knew* as a struggle for the possession of Maisie badly misrepresents the case. Maisie, for the parties with a 'claim' to her, is a burden to be shifted, or a means (if retained for a limited period) of annoying the other, or a possible convenience. In the final act at Boulogne she is for Mrs. Beale a mere convenience; and we need not suspect Sir Claude, for all his playful description of himself as a born nurse, of being moved by any overbearing maternal, or paternal, passion. He is kind, he has a sense of decency and a conscience, and he likes Maisie; but he clearly has doubts about the convenience her presence in a *ménage à trois* would in sum be, as well as about the decency. The only party who may be supposed really to want Maisie is Mrs. Wix, as Maisie has sufficiently ascertained—to note which fact is to complete the explanation why, when it has become plain that kindness and sense of decency will not avail to separate Sir Claude from Mrs. Beale in order that he may perform his assumed duty by his stepchild, she opts for Mrs. Wix.

The reason that Mr. Bewley gives for that choice—it would surely have to be thought of as James's reason rather than Maisie's—is that (it being 'Maisie's mission in life to educate her elders') 'of the people struggling for possession of Maisie in the concluding chapter only poor Mrs. Wix remains amenable to education'. This suggestion seems to me to be jarringly out of resonance with the whole distinctive tone and spirit of the tale, which, for all its preoccupation with triumphant goodness, is so convincing in its realism. I see no reason at all for supposing that Mrs. Wix's ' "moral sense" is capable of being educated into fineness'. She will go on in her honest muddled conventionality; affectionately admiring Maisie's 'goodness' on the one hand, and knowing, on the other, that nothing matters more than a 'moral sense' in her own sense. And perhaps—may we not reflect?—it is as well that Maisie, after the childhood that has provided us with James's comedy, should enter adolescence under that kind of respectable tutelage.

7

MAISIE, MILES AND FLORA
THE JAMESIAN INNOCENTS

A REJOINDER

I DOUBT if a point-by-point reply to Mr. Leavis's 'Dis-agreement' on *What Maisie Knew* and *The Turn of the Screw* would be profitable. I think that a part of our disagreement over these two novels has its origin at levels not readily access-ible to critical persuasion. I shall try to suggest later what I mean by saying this. But I think the 'Disagreement' does provide an unusual opportunity of examining the exact nature of our divergence. Beyond correcting those minor and unavoidable distortions of emphasis with which Mr. Leavis's comments, concerned as they were with advancing his own analysis, have underscored my essay, the further advantage I see in offering a Rejoinder is this: our disagreement occurs, I believe, in an area where the same critical language is spoken, and where one may presume the same critical postu-lates more or less govern. With this advantage it may be possible to isolate the terms of our difference in a clearer medium than the murky atmosphere of discrepant critical languages and intentions usually allows. To do so will hardly lead us into agreement on these two novels, but I think it may serve to illuminate our respective positions.

Mr. Leavis begins by saying that 'For Mr. Bewley, of the two tales, *The Turn of the Screw* might almost seem to be the major concern.' Mr. Leavis would not, of course, maintain that I make artistic claims for *The Turn of the Screw* compar-able to those I make for *Maisie*, although I do esteem it much more highly than he does. But I think the remark ignores the intention of my essay as a whole, which was not at all to present a detailed critique of either novel as such (although an evaluation, it goes without saying, is necessarily every-where implicit), but to isolate and consider in its effect on

James's art a basic preoccupation which, I think, constitutes a radical and recurrent flaw in much of his work. I defined this preoccupation—or call it rather a defect, a tic, of the sensibility—as a precarious balance, sometimes disastrously lost, between appearance and reality. The preoccupation is imperfectly visible *as such* in any given work, and I believe it must be sought out and defined by considering a number of James's works together. Mr. Leavis would call this concern of mine a 'distorting preoccupation', but I believe some of the persuasiveness of his charge arises from the fact that he discusses my analysis of *The Turn of the Screw* quite apart from the central argument in my essay as a whole. This argument does not interest Mr. Leavis, for he is intent on something else; and yet I intended my remarks on *The Turn of the Screw* to mark the culminating point of my discussion of *The Golden Bowl*. While drawing a limited parallel between *The Turn of the Screw* and *Maisie*, I did so for the purpose of exhibiting, not their similarity as much as their radical difference: for if the tension which forms the subject of my paper is centred, among all of James's works, in *The Turn of the Screw*, it is precisely *Maisie* from which it is most conspicuously absent. In the light of my subject, *The Turn of the Screw* was indeed my major concern, although it is so much less interesting, and so much smaller, than the other novel. I insist on this point because it is here that I think Mr. Leavis's and my disagreement begins. I believe that he is really questioning the legitimacy of the problem I had undertaken to examine, and is indirectly expressing here his regret that I did not write a different *kind* of essay altogether. I can understand this objection (if I have interpreted it correctly), although I don't agree with it here, and my only complaint is that in excerpting what I had to say about *The Turn of the Screw* from its larger context, Mr. Leavis reads my intentions in an extremely limiting perspective.

When I called *The Turn of the Screw* 'appalling' I had in mind something different from the mere Gothic horror which, I believe, Mr. Leavis credits me with. Perhaps I should have used the phrase 'metaphysically appalling' (although that sounds pretentious) to have been exact, for what I meant was that the dissolution of the ties between appearance and reality which threatens in many of James's stories was here realized with peculiar violence and intensity, and that what it signified was a lack of faith in the grounds of creation and hence a denial of the possibility of strict moral action. In one guise or another this is a theme of many American writers. Melville wrote a variation on it in *The Confidence Man*, which is not a story of horror in the sense that *The Turn of the Screw* is because the supernatural is nowhere invoked in that novel, except ironically, and the intolerable tension between appearance and reality which Melville makes the theme of *The Confidence Man* therefore threatens only the material plane with disintegration and collapse. When in his 'Preface' James called *The Turn of the Screw* an 'excursion into chaos' I am convinced that he did so with complete fullness of meaning. It was under that text from the 'Preface' (although I did not quote it) that I conducted my examination of the story.

At one point in his essay Mr. Leavis says that one part of my interpretation is due to 'an ignorance of English possibilities'. I hope that I am not immodest enough to deny this, and I am grateful to Mr. Leavis for the phrase, for I think that *The Turn of the Screw* is peculiarly rich in American possibilities. It was these—the tensions and the frame of mind which I designated as American in my essay—that I undertook to examine. Mr. Leavis expresses his surprise that so many critics have made heavy weather of *The Turn of the Screw*. Most, if not all, of the critics who have done so have been American, and this is in itself suggestive to me that the story does indeed contain possibilities that the American may respond to more strongly, and take up more readily than others. As Mr. Leavis points out in his essay, James referred to the story as 'an *amusette* to catch those not easily caught'. Even if I am to take James perfectly literally here, I will not impudently assert that, in that case, I think he was the first to be caught in it; but I do think that he constructed his '*amusette*' out of some of the deepest materials of his experience. 'It is an excursion into chaos while remaining, like *Bluebeard* and *Cinderella*, but an anecdote.' I readily conceded the anecdotal ingenuity in my essay, but it was the 'excursion into chaos' that engaged my attention.

There is no point in rehashing here my case for Miles's and Flora's innocence, or for the governess's guilt. It seems to me to have been adequately presented, and to stand in no pressing need of enlargement. But Mr. Leavis makes three points which I should like to comment on here briefly because I think they leave my own position open to some misunderstanding.

First, speaking of my obligations to Mr. Edmund Wilson, Mr. Leavis says:

> From Edmund Wilson he takes over too that remarkable misrepresentation of the 'authority' that James, in the Preface, tells us he has given the governess. . . . All he means (as Oliver Evans points out) is that he has invested her with authority for the reader, who will know that he is to trust her implicitly.

I think I can see why Mr. Leavis makes this interpretation of my meaning, although I make no direct mention of the passage in my essay, and am unaware of having referred to it indirectly. But so far from having taken up Mr. Wilson's position on the matter, the whole point of my interpretation is that it is the *reader* with whom the governess has authority. 'The reader and the housekeeper at Bly', I wrote, 'are equally helpless in her hands.' This may be perversity, but I think it is James's perversity and not mine, and I think James has played the same trick elsewhere. When he collected his stories for the definitive edition he included *The Liar* with *The Turn of the Screw*, a fact of some significance. In my essay I tried to show in considerable detail how Oliver Lyon, the painter, who also has complete authority with the reader, uses it to lead the reader up the garden, and so successfully that, as far as I know, no one has ever advanced my own reading that he is the liar after whom the story is named. He has taken himself in completely, of course; but that doesn't, as I tried to show in my analysis, mean that he is innocent. I said that Mrs. Capadose in that story was an early forerunner of Maggie Verver; but it seems to me no less true to say that Oliver Lyon is an early type of the governess in *The Turn of*

135

the Screw. One of my chief concerns was to investigate the nature of the lie in Henry James. It occurs very ambiguously in his work, but I think the intention James is usually aiming at, to put the matter simply, is to depict the very substance of society as so perverted and warped that an apparent lie, in such a context, is often the shortest way to truth, and what looks like truth is often the most egregious lie. The reader trusts the governess implicitly, but that trust is the measure of his participation in what, taking Hawthorne's phrase, I called 'the world's artificial system'. I believe that the effectiveness of *The Turn of the Screw*, its haunting and disturbing quality, arises from the fact that the reader uneasily suspects that he is aiding and abetting the governess in her persecution of the children, and yet her authority with him is real because he is, in his adherence to the world's false proprieties, guilty in the same way. This was what I meant when I called *The Turn of the Screw* a 'destructive foray into the grounds for moral judgement'. That the trap James constructed should be of this nature seems to me wholly in accord with the preoccupation I discussed in some of his other works, and to count it anything less hardly seems to me to leave it a trap at all. James said that his values were all blanks, but this seems to me essential to the trick since they must be filled in with figures drawing on the pooled resources of the reader and the governess, working together. Hawthorne wrote that we could never know how much of the world was 'merely the interpolation of the perverted heart and mind of man', and James's 'blanks' have the effect of taking the ceiling off the possibilities in that direction. While Mr. Leavis and I disagree in believing that James meant this, I do agree that such a meaning is perversity—or in another context, it might even be called arch-heresy.

The second point of Mr. Leavis's I should like to comment on concerns Flora. Mr. Leavis writes: 'As for Flora's depravity, the housekeeper (will Mr. Bewley argue that she is bullied into it?) bears fully explicit testimony to that in her talk with the governess after the scene by the lake.' This is, of course, Mr. Leavis's view of the episode, but his parenthetical question implies a dismissal of my own very full discussion of that scene which, whether one finally agrees with it or not, seems to me to do it less than justice. Mr. Leavis's question (if I read him rightly) really comes to this: How does the governess communicate her guilty knowledge to Flora at the lake's edge? I can only refer back to my discussion of it, which seems to me adequate, but I frankly say that I am unwilling to answer the particular question couched in this way because it seems to me to be answerable *only* in terms that are at variance with the mode in which I conceive the story to have been written. But I add that I may be responsible for a misunderstanding here. I have insisted on the innocence of Miles and Flora, but in doing so I have been speaking of their relations with Quint and Miss Jessel. There is no doubt that Flora is at last corrupted (as I hope I made clear)—thoroughly immersed in the governess's guilty vision of life.

The last particular point I wish to discuss apropos of this novel concerns the nature of the ghosts. In my article I quoted from James's 'Preface':

> . . . Peter Quint and Miss Jessel are not 'ghosts' at all, as we now know the ghost, but goblins, elves, imps, demons as loosely constructed as those of the old trials for witchcraft; if not, more pleasingly, fairies of the legendary order, wooing their victims forth to see them dance under the moon.

I agree with Mr. Leavis that James is explaining here how Quint and Miss Jessel have the function of producing a given effect in *The Turn of the Screw*, but as James has just finished explaining, that effect could not have been achieved with orthodox ghosts. There are some things, as he points out, that 'correct' apparitions don't do. The kind of demon I suggested as a possibility is a conventional, and not very odd, member of that 'legendary order' to which James asserts his 'demon-spirits' belong—and his choice of that phrase 'demon-spirits' seems to me conclusive evidence that they aren't, after all, human-spirits, for if James is speaking with any strictness at this point, the two terms are mutually exclusive. James's reference later in the same paragraph to 'the bad dead' strikes me as unpersuasive. It is ostensibly *as* 'the bad dead' that the demons make their appearance in the story, and it seems to me the natural way for James to refer to them at this point, which he is the freer to do because he has just finished explaining at some length that they are not 'correct' apparitions—not 'ghosts' at all. And in any case James is explaining when he uses that phrase the limiting conditions that prevail in a work of art when 'the bad dead' are brought back to do evil. Whether the demon-spirits are 'the bad dead' or not, those limiting conditions would still govern if the story was to be successful unless it was James's intention to show them up as impostors. I think, then, that James is discussing the artistic problem here and not the demon-spirits in their own identities at all. But I also think this discussion puts a false emphasis on my meaning as I expressed it in my article. I am not much concerned about the exact nature of the apparitions. James tells us they are 'evoked', and that is the important thing. The second thing I would insist on is that one cannot make a judgment on the friendship between Miles and Flora and the two living servants on the basis of what we know of the 'ghosts'. I think my explanation the most probable one (insofar as an 'explanation' should be sought for at all), but once the two points I have mentioned are safeguarded, I am not much further concerned.

I am less interested here in Mr. Leavis's disagreement with me over *What Maisie Knew*, not because I think it less important, but because it seems to me to be a more simple and straightforward divergence between our readings than was the case with *The Turn of the Screw*, complicated as that was by being part of a larger argument. First of all, I endorse whole-heartedly Mr. Leavis's assertion that *What Maisie Knew* is a comedy, but I see no conflict between this fact and the atmosphere of horror which I believe one encounters in *Maisie*. I cannot abstain from quoting two sentences from an earlier article of mine on James, for they make my position clear. Speaking of another of James's novels, I said:

> To call its comedy 'brilliant' would be to insist on the moral illumination that reveals the dimensions of its meaning rather

138

than the mere glitter of surfaces that is usually accepted as justification for that adjective when applied to comedy in the social mode. The shifting distinction between comedy and tragedy is, perhaps, finally dependent on a radical ambiguity in the nature of moral experience itself, but whatever the explanation, the comic effects that James brings off on his carefully plotted stage frequently seem to be performed on trap-doors opening immediately into subterranean regions of a vastly different character.

There is much beautifully controlled comedy in *Maisie*, but the trap-doors are more yawning there, it seems to me, than in any other of James's novels. But it is exactly against my 'projecting Evil' into *Maisie* that Mr. Leavis vehemently protests. Our contemporary novels specializing in theologically romanticized Evil ('the grandeur of the damned' as a recent American book blurb has it) have not created a prejudice in me in favour of the term I am obliged to use here; but it seems to me that to eliminate evil from Maisie's world is to deprive her of the peculiar grace of her triumph and a good deal of her stature.

I did not analyse the atmosphere of horror I found in *Maisie*, but I did suggest what I thought was the essence of the vibration I detected:

> . . . the essence of that horror consists in the way we are able to isolate the *grotesqueness* of moral evil as it caricatures and distorts human action and motive—to isolate it through the innocent eyes of a little girl whose vision is not sufficiently dulled by conventional experience to absorb the singularity of the irregular world in which she lives.

I meant that through Maisie's eyes the characters of her adult world, and their conduct, are frequently reduced to appearances that correspond physically to the moral qualities they embody—and the picture is profoundly disturbing. Mr. Leavis mentions Mrs. Cuddon in his essay, 'the American Countess' who pays Maisie's father to be her lover, and he singles out one passage from Chapter XVIII in which she figures as an example of James's comedy. I agree that it is superb comedy, but if Mrs. Cuddon is kind, she is also a freak of sorts, a kind of Goya grotesque. We first see her at an Exhibition or Carnival coming out of a sideshow called the Flowers of the Forest which exhibits on its posters 'a large presentment of bright brown ladies—they were brown all over—in a medium suggestive of tropical luxuriance'. The sideshow is the perfect comment on the nature of the 'romantic' relation between Mrs. Cuddon and her lover, and this note of the extravagant and fantastic, of the perversely debased and demoted, sounds for me throughout all her scenes. Mrs. Cuddon becomes progressively less human in Maisie's eyes: 'She literally struck the child more as an animal than as a "real" lady; she might have been a clever frizzled poodle in a frill or a dreadful human monkey in a spangled petticoat.' What Maisie's rejection of Mrs. Cuddon's kindness amounts to is a discriminating rejection of her sordidness—for Maisie's rejection, although she herself would not express it so, really comes down to that. Mrs. Cuddon's kindness is impossible for Maisie because it is part of the fabric of a world she is slowly preparing to cast from her. Mr. Leavis at one point compares Mrs. Cuddon's kindness with that of the Captain. The scene in Kensington Gardens in which Maisie talks with the dashing Captain, her mother's latest lover, impresses me as one of the finest in the book; but for me it also seems one of the most harrowing exposures of childish innocence and goodness to a monstrous selfishness that occurs in literature. The Captain is kind, but the springs of his kindness are contaminated. The source of the atmosphere of horror in this scene isn't, of course, the Captain, although his defection of moral sensibility provides a suitable resonance, but Maisie's mother, Ida, who all during the conversation is quarrelling with Sir Claude in the background. I find it difficult, in view of the achieved rankness she so startlingly embodies, to confine my sense of Maisie's situation within terms of social comedy alone, however brilliant it may be. The essence of Mr. Leavis's and my disagreement is this: that for me the comedy still has something of the infernal about it. I am reluctant to mention a masterpiece like *Maisie* in the same breath with Sartre's *Huis Clos*, and yet the men and women who people Maisie's adult world, parasitically feeding on each other's vices, and trapped in each other's orbits, generate for me that kind of atmosphere with an intensity immeasurably beyond anything in Sartre's range. I think that if one denies evil in this novel one will be depriving Maisie's triumphant escape of a good deal of its significance. As Mr. Leavis reads the novel, Maisie's escape is a chance to enter adolescence under respectable tutelage. I agree that is important, although I am less sanguine about the possibilities with Mrs. Wix than he. The benefits as far as she is concerned seem to me entirely negative at best. Maisie's escape also exists, I think, at a more important level. She has literally saved herself spiritually, and it has been all her own doing with the exception, perhaps, of some help from Sir Claude. As I read it, the pathos of *Maisie* does not exist *only* in the little girl's situation, although it is, of course, centred there. It seems to me that there is a subtle and profound sympathy and understanding between the young man and the child that has meaning only because the danger that confronts Maisie (making due allowances for the differences in their roles and ages) is to a large degree the danger that Sir Claude does *not* escape. It is, I think, this instinctive sympathy arising partly from their shared 'danger' which explains Sir Claude's remarkable attachment for Maisie, and I am far from attributing to him the 'overbearing maternal, or paternal, passion' which, to Mr. Leavis, seems the upshot of my position. Unless evil is a permitted term, this 'danger' (upon the existence of which I am far from wishing to imply Mr. Leavis and I agree) is unintelligible. As I see it, the impressiveness, as well as the deeply moving poignancy of the last pages of the novel is heightened by the fact that if Maisie is saved, Sir Claude is (if I may use a charged word) lost. It seems to me that this interpretation of the nature of their relationship is confirmed by their last farewell:

Sir Claude had reached the other door and opened it. Mrs. Wix was already out. On the threshold Maisie paused; she put out her hand to her stepfather. He took it and held it a moment, and their eyes met as the eyes of those who have done for each other what they can. 'Good-bye,' he repeated.

'Good-bye.' And Maisie followed Mrs. Wix.

Before concluding I wish to make a comment on my remark that Maisie lies. Mr. Leavis is in a strategic position here, for he denies my earlier point that Miles and Flora did not lie nor practice cunning and deceit in any culpable way. Since I had discussed the ambiguous nature of the lie in James's work at length, I felt free to suggest, as a way of stating the essential innocence of all three children, that Maisie lied as much as Miles and Flora. Naturally if one believes in the guilt of Miles and Flora my statement requires revision, but in its context I think it is clear.

To sum up, then, my attitude to *Maisie*: the adult characters of Maisie's world seem to me demonstrably a horrible set of people, far beyond any conventional late-Victorian or Edwardian fast set. Their viciousness does not seem to me to reside so much in their overt physical acts as in a subtly communicated taint of the spirit—a prevailing corruption which I strongly sense in every part of the novel. I believe that comedy is often able to absorb the shock of merely carnal evil, as Restoration comedy might be said to do. But the comedy of Maisie seems to me much nearer to *Volpone*, and if Jonson's dance of the hermaphrodite, the eunuch, and the dwarf is comedy, it is also horror. For me, the comedy and the horror of *Maisie* is closely akin to that.

In the beginning of these remarks I expressed my belief that our disagreement over these novels had its origin in areas not readily open to literary-critical persuasion. I believe I may now define these areas as: the relationship between James's sensibility and the idea (so deceptively abstract in sound when formally stated) which formed the central theme of my paper; the meaning and function of evil in *Maisie*; as a consequence of that, the significance of the atmosphere of horror. These three items are, as I see it, intrinsically related, and although the last two appear to be primarily critical considerations, I think the way one senses their presence in the novels may be due to one's conception of them *outside* the novels. I would agree, I hope it goes without saying, that these terms can have significance in *The Turn of the Screw* and *What Maisie Knew* only insofar as they are validated in the actual texts themselves, but I think the cross-reference works in both directions simultaneously. It would of course be Mr. Leavis's point that I have not sufficiently disciplined the cross-references between my values and the novels—that I have allowed the former to make some egregious contributions of their own. I do not see it myself, but if it is so I believe it will be the more apparent for having tried to clear away some of the hidden treacherous roots that always make discussion and mutual understanding difficult where such problems are considered.

8

COMMENT by F. R. Leavis

ALL James means (doesn't the whole context of the Preface make it plain?) by calling *The Turn of the Screw* an 'excursion into chaos' is that 'this piece of ingenuity pure and simple' is a creation won from the void and formless infinite: he is stressing the extreme freedom of improvisation that constitutes the trap or difficulty of the 'fairytale' for a serious artist. The apparitions are 'not "ghosts"' at all, as we now know the ghost'—in these days of 'psychical research', with the pointless trivialities it deals in: 'I had to renounce all attempts to keep the kind and degree of impression I wished to produce on terms with the to-day so copious psychical record of cases of apparitions.' I cannot see why Mr. Bewley should suppose that by 'evoked predatory creatures' (see Preface, p. xxiii) James can mean anything but that they are evoked by the calculating author. As for the governess's 'authority', I contended—and contend—that James clearly means by it, not that she has the power of making the reader, or the housekeeper, 'helpless', but that we are to accept her in unquestioning good faith as a wholly credible witness—a final authority.

Maisie's 'discriminating rejection of Mrs. Cuddon's sordidness'?

> 'Your father's temptress?' Mrs. Wix gave her a sidelong squint.
> 'Perfectly. She pays him!'
> 'Oh *does* she?' At this the child's countenance fell: it seemed to give a reason for papa's behaviour and place it in a more favourable light. She wished to be just. 'I don't say she's not generous. She was so to me.'

But I must not take up the argument again. I find no 'horror' in *What Maisie Knew* and nothing 'metaphysically appalling' in *The Turn of the Screw*: Mr. Bewley and I have not shaken each other. We must submit the case to others.

9

THE RELATION BETWEEN
WILLIAM AND HENRY JAMES

I DO not raise the following point for the purpose of con-
tinuing the discussion of *The Turn of the Screw*. Both Mr.
Leavis and myself have pretty fully defined our respective
positions, and there is little to be gained by going on indefinitely offering interpretations and counter-interpreta-
tions of the details of the story. However, Mr. Leavis makes
a remark in his reply to my rejoinder which provides an
opportunity to introduce a new topic which will serve to
sharpen the definition of my argument. The terms 'appearance and reality' which I have used in the foregoing pages
may have seemed unconvincingly elusive to some, but the
'tension' is capable of being discussed in a much tighter
vocabulary than I have so far chosen to use. The 'tension'
itself has undergone a long historical development in the
American scene, and the moment at which it becomes subject
to formulation in a philosophical vocabulary suited to the
American temperament is comparatively recent. The terms
'appearance and reality' have the advantage of aligning
James's work with the American artistic past in which this
tension has frequently been (as I have tried to suggest) an
emotive driving force. The employment of the later terminology would have implied that James was a 'philosophical' novelist in a sense which I think would have been
unfortunate and misleading.

By 'excursion into chaos' Mr. Leavis says James only
means 'the extreme freedom of improvisation that constitutes the trap or difficulty of the "fairytale" for a serious
artist'. This 'freedom of improvisation' is, I agree, partly a
freedom of technical improvisation. But I do not think James
belonged with those Americans for whom technique 'pure
and simple' was capable of becoming an end in itself. The
emphasis on technique in James is usually accompanied by,

and is, indeed, the very means by which he usually expresses, his moral interests. I think it goes without saying that Mr. Leavis would agree with such a statement, although he would make an exception of *The Turn of the Screw*: 'the story has no ponderable significance; it is a mere thriller'. In my discussion of *The Turn of the Screw* I was not primarily interested in James's freedom to improvise technically, although I think I did not neglect that aspect of the story. I was chiefly interested in James's freedom to improvise on the moral plane, which I did not see as ultimately separable from his technical freedom. This kind of 'extreme freedom of improvisation' seemed possible to me because James *apparently* conceived no inherent or overriding law as governing the terms of human experience. This kind of freedom of moral improvisation seems to me to constitute an 'excursion into chaos' in the sense in which I interpreted the phrase, and since such a freedom constitutes an intellectual and philosophical position, the story acquired in my eyes a significance that was ponderable in that degree in which it revealed something about James's attitudes to life which might ultimately prove relevant to understanding his fictions as art. This story, taken with others which I discussed, seemed to suggest that for James the universe was pragmatically plastic, both for good and for evil. In that word 'pragmatic' I get to the real purpose of my present remarks.

There has been no opportunity for discussing here the relationship between William and Henry James. To say that either has any direct influence on the work or thought of the other would be a stronger statement than one might be able to substantiate. But each brother, in his own peculiar set of terms, represents a development frequently parallel with the other. What the origin of this similarity in their development is I am not much concerned with here. But I think the tension between appearance and reality which I have discussed in Henry James's novels becomes immediately intelligible from a different point of view when it is discussed in terms of his brother's Pragmatism. Pragmatism really existed in America long before William James formulated it into an intellectual position. The whole historical situation conspired to make

America into a nation of pragmatists, and all William James had to do was to take the temperature of the air around him and give it a name and definition. From the eighteenth century or earlier Americans had remodelled ancient European reality to meet their own needs, and their sense of having done so successfully left them with a great feeling of optimism about their ability to continue remodelling in the future. The norm by which they had lived was one of comfortable, and sometimes luxurious, expediency, and expediency had come, in their eyes, to be the good and true. Consequently, when William James formulated his pragmatic conception of truth, the definition was likely to be more satisfying than startling to the bulk of Americans:

> Grant an idea or belief to be true, what concrete difference will its being true make in anyone's actual life? How will the truth be realized? What experiences will be different from those which would obtain if the belief were false? What in short, is the truth's cash value in experiential terms? The moment pragmatism asks this question, it sees the answer. *True ideas are those that we can assimilate, validate, corroborate and verify. False ideas are those that we can not.* That is the practical difference it makes to us to have true ideas; that, therefore, is the meaning of truth, for it is all that truth is known as.

Or, even more pointedly:

> The truth of an idea is not a stagnant property inherent in it. Truth *happens* to an idea. It *becomes* true, is made true by events: its verity *is* in fact an event, a process: the process namely of its verifying itself, its veri-*fication*. Its validity is the process of its valid-*ation*.

Henry James was wholly in sympathy with this pragmatic philosophy of his brother. In a letter to William James written from Lamb House on October 17, 1907, Henry James said:

> Why the devil I didn't write you after reading your *Pragmatism*—how I kept from it—I can't now explain save by the very fact of the spell itself (of interest and enthralment) that the book cast upon me; I simply sank down, under it, into such depths of

submission and assimilation that *any* reaction, very nearly, even that of acknowledgement, would have had almost the taint of dissent or escape. Then I was lost in the wonder of the extent to which all my life I have (like M. Jourdain) unconsciously pragmatised. You are immensely and universally *right*, and I have been absorbing a number of your followings-up of the matter in the American (journal of Psychology?) with which your devouring devotee Manton Marble . . . plied, and always on invitation does ply, me with. I feel the reading of the book, at all events, to have been really the event of my summer.

The Golden Bowl had appeared three years before James wrote this letter. The interpretation which I offered of *The Golden Bowl* demonstrates, I think, exactly what James meant when he said 'I was lost in the wonder of the extent to which all my life I have . . . unconsciously pragmatised.' In Maggie Verver I think we have the greatest pragmatist in literature. She shows how truth can be constructed out of lies, and the verity of that truth '*is* in fact an event, a process: the process namely of its verifying itself . . .'. This pragmatic base of James's art could be traced, I think, in a large number of short stories, although I only dealt with two, *The Liar* and *The Path of Duty*. It is this pragmatic bent in James, this 'extreme freedom of improvisation' in the world of human behaviour—this belief that there is no immutable reality behind appearances, but that appearances can always be twisted into new and convenient realities which constitutes so much of Henry James's American flavour.

This 'extreme freedom of improvisation' as it exists in *The Turn of the Screw* amounts, I think, to a peculiarly perverse rendering of the doctrine of 'truth' which is discoverable in *The Golden Bowl*. It is the Credo of Pragmatism read backwards. It is easy enough to read the following quotation from *The Turn of the Screw* as a reference *only* to the artistic process, the technical method by which the story was created. But underneath that reference to a technical or artistic process there is a profounder reference to a habit of thinking, a way of intellectual and spiritual life without which I do not think this story would have been successful.

148

There is for such a case [James wrote in the Preface] no eligible *absolute* of the wrong; it remains relative to fifty other elements, a matter of appreciation, speculation, imagination—these things, moreover, quite exactly in the light of the spectator's, the critic's, the reader's experience.

There is no doubt that James is referring to the ingenious artistic solution here—but I believe such a solution would have occurred as a possibility *only* to a writer (and would certainly have been used successfully *only* by him) who was capable of approving William James's Pragmatism in such terms as were quoted above. In the quotation from the Preface which I have just given I think it is possible to discern the point at which technical and moral improvisation become one in *The Turn of the Screw*. In *The Golden Bowl* Maggie Verver constructs her Truth out of lies, but I believe that in *The Turn of the Screw* the Governess constructs her Evil out of truth, the truth that resides in what I have contended is the innocence of the two children.

I said in my rejoinder that *The Turn of the Screw* contained possibilities that the American could respond to more readily than other people. I could now phrase this more intelligibly, perhaps, by saying that *The Turn of the Screw* is ingeniously calculated to exploit, albeit in a perverse way, that native pragmatic bent which pre-eminently characterizes, above all others, the American sensibility. One value at least I hope will be conceded to my reading of *The Turn of the Screw*: Pragmatism is said to be the most amiable of all philosophies, but I think my conception of the Governess may suggest that it is also capable of proving a very nasty spoonful of bitters indeed, a veritable 'excursion into chaos'.

II

Some Aspects of Modern American Poetry

(i)

IT is easier to admit a difference between English and
American poetry than to analyse what the exact nature
of that difference is. Poets and critics frequently speak of
vocabulary, metric, syntax, and punctuation as though such
things explained the difference between the two poetries.
Certainly one would not wish to underestimate their importance. But ultimately such considerations are the expression of
a divergence in attitude which is ulterior to themselves. They
are secondary rather than primary characteristics. But to get
behind such characteristics, obtrusive as they are, to something essential and final is extremely difficult. I believe it
may be possible to move a little way in the right direction by
considering the different conceptions which now prevail in
England and America of what the function of a poet in
society is. I do not necessarily mean the consciously held
idea, for that frequently seems identical in both countries;
rather, I mean the function that is involuntarily served when
the poet is actually practising his art: that is to say, the kind
of relationship envisaged between his art and the community
in which, and for which, he writes, and the range and
efficacy of possibilities which he instinctively sees as inhering
in the exercise of the creative faculty. Whatever his particular
conception of function may be, it plainly cannot sustain itself
in an exclusively literary atmosphere. In the nature of the
case it is immediately dependent on the energy, direction,
and general health of the society in which it occurs. For a
poet is a man in whose creative talent the energy of a society
becomes momentarily focused.

Before considering the present state of American poetry it
will be well to recall, however briefly, the principal verse
writers in America during the nineteenth century. The
names that come first to mind are Poe, Whitman, and Emily

Dickinson. In the case of Poe our indebtedness, such as it is, is indirect, by way of his influence on the French Symbolists. But it is difficult not to doubt that if Baudelaire had known English better he would have liked Poe less. Emily Dickinson established a line that emerged in the twentieth century in Edna St. Vincent Millay, and since her in a school of coyly baroque poets of whom Mr. Dunstan Thompson might be taken as the representative example.[1] In the case of Walt Whitman, whose impact has been so great, it may appear foolhardy to depart from the conventional estimate of him without offering a detailed discussion, but even such a glancing reference as this can afford to suggest that the effect of Whitman's poetry has not been entirely fortunate on the development of American writing. His poetic discoveries were real enough in their way, but they had an effect on American art somewhat similar to the effects of the New World on Spain. The sudden acquisition of all that gold to be had with so little effort undermined everybody's morale, and in the end the losses may well have exceeded the profit. What seems to be clear is that the best American intelligence during the nineteenth century went into the production of prose. It has only been with the twentieth century that the American achievement in poetry has begun to assume impressive characteristics. The energy which, under Whitman, dissipated itself in fusillades of patriotic and expansive metaphor, is now more surely co-ordinated with critical intelligence, and placed at the disposal of an American sensibility which, if not entirely at its ease in verse, is admirably intent on learning discipline and poise.

It is precisely at this point of 'energy' that one may begin to differentiate between English and American poetry today. The energy of poetry and the energy of society are ultimately embedded in each other, and the effects of the War on the general life of England, together with the comparative escape of America, are considerations that cannot be neglected. And they do point to a situation or state in English poetry that is undeniable—a state which Mr. Cyril Connolly described for an American audience as one of 'exhaustion'.

[1] Mr. Dunstan Thompson's *Poems* were published in England in 1946.

The tradition of poetry flows unevenly, and at times dwindles, not even to a tiny trickle, but to a series of little stagnant ponds in which all life appears on the point of expiring. The reason seems to be that at infrequently spaced intervals a generation of poets is born which mobilizes speech and energy in such quantities, and under such new aspects, that the poets who occur between two such periods depend largely on the idiom and modes of feeling developed by their predecessors to express their own ideas. This is not usually owing to the lack of original talent in the later poets, but to the fact that the sensibility of the age has not yet changed sufficiently to justify that modification which an original poet must impose on old forms. The time has not yet developed those new requirements and urgencies which would make any such modifications intelligible to any envisaged public, or even to the poet himself. For if poets create the speech of their time, they cannot create it out of improper materials. They have to await the moment at which creation becomes possible. The 'exhaustion' of English poetry today is obviously part of that more general exhaustion which inevitably followed the War, for the energy of literature and society is, to a large extent, one energy. The listlessness which settled down on art was not entirely the listlessness *of* art.

On the other hand, it would appear that American poets have come through the War with an emboldened sense of function and responsibility. If, in view of the quality of much of their work, the conviction seems a little naïve, I am trying to point here to an attitude, a psychological situation, rather than offer a critical examination of individual writers. This conviction of function, of important work to do, arises first of all from the material circumstances of American life, its overwhelming activity on every side, its mere physical appearance of abundance and directed energy. Since the War there has been an intensification of the desire to explore and define American experience, not in itself only, but in its relations with the world. And the fact that the American poet, unlike the English poet, is not inclined to resent his present government, permits him to feel functionally associated with that experience. What the vast horde of American poets mean by

American experience is, of course, something that cannot safely be generalized about for more than one poet at a time, but all the poets have this—and perhaps only this—in common: each is aware that his own experience is American, and the sense of it gives him confidence and a feeling that what he has to say is important. The result may often be extremely bad poetry, but it is something very different from 'exhaustion'. For example, opening a recent anthology I find this poem by Mr. James Laughlin, the editor of *New Directions*. I am tempted to quote it entire because I cannot quite imagine the attitude expressed in it transposed over into the English scene under any circumstances whatever, and it illustrates in a disarmingly frank-faced manner the attitude I have been speaking of, even to its title, 'Go West Young Man':

> Yessir they're all named
> either Ken or Stan or Don
> every one of them and
>
> those aren't just nick-
> names either no they're
> really christened like
>
> that just Ken or Stan or
> Don and you shake hands
> with anybody you run into
>
> no matter who the hell
> it is and say 'glad to
> know you Ken glad to
>
> know you Don' and then
> two minutes later (you
> may not have said ten
>
> words to the guy) you
> shake hands again and
> say 'glad to have met

L

you Stan glad to' and
they haven't heard much
about Marx and the class

struggle because they
haven't had to and by
god it makes a country

that is fit to live in
and by god I'm glad to
know you Don I'm glad!

Whatever one might say about a piece like that, it does rest amazingly secure in its sense of the goodness of its own experience. It shows no doubts. Like a great deal of American writing, it is pure and emphatic assertion. Whether it has logic or not, it has a good deal of will in its make-up, and one is really surprised at the strength of the conviction behind it. Now these elements that are so apparent here—security and faith in its own experience (whatever that experience may be), a reliance on will and assertion, and a feeling that it is pretty important, are the most reliable signs by which to identify an American poem today. They are not infallible, but they are better signs than syntax, vocabulary and rhythm. They rarely exist as openly and simply as in 'Go West Young Man'. Sometimes the disguise is very deep indeed, but under whatever tropical growth of cynicism or tortuous self-questionings the poet may hide, if one listens carefully enough the voice of the American is heard at last expressing his satisfaction in his own being. To take a fairly obvious example of this disguised security, Mr. Delmore Schwartz ends a recent poem in which he carefully delineates the successive disillusionments of his life in these three verses:

Illusion and madness mock the years
    (A Godforsaken farce at best),
And yet through all these mounting fears
    How glad I am that I exist!

154

How strange the truth appears at last!
I feel as old as outworn shoes,
I know what I have lost or missed,
  Or certainly will some day lose,

And yet this knowledge, like the Jews,
Can make me glad that I exist!
    with a hey ho, the foolish past,
    and a ho ho and a ha ha at last.

Any English reader would probably have some difficulty
in distinguishing this tone from the bravado of Henley, but
nevertheless (and I am not thinking merely of the Elizabethan decor) it is something quite different. The attitude
behind it is a reflection of an important part of American
character—an ability to see-saw from cynicism into optimism
and enthusiasm, and a moment later, rigorous conviction.
Whatever disabilities may attend it, its chief virtue is quick-
ness of recovery. Americans could hardly get on without it,
and it is therefore not to be dismissed as a merely shallow or
silly or insubstantial attitude. Mr. Schwartz's poem is trivial
enough, but I say all this because it is not a bad poem in the
way I am fairly certain most English readers will conclude.
And this attitude which is behind it is an important part of
that larger complex of qualities which I am trying to suggest
is one of the chief distinctions between the quality of English
and American poetry.

But perhaps I may make my point more clearly by glancing at an essay by Mr. Schwartz which he calls *The Grapes of
Crisis*. Mr. Schwartz presents some evidence in this article
to suggest that since the First World War, but gaining
incredible momentum since the Second, a change has been
occurring in American character—a change which is registered in American art, particularly in literature and films.
New books have sorrowful titles: *Lord Weary's Castle*, *The
Dispossessed*, *The Victim*, etc. New films have unhappy end-
ings. And the Daisy Millers of American literature have
given place to the nymphomaniac of *A Streetcar Named Desire*.
All this Mr. Schwartz sees as evidence of a crushing dis-

illusionment—an abandonment of traditional American optimism. But however persuasive the evidence may seem, Mr.
Schwartz's own conclusions indicate that the change has so
far been confined to the surface. Pointing to the cynicism
which, in some respects, has overtaken the American literary
scene, Mr. Schwartz accepts it as the basis of a real advance
—the creation of

> the possibility of a genuinely tragic art. Nobility is quickened by
> tragedy and nurtured by necessity. Once the mind is capable of
> regarding the future with a sense of tragedy and a sense of
> comedy, instead of requiring the forced smiles (and the whis-
> tling in the dark) of dogmatic optimism, the awakened con-
> sciousness is prepared to respond to existence with courage and
> intelligence.

Thus the strategy of Mr. Schwartz's criticism follows the
strategy of his poem, quoted above. At the last moment a
joyful and unexpected reversal assures us that the American
has come through. This is a deeper kind of optimism than
the one which Mr. Schwartz has made the subject of his own
paper. I doubt if it can ever lead on to genuinely tragic art,
but it represents a valid resilience which may ward off
tragedy outside the realm of art.

(ii)

I wish in these remarks to examine rather closely the work
of only one young American poet. There is good reason for
such abstinence. The great number of American poets, all
with established reputations, is itself discouraging for anyone
attempting a 'survey'. Any attempt to deal with them com-
prehensively could hardly be anything but confusing in a
brief essay. But one should not be misled by mere multitude
into supposing that Americans are essentially more interested
in literature than the English. Although the details of
Tocqueville's analysis of American writing have changed
since he wrote *Democracy in America* over a century ago, the
greater number of American poets may still be explained as
the product of peculiarly democratic processes of thought:

Taken as a whole, literature in democratic ages can never present, as it does in the periods of aristocracy, an aspect of order, regularity, science, and art; its form will, on the contrary, ordinarily be slighted, sometimes despised. Style will frequently be fantastic, incorrect, overburdened, and loose—almost always vehement and bold. Authors will aim at rapidity of execution, more than at perfection of detail. Small productions will be more common than bulky books; there will be more wit than erudition, more imagination than profundity; and literary performances will bear marks of an untutored and rude vigour of thought—frequently of great variety and singular fecundity. The object of authors will be to astonish rather than to please, and to stir the passions more than to stir the taste. Here and there indeed, writers will doubtless occur who will choose a different track, and who will, if they are gifted with superior abilities, succeed in finding readers, in spite of their defects or their better qualities; but these exceptions will be rare, and even the authors who shall so depart from the received practice in the main subject of their works, will always relapse into it in some lesser details.

There are ways in which this description no longer applies. For example, there is a growing emphasis on technique among American poets, and a taste for complicated metrical forms, which is replacing the older hackneyed emphasis on experimentalism that predominated in the 'twenties and held on tenaciously through the 'thirties. But Tocqueville's passage is still true enough to suggest why being a poet comes more easily in America than in England. Many modern American poets have acquired great skill in writing in intricate metrical patterns, but the complications of form which they pursue frequently seem to be achieved with facility rather than sustained with conviction or an unbrittle poise. There is a disquieting tendency on the part of many American critics to refer to such poets as 'great technicians'. I say it is 'disquieting' because a highly ordered form in poetry ought to relate to patterns of living, to organizations of feeling and thinking, somewhat less technological than the favoured term implies. It is difficult to imagine an early critic reading 'Alexander's

Feast' for the first time and exclaiming, 'What a great technician Dryden is!' 'Technician' in such a context means nothing more than 'verbal engineer', which may be why the critics of a highly technological civilization have come to favour it so much.

The 'technicians' among modern American poets may be divided into several categories, but perhaps those who take religion as their theme, no doubt seeing in the order of their verse a correspondence to the order of their theology, are the most important. To this group the young American poet belongs whom I earlier mentioned as the one poet whose verse I should consider with some care in this paper: I mean Mr. Robert Lowell.[1] There are several reasons for selecting Lowell's verse in preference to that of other writers of his generation (Mr. Lowell was born in 1917). First of all, he has received a degree of recognition far beyond that accorded any other new writer during the 'forties, and the tributes have ranged from publicity in *Time* to accolades from T. S. Eliot and Santayana. From the first the most distinguished American critics appeared to enter a conspiracy for the purpose of establishing Lowell's literary reputation on as sound a base in as short a time as possible. The enthusiasm of his admirers has been equalled on this side of the Atlantic only by the boosters of Dylan Thomas. And undeniably Lowell's verse has a great deal of intrinsic interest. It is integrated with the American background and the New England tradition to a degree unique among contemporary poets; while traditional, it also represents something new, though not perhaps quite as new as critics have claimed; and it is intensely serious—sometimes over-reachingly so. In its own distinctive way it is alive with that sense of responsibility and function I have predicated of American poets in general.

But since my own criticism of Lowell's poetry will be considerably less enthusiastic than the prevailing view, I should like to say at once what I believe its virtues are. In several of his poems there is an immediacy of relation between his sensibility and the old New England of shipping and the sea

[1] *Poems: 1938–1949.* Faber and Faber.

that comes off with great distinction. 'The Quaker Grave-
yard in Nantucket' which begins,

> A brackish reach of shoal off Madaket,—
> The sea was still breaking violently and night
> Had steamed into our North Atlantic Fleet,

is as original and fine a poem as America has lately produced.
There is a kind of enduring newness in the evocations of the
poetry that assert themselves more solidly with time. Speaking
of a burial at sea,

> We weight the body, close
> Its eyes and heave it seaward whence it came,
> Where the heel-headed dogfish barks its nose
> On Ahab's void and forehead . . .

But it is difficult to quote piecemeal from such a poem.

An important element in Mr. Lowell's poetry is his feeling
for Puritan New England. At the time most, if not all, of
these poems were written, Lowell was a convert to the
Catholic Church, and the Church forms a large part of their
subject matter; but Lowell is not, as Mr. John Berryman has
called him, 'the master of the Catholic subject without peer
since Hopkins'. The quality of Lowell's sensibility depends
almost entirely on its intractable Protestant puritanism, and
it is never at its ease in Catholic images. The very structure
of his sensibility is centred in considerations that were of overwhelming importance to the early New Englanders, but
which are alien to Catholic feeling—ideas of innate depravity,
the utter corruption of human nature and creation, regenera-
tion, damnation of the non-Elect, and a habit of tortuous
introspection to test the validity of grace in the soul. All these
doctrines have in Lowell's poetry professedly undergone con-
version to Rome, but on the face of it they still look very
much their old Protestant selves. One critic wrote of Lowell's
poetry that it exposed 'the full force of the collision between
a long heritage of New England Calvinism and the tenets of
the Roman Catholic Church'. Although the critic did not use
the description in an unfavourable sense, it remains a very
good one of what happens in Lowell's verse. A head-on

collision between the Catholic tradition and an Apocalyptic Protestant sensibility is exactly what occurs in a verse like the following from 'Where the Rainbow Ends':

> In Boston serpents whistle at the cold.
> The victim climbs the altar stair and sings:
> 'Hosannah to the lion, lamb, and beast
> Who fans the furnace face of IS with wings:
> I breathe the ether of my marriage feast.'
> At the high altar, gold
> And a fair cloth. I kneel and the wings beat
> My cheek. What can the dove of Jesus give
> You now but wisdom, exile? Stand and live,
> The dove has brought an olive branch to eat.

The poem of which this is the third verse has a certain impressiveness, but it is characteristically reluctant to yield up its meaning. It contains some extremely awkward images which need not be examined here as this quality of awkwardness can be better studied in some other verses, and a good many of the lines are far from being inevitably precise in their meaning. For example, the first line above may mean that in Boston sin is non-sensuous and chillblained, being the result mainly of the more frigid spiritual vices. But I should hesitate to stake anything of value on such a reading being the correct one. As for the remainder of this verse, it appears likely that the poet has just received Holy Communion, but if so, he celebrates it in an Apocalyptic terminology that seems unsuitable for such a subject. In this poem the two traditions collide, but it is a collision only—the metaphorical impact of staunchly opposed opposites. Mr. Lowell himself seems not even to be aware of the polarity involved, and none of the struggle of the opposing traditions get through into the texture of his verse.

The Puritan saints, so far from resting on assurances of their election, gave themselves up to some of the most agonizing soul probing ever encouraged by any religion. They examined endlessly the nature of the grace they felt in their souls that they might be sure it was authentic and not a temptation from the Devil; they searched the Scriptures for confirmation, and analysed endlessly the movements of their hearts. All this developed a tone, an attitude—and despite the Catholic gesturing, it is an attitude one finds in Lowell's poetry. This attitude or tone sometimes becomes feverishly tortuous, and leads Lowell into attenuations so rarefied, and through logical transitions so slippery and concealed, that it is frequently impossible to follow him all the way. The poem 'Colloquy in Black Rock' is an example of one of these dialogues between Lowell and his own heart as a preparation for its fuller possession by Christ. It is a dull poem, but nevertheless it is worth considering as a way of approaching his most serious defect—the conviction that he is being, not only intelligible, but highly ordered and logical in the disposition of his images and the structure of his thought when, in reality, his experience is claustrophobically private and subjective. Despite the rigorous appearance of an objective framework of logic 'The Ferris Wheel' is such a poem, and it could be duplicated in this quality by many other of Lowell's verses.

A number of Lowell's poems can be interpreted in purely Protestant terms—for example, 'The Drunken Fisherman', which is one of his best pieces. And no doubt it would be fairer to Lowell if one were to concentrate on these. But Lowell was specifically acclaimed as a Catholic poet, and to this fact he no doubt owes a good deal of his recognition. But whenever the subject is pointedly Catholic there is something disturbing in the tone. Turning to 'A Prayer for My Grandfather to Our Lady', Lowell's uncertainty or awkwardness is unmistakable under the boldness of feeling in a passage like this one addressed to the Blessed Virgin:

> O Mother, I implore
> Your scorched blue thunderbreasts of love to pour
> Buckets of blessings on my burning head
> Until I rise like Lazarus from the dead:
> *Lavabis nos et super nivem delabor.*

This is a network of conflicting connotations that operates at cross-purposes. 'Thunderbreasts', I presume, is meant to suggest the mythical Thunderbird of various Indian tribes, which was supposed to bring rain, and so the word may imply the life-giving qualities of Our Lady's love. But Our Lady and the Thunderbird (if it *is* intended, and I don't see what else could be meant here) belong to traditions too remote from each other to coalesce imaginatively at the low pressure to which they are submitted. Blue, of course, is Mary's colour. And perhaps 'blue thunderbreasts' is meant to emphasize the blue heavens from which rain and grace come. But the quality of Lowell's sensibility is such (and I am thinking of the poem in the full context of the volume) that the word seems likely to start a train of disease images. 'Buckets of blessings on my burning head' is breath-takingly infelicitous. Apart from the ugly sound of it, and the almost Gilbert and Sullivan visual image it presents, it suggests that Our Lady is dousing a halo, which can hardly be what is meant. I am not merely trying to be difficult, but I find this passage typical in the awkward qualities I have mentioned. It frequently happens that when Mr. Lowell is dealing with a religious subject something seems to go wrong with his verse—not inevitably so, for 'The Holy Innocents' is a very good poem. But a religious theme is usually a signal for intolerable strain.

This strain is not lessened when Mr. Lowell relates human action to religious significance. His sequence of four poems, 'Between the Porch and the Altar', is a melodramatic narration of a man who deserts his wife and two children for another woman, gets killed in a motor accident, and goes to Hell. At any rate, that is the action as far as I can follow it, but the character of the seducer seems strangely uneven. In the first poem he is a son with a mother fixation. In the second he is a Concord farmer who, in the closing image, is identified with Adam in the act of committing Original Sin. In the fourth poem he turns up, rather sportily, in a night club shortly before his fatal mishap. Here is the opening of the fourth poem, and it illustrates the recurrence of that strain or awkwardness that I have just noted elsewhere:

> I sit at a gold table with my girl
> Whose eyelids burn with brandy. What a whirl

Of Easter eggs is coloured by the lights,
As the Norwegian dancer's crystalled tights
Flash with her naked leg's high-booted skate,
Like Northern Lights upon my watching plate.
The twinkling steel above me is a star;
I am a fallen Christmas tree. Our car
Races through seven red lights—then the road
Is unpatrolled and empty, and a load
Of ply-wood with a tail-light makes us slow.
I turn and whisper in her ear. You know
I want to leave my mother and my wife,
You wouldn't have me tied to them for life. . . .

Apparently at that moment the accident occurs which, in view of the sentiments he is expressing just then, sends him straight to the Devil.

The first thing one notices about this passage is a characteristic wooden ugliness that is related to the rhythm—particularly to Mr. Lowell's flattening habit of placing a cæsura just before the last foot of every line. It is a common practice with him, and can be better observed in a poem like 'After the Surprising Conversions':

I preached one morning on a text from Kings;
He showed concernment for his soul. Some things
In his experience were hopeful. He
Would sit and watch the wind knocking a tree. . . .

But to return to the earlier quotation—the rhythmical flatness is matched by an unsatisfactoriness in the images themselves. Anticipating the descent into Hell in the last part of the poem, the second line strains too hard to get as much sordidness as possible out of a few glasses of brandy, and the sense of strain is not reduced by the absurd image of the Easter eggs, which is obviously introduced for the purpose of recalling the Redemption, quite as if by accident. Again, I wonder why the nationality of the fancy skater is insisted on since the only purpose that particular exactness can serve is to start the American reader thinking of Sonja Henie. Nor can I understand in what relevant sense the speaker's plate may be said to be 'watching', unless, indeed, he is speaking, not of the plate on the gold table, but of his retina which he compares to a photographic plate. In the next line it is extremely difficult to know what the twinkling steel is. It may possibly mean that a sword is hanging above the poet's head, and that the consequent feeling of uncertainty which it engenders is a warning which might, if heeded, save him, and which for that reason he compares to the star of Bethlehem. But it is asking more than reasonable co-operation from any reader to put any very precise sense in the lines at all. The same kind of muzziness attends the next image into which the figure of the twinkling star naturally moves, 'I am a fallen Christmas tree'. This could, no doubt, mean a number of things, but it hardly seems to mean anything with much certainty. The action which is recorded in the last lines is handled laboriously and jerkily, and the closing bit of 'wickedness' is blurted out in an extremely youthful way.

Most critics have referred to Mr. Eliot as among Lowell's chief influences, but he seems to be much nearer Edwin Arlington Robinson. Both poets are disconcertingly fond of classic allusions, and they both present little tin-types of unusual American characters and episodes. And both have a disastrously 'literary' taste for the more romantic and ancient themes. We find Mr. Lowell writing exotic little set pieces (but on the surface quite 'modern' and difficult to read): 'Napoleon Crosses the Berezina', 'Charles the Fifth and the Peasant', or 'The Fens' (after Cobbett). As for Mr. Lowell's rhythm, a passage like the following from Robinson is much nearer a good deal of Lowell's verse than anything in Eliot:

> Now I call that as curious a dream
> As ever Meleager's mother had—
> Æneas, Alcibiades, or Jacob.
> I'll not except the scientist who dreamed
> That he was Adam or that he was Eve
> At the same time; or yet that other man
> Who dreamed that he was Æschylus, reborn
> To clutch, combine, compensate, and adjust
> The plunging and unfathomable chorus

> Wherein we catch, like a bacchanale through thunder,
> The chanting of the new Eumenides,
> Implacable, renacent, farcical,
> Triumphant, and American.

I should find myself hard-pressed if I were asked to put a particular passage from Lowell against that to demonstrate my point, but with the exception of several poems that seem to me highly distinguished, the volume as a whole is alive with echoes of that kind of writing. Yet Lowell's two or three really successful poems are strikingly original; but original also is a peculiar kind of ugliness which runs through much of his verse. Some of his lines remain in the memory as classic examples of verbal and visual infelicity, for example:

> Her Irish maids could never spoon out mush
> Or orange juice enough . . .

In the most literal sense Lowell's world is astonishingly without colour. His images are nearly all grey or black or white, and they gravitate towards such unpleasant items as snow, ice, snakes choking ducklings, melted lard, dead cats, rats, coke barrels, iron tubs, fish, mud, Satan, rubble, stones, smoke, coke-fumes, hammers, the diseases of old age, and every possible variation on the most depressing aspects of winter. Except in a few poems I cannot see that Lowell transcends the dreary materials he builds them with. On the few occasions he achieves beauty in his poetry the sea is likely to be beating coldly and sombrely in the background.

And yet, under these disagreeable surfaces, Lowell's poetry does give evidence of an unusal integrity. It proves, I think, that the sense of function which I earlier predicated of the American poet, is not wholly, and in all cases, a product of America's material activity. Among its deeper historical roots one may point to the New England puritanism of the seventeenth century, which regarded logic and rhetoric as a means of knowing and communicating Divine Truth. It is under the banners of logic and rhetoric, although these are subsumed in the name of poet, that Mr. Lowell undertakes his work. And it makes little difference from the viewpoint of

165

his intention that the logic is often elusive and the rhetoric unappealing. No poet could well conceive of a greater function than this religious onslaught on Truth, and it is, as I have tried to indicate, a function made wholly valid by the tradition from which Mr. Lowell emerges.

(iii)

There is not much doubt that, historically, Robert Lowell is the most important figure in American poetry among those who came to prominence during the 'forties. But he must still be reckoned a comparatively young writer, with a very limited amount of work behind him, and one must not hesitate to ask who is the most intrinsically important poet now writing in America. There are only three possibilities: Robert Frost, Ezra Pound, and Wallace Stevens. The poetry of Frost, however sensitively related in its colloquial rhythms and its subject matter to its New England background, is hardly of a stature to give decisive orientation or a very considerable new impulse to American writing. Despite its rhythmical distinction and beauty it is yet more parochial than befits the work of a nation's first poet. Much of Frost's later writing gives the impression that a sensibility equipped to deal effectively with such subjects as Edward Thomas took as his province has tended to overload itself with material no longer intimately related to those central springs from which his earlier poetry issued.

Pound is the most difficult of all to assess. He is a monumental fragment of a city that may, or may not, have been there, and it is no part of the purpose of these present notes to consider the evidences. But it is probable that he will continue to preoccupy the Americans more than the other two. Pound's relative looseness of erudition, the apparent flow and volume of his writing, the easy American strut of his assurance, may merely duplicate, on a higher and tighter level, the effects of *Leaves of Grass* on American poetry. Of the three poets mentioned it is Pound, paradoxically, who seems closest to his countrymen. His Americanism is of an orthodox variety merely turned wrong side out. His dogmatic assertiveness, his sense of importance and function, his speedy acquisition of foreign cultures, are all of a kind that is characteristically American. With much less ability and a different orientation he might easily have stayed at home and become another William Carlos Williams.

Wallace Stevens is less understandable to the American literary scene, and his poetry will have less direct influence than Pound's. And yet it is probable that he is the greatest of the three—certainly, he seems the only American poet whose work might be able to counteract the spiritually loose-jointed, tragic influence of Whitman. The poetry of Stevens is frequently painfully difficult:

> The poem must resist the intelligence
> Almost successfully.

But this difficulty inheres in his profound recognition of the inexplicable quality of experience. He has created his poetry out of images and phrases the meaning of which has to be learned in the same painstaking way one might learn a foreign language. It is only after the reader has become thoroughly familiar with this vocabulary that Stevens' images and phrases assert their intimacy with the American language, and that he begins to discover how importantly and intensely Stevens' central meaning inheres in the heart of all his poetry. Imaginative insight, the intuition of art (by which Stevens means the creative, synthesizing insight of any human being at his moments of most intense awareness) become, in one way and another, the subject of all his poetry, and the essence of its form. Stevens' poetry has an appearance of highly coloured artificiality. It is filled with images of art, and the appearances in the world it offers correspond to the appearances of the real world only in the most esoteric of ways. But these appearances express that central meaning and take fire from it so that what in the beginning appeared to us as artificiality ends, by virtue of that very quality, in showing forth and emphasizing the life-giving power of the legend with which Stevens is concerned. But it is impossible to discuss Stevens' poetry within the limits prescribed by the present discussion. I have only wished to indicate here his relative position in the larger group of American poets. A fuller examination of his poetry must be postponed till the following essay.

(iv)

I have been concerned with pointing to the existence of an attitude to poetry which, if properly protected and developed, might become a satisfactory foundation for a highly productive period in American literature. It has been necessary to keep in mind some of the dangers that such an attitude runs; and they are numerous in a commercial society such as America's in which any enthusiasm or conviction is likely to be at the mercy of the exploiter. But, after all, such dangers are extraneous. Before bringing these notes to a close I should like to probe a little deeper into the nature of the American's sense of function and responsibility where poetry is concerned, and endeavour to see if it carries any specific principle of limitation inherent in itself, and, if so, how this affects the nature of the poetry produced.

It is possible to approach the problem by considering the American emphasis on the positive affirmation, on the exercise of will, and on the belief that the future can be engineered profitably if one only has the engineers and the materials— in short, by examining the largely activist modes of American feeling and thinking. It is doubtful if the greatest poetry is ever written in these modes, which are never wholly disinterested. If poetry is a fiat, it is never mere assertion, however brave; and if it is a source of truth, it is yet never praiseworthy for its dogma. Probably the greatest poetry of our time is Eliot's *Four Quartets*. Possibly the Quartets owe some of their popularity to the fact that dogma can be extricated from them, but that is by the way. If Mr. Eliot was once an American poet (and he may still not be an *English* poet), he never expressed the distance of his sensibility from American modes more fully than in these poems. A measure of that distance may be found in such lines as,

I said to my soul, be still, and wait without hope
For hope would be hope for the wrong thing; there is yet faith

But the faith and the love and the hope are all in the waiting.
Wait without thought, for you are not ready for thought:
So the darkness shall be the light, and the stillness the dancing.

That great poetry and intense experience should come out of something undergone or suffered in this way is not the first lesson one learns from American poetry. It fails to understand that element of passivity which is part of the base of great art, and it frequently mistakes the turmoil for the reality. Americans are supposed to like—or to have liked in the past—classical art. But it is the rhetorical gesture and not the moment of repose that they are inclined to value most. Mr. Eliot's lines express their remoteness from the American sensibility in a number of ways. The American would not snub Hope (which in his heart at least he would surely capitalize) in the way that Mr. Eliot does. He knows that Hope literally cleared the wilderness, and confronted with the solid monuments she has erected across the continent, the most critical of poets would hesitate to question too radically whether or not it was, after all, hope of the wrong thing. I do not mean that the American poet might not be as critical on the surface as the English poet, but he is too much a part of the fabric to question too radically unless he should also be willing to remove himself from the scene for good. There is a profundity of questioning possible in these matters which is irreconcilable with the term 'American' being still applied to the questioner in any sense that is significant in such a discussion as the present one. Nor would the American sensibility, which is nervous and impatient, understand the goodness of waiting. To be up and doing, even in matters of spirituality—to say nothing of poetry—is its sweetness and joy. Nor could it suppose it was not ready for thought, for too many fragments of eighteenth-century rationalism still inhere in its composition. And it would have some difficulty in distinguishing thought from the processes of technology, with which it has enjoyed great success. Above all, it could not accept the resignation of the last line.

The sense of function in the American poet is deeply influenced and essentially modified by this activism. This activism is likely to discourage the greatest poetic achievement, but this, at least, can be said for it: it conceives poetry in a public capacity, and the poetry it produces frequently has something of the forum in it. It is not likely to enlarge experience by the insights of original genius operating at the highest level of the imagination, but it is able to explore and define experience deliberatively or imaginatively within certain set boundaries and propositions. Such poetry will tend to have a validity in the American scene that it will not always be able to carry over into other contexts. If we can say that this is a serious criticism, we should not lose sight of the more difficult point that the very limitation carries its intimate importance for the American tradition itself, which is still in a formative stage.

III

The Poetry of Wallace Stevens

(i)

A GOOD deal of criticism has been written by this time on the poetry of Wallace Stevens; and it is poetry that requires extensive analysis in the beginning if it is finally to be read with much intelligence. But that criticism has not been consistently accurate or helpful, and some of the best of it—an essay by the late Hi Simons in *Sewanee Review*, for example—is now forgotten in the files of literary periodicals. R. P. Blackmur's essay in *The Double Agent* is still illuminating, and, fortunately, still available; but the only other easily accessible extended essay is Yvor Winters' acrid attack, *Wallace Stevens, or the Hedonist's Progress*, which is extremely misleading in its conclusions. And even these articles (Blackmur's and Winters') were written early, and deal almost exclusively with *Harmonium*. The result of this critical situation is that there has been a persistent bias in favour of Stevens' first volume, and this has led to an underestimation of the importance of meaning in his work as a whole. Yet Stevens deserves his reputation partly because his meaning is an important one, and because that meaning has been consistently developing from *Harmonium* towards the maturity of the late work. I do not wish to imply that the central meaning in Stevens' poetry is not present in *Harmonium* just as much as in *Transport to Summer*, but it is present in a hidden way, and also in a less mature way, and it is sometimes extremely difficult to come by. Marianne Moore once wrote: 'Wallace Stevens: the interacting veins of life between his early and late poems are an ever-continuing marvel to me.' It is only by tracing out some of these veins of interaction that one can ever be *quite* sure, at least in the early poems, that one knows in fullness of detail what Stevens is talking about.

The relation, then, of Stevens' late work to his early work is not one of conflict or supersession. But neither would it be correct to say that the late work relates to the early as the sum of a problem relates to the digits it totals, for something has been added in the late work that was not present, in however piecemeal a state, before. What this addition is may be only a complex balance, an infusion of remarkable poise, but it *is* new. And despite those critics who think *Harmonium* the best of the volumes, it was needed. Its presence may have contributed to that sense of change in Stevens' work that led some critics in the late 'thirties to think he had taken up the social burden; but actually what was being taken up were the familiar meanings of the early verse, but taken up in a new way by the imagination—taken up, in fact, into what was sometimes a new dimension of poetic reality (new, at any rate for Stevens), and occasionally one could turn aside and look downward from the new use to the old use of an identical image, and realize with a sense of delicious discovery that one now, perhaps, really read the earlier poem for the first time. Stevens' poetry shares this ability to be read profitably both forward and backward with Eliot's poetry. When the 'Preludes' were first printed in *Blast* in 1915 they must have seemed little more than remarkable Imagist poems, yet Eliot had showed almost uncanny prevision in naming them, and returning now from the *Quartets* to those early opening themes, their images acquire, through the resonance of all the later work, a depth and meaning that was surely not present to their earliest readers.

In a somewhat similar manner Wallace Stevens can write in 'Six Significant Landscapes' (*Harmonium*) what appears, what undoubtedly is, a charming little Imagist piece hardly beyond Amy Lowell's prowess:

> Rationalists, wearing square hats,
> Think, in square rooms,
> Looking at the floor,
> Looking at the ceiling,
> They confine themselves
> To right-angled triangles.
> If they tried rhomboids,
> Cones, waving lines, ellipses—
> As, for example, the ellipse of the half-moon—
> Rationalists would wear sombreros.

This contains the possibilities of a complex idea, no doubt; but in itself there is little to invite the exploration of those possibilities. Yet nearly twenty years later in another poem called 'The Pastor Caballero' (*Transport to Summer*), Stevens took up the same idea, and the poem became a reflection of his deepest attitudes:

> The importance of a hat to its form becomes
> More definite. The sweeping brim of the hat
> Makes of the form Most Merciful Capitan
>
> If the observer says so: grandiloquent
> Locution of a hand in rhapsody.
> Its line moves quickly with the genius
>
> Of its improvisation until, at length
> It enfolds the head in a vital ambiance,
> A vital linear ambiance. The flare
>
> In the sweeping brim becomes the origin
> Of a human evocation, so disclosed
> That, nameless, it creates an affectionate name,
>
> Derived from adjectives of deepest mine.
> The actual form bears outwardly this grace,
> An image of the mind, an inward mate,
>
> Tall and unfretted, a figure meant to bear
> Its poisoned laurels in this poisoned wood,
> High in the height that is our total height.
>
> The formidable helmet is nothing now.
> These two go well together, the sinuous brim
> And the green flauntings of the hours of peace.

The bouncy observation of the first poem has gradually moved towards this subtle statement of spiritual poise, and that Stevens is consciously aware of the transition is strongly suggested by the 'becomes' of the first line. The form of a deeply complex attitude or grace is metamorphosed into the

173

form of a particular hat, and the images that cluster around this central symbol do a good deal towards elucidating other poems in *Harmonium*. But first take the hat itself: by this time we have a somewhat elaborate idea of what it stands for, and can turn back to the last verse of 'Palace of Babies' (*Harmonium*):

> The walker in the moonlight walked alone,
> And in his heart his disbelief lay cold.
> His broad-brimmed hat came close upon his eyes.

This was certainly never one of the more difficult poems, but it had seemed a little thin. Years later Stevens enunciated a luxuriant connotation for the walker's broad-brimmed hat (a hat that obviously had no flare) and so he enabled his earlier image to explore in a more significant way the nature of the moonlight walker's disbelief. The day 'The Pastor Caballero' was written the 'Palace of Babies' became a better poem than it had been the day before: one might even say that it had been revised. This is not as odd as it may sound, for if a poet creates his own language he does not cease to create it until he has ceased to be a poet—and there is a sense in which a poet rewrites his collected works every time he writes a genuinely new poem.

But 'The Pastor Caballero' offers relevant insights into other early poems as well. If one reads it together with Stevens' well-known 'Bantams in Pine-Woods', for example, one senses how closely united Azcan is to the more faintly evoked Most Merciful Capitan:

> Chieftain Iffucan of Azcan in caftan
> Of tan with henna hackles, halt!
>
> Damned universal cock, as if the sun
> Was blackamoor to bear your blazing tail.
>
> Fat! Fat! Fat! Fat! I am the personal.
> Your world is you. I am my world.
>
> You ten-foot poet among inchlings. Fat!
> Begone! An inchling bristles in these pines,

Bristles, and points their Appalachian tangs,
And fears not portly Azcan nor his hoos.

The rather brassy appeal of this poem exists at a more superficial level than its meaning, which is extremely difficult to excerpt. The poem has been relatively overpraised within the body of Stevens' work, and it would hardly be worth the trouble of interpreting, except that it provides one of the most admirable opportunities in Stevens for studying the interaction of imagery between his early and late poems. Two extreme interpretations which would contradict each other seem possible, depending on whom one chooses as the villain of the piece, Azcan or the inchling. An interpretation internally consistent, and more or less in harmony with the context provided by Stevens' poetry as a whole, can be worked out in either direction. But in actual fact, I believe that the real meaning is complex enough to release them both from the glory or responsibility of being either wholly hero or wholly villain. The poem seems to be, more than anything else, an investigation of the relationship between the imagination and reality in an anti-imaginative society. Read in this light it offers a comment on one of the more complex facets of Stevens' belief.

To begin: there is some evidence that Azcan is a symbol of the imagination. His height alone associates him with the 'tall and unfretted' Capitan of the other poem, who was 'high in the height that is our total height', and it associates him also with that 'giant, on the horizon, glistening', who is used as a symbol for imagination in Stevens' recent poem, 'A Primitive like an Orb'.[1] But there are important differences. The Most Merciful Capitan is so successfully a state of mind that he can be visualized only as the elegant sweeping flare in the brim of a quite irresistible hat—the sort of sombrero that rationalists would wear if they studied the ellipse of the half-moon. But what is most noticeable is that the relationship of Azcan and the Capitan to their respective environments is dissimilar. Azcan is not on friendly terms with the inchling, who represents his environment, and therefore

[1] Reprinted in *The Auroras of Autumn*, Knopf.

reality; but the Capitan has evidently culminated a successful resistance ('The formidable helmet is nothing now') which
leaves him free to look forward to 'the green flauntings of
the hours of peace'.

If at this point one opens Stevens' Princeton lecture, 'The
Noble Rider and the Sound of Words', printed in Allen
Tate's *The Language of Poetry*, the following passage proves
helpful in distinguishing between the plights of Azcan and
the Capitan. Stevens says there that the possible poet of
today

> will consider that although he has himself witnessed, during the
> long period of his life, a general transition to reality, his own
> measure as a poet, in spite of all the passions of all the lovers of
> the truth, is the measure of his power to abstract himself, and to
> withdraw with him, into his abstraction, the reality on which
> the lovers of the truth insist. He must be able to abstract him-
> self, and also to abstract reality, which he does by placing it in
> his imagination. He knows perfectly that he cannot be too noble
> a rider, that he cannot rise up loftily in helmet and armor on a
> horse of imposing bronze.

Now the Capitan is a successful exponent of the imagination
because he is able to dispense with the 'formidable helmet'.
He knows how to deal with reality, how to subjugate it to
himself by his abstracting genius. Azcan, on the other hand,
is imagination mounted on too high a horse; his henna
hackles are too impressive an armour, and he is out of touch
with reality. 'There are degrees of imagination,' Stevens had
said in the same lecture, 'as, for example, degrees of vitality,
and therefore of intensity. It is an implication that there are
degrees of reality.' And he further remarked that poetry
represents an 'interdependence of the imagination and reality
as equals'. But the hostile, military bearing of the inchling
towards Azcan signifies that reality, in the world of this
poem, is militantly out of sympathy with the imagination,
and each is thereby revealed as incomplete in itself because
of that hostility.

Stevens wrote in *Notes toward a Supreme Fiction* (reprinted in
Transport to Summer):

176

How clean the sun when seen in its idea,
Washed in the remotest cleanliness of a heaven
That has expelled us and our images.

Because of the distorted dealings between them, Azcan cannot abstract from reality towards that pure idea of the sun:
the sun is only a blackamoor to him, smeared over with the
grimy limitations of physical fact. And yet, although prevented from functioning properly, Azcan remains a good
giant at heart. When the inchling screams 'Fat!' at Azcan,
he applies the word in a derisive manner; but 'fat' is an
adjective with consistently benign connotations in Stevens'
poetry. He uses it typically in *Notes toward a Supreme Fiction*
(Part III, poem 10) to describe the symbolical female embodiment of 'the fiction that results from feeling', and that, as
every reader of Stevens knows, is his chief reality (reality, that
is, in its final, completed sense)—the synthesizing imagination
itself.

It is characteristic of the elaborate conflicting connotations
in this poem (representing the inchling's confusions) that the
favourable word 'fat' is qualified in the last line by the unfavourable adjective 'portly'. In *Harmonium* the page adjoining
'Bantams in Pine-Woods' is occupied by 'Anecdote of the
Jar', in which a jar is placed on the top of a wilderness-
encircled hill in Tennessee:

> The wilderness rose up to it,
> And sprawled around, no longer wild,
> The jar was round upon the ground
> And tall and of a port in air.

It has been pointed out before that the good, untrammelled
wilderness is subdued by the presence of that jar to a conventional and man-made drabness ('It took dominion everywhere'), and like Azcan the jar was of a port in air. It had
style (more properly, manner or affectation) rather than
reality. When the inchling uses 'fat' and 'portly' inter-
changeably he serves notice that he is unable to make the
necessary distinctions (connoisseur of the hard-surfaced fact
that he is).

And he reveals his incapacity even more remarkably by conjoining 'portly' and the Chieftain's hoos. One would hardly guess it from the poem itself, but these hoos are a symbol of Azcan's innate vitality. In *Notes toward a Supreme Fiction* we find these verses:

> We say: At night an Arabian in my room
> With his damned hoobla-hoobla-hoobla-how
> Inscribes a primitive astronomy
>
> Across the unscrawled fores the future casts
> And throws his stars around the floor. By day
> The wood-dove used to chant his hoobla-hoo
>
> And still the grossest irridescence of ocean
> Howls hoo and rises and howls hoo and falls.
> Life's nonsense pierces us with strange relation.

Stevens always uses 'primitive' to indicate the natural sources of vitality and insight which are suppressed by the academic and the insistently rational; and the stars and ocean (it is interesting to note that the ocean's 'irridescence' is 'gross', a synonym for 'fat') are merely two items from his usual landscape that serve the same function. The Arabian, then, is seen, like Azcan and the Capitan, to be the symbol of imaginative knowledge; but it is necessary to remember that these three are not identical for they exist under different circumstances. (Incidentally, it is rather amusing to note the diverse implications carried by Stevens' Arabian astrologist and Eliot's Madame Sosostris, whose name, oddly enough— to say nothing of dear Mrs. Equitone—might have been invented by Stevens.) It was not difficult to pass Azcan's hoos off as utter nonsense the first time one heard them, but now it is clear that Azcan and the Arabian both learned their hoos from nature itself, from the wood-dove and the ocean. And in another early poem, the frequently antholo- gized 'Tea at the Palaz of Hoon', that exalted Personage with whom the purple-gowned and fragrant tea guest (the state of guesthood, it should be said, is not explicit in the poem, but the hospitable social implications of the title are inescapable, and are directly related to Stevens' conception of the relation between imagination and society[1]) found himself more 'truly and more strange', and proceeded to create an imaginative synthesis of the world, may very well be merely the personification of Azcan's wild woodnote, which the inchling with his preference for hard facts scorns so much.

In proclaiming himself to be 'the personal', the inchling has merely mistaken the part for the whole, for it is clear that a true 'personal' could not tolerate a dichotomy between the sensuous experience of external reality and imaginative knowledge any more than the person could be defined in terms of a single faculty. But the 'scientific' bias of the inchling with his insolent cry to the imaginative life, 'Begone!' reveals him content with fragmentary existence and its consequent moral isolation. When the tea guest of Hoon proclaimed:

> I was the world in which I walked, and what I saw
> Or heard or felt came not but from myself;
> And there I found myself more truly and more strange,

he meant that he had recreated the external world in his imagination, and in doing so had elevated it onto a plane in which the world of fixed objects escaped its static and excluding definition in space. And so in the world of his imagination he was at last able to emerge from his moral isolation in himself. But the inchling, being the enemy of Azcan, although he may mistake his servitude for something else, is really held incommunicado in his own identity.

Apropos of this moral isolation in the material world, it is relevant to turn back to another early poem, 'Metaphors of a Magnifico' (*Harmonium*), which Mr. Winters described as 'willful nonsense':

> Twenty men crossing a bridge,
> Into a village,

[1] Stevens has written: '. . . reality is life, and life is society and the imagination and reality, that is to say, the imagination and society are inseparable'.

Are twenty men crossing twenty bridges,
Into twenty villages,
Or one man
Crossing a single bridge into a village.

So far from being 'willful nonsense', this is a deeply penetrating statement about the horror of such isolation. It means
much the same thing as Eliot's

> *Dayadhvam:* I have heard the key
> Turn in the door once and turn once only
> We think of the key, each in his prison
> Thinking of the key. . . .

The key for Eliot is Christianity, the key for Stevens is
imagination, and in *Dayadhvam* (meaning 'sympathize', as
Eliot has told us) both keys fit the same lock. For sympathy
is a kind of common ground between the 'vivid transparence'
of the imagination in which Stevens meets his friend in the
poem quoted below, and the Christian charity of Eliot's later
work. The poetry of both is an attempt to overcome the
moral isolation imposed by the modern world: and if Stevens,
Azcan, the Capitan, and the Arabian are all tea guests at the
Palaz of Hoon, there is no reason to suppose that Eliot with
the third walking by his side is not also on friendly calling
terms with that tremendous Personage. Only the inchling
must go without his tea.

So we conclude that however much Azcan seems to fail
the function he ought to be performing, the blame lies with
the truculent inchling, who is a most unco-operative reality.
And one should note that he turns away from insulting
Azcan to point the Appalachian tangs of the pines, thereby
bringing the good wildness of nature under control in the
same way that the grey and bare jar on the Tennessee hill
domesticated the wilderness. His 'Begone!' is, in a sense, self-
defensive, for he instinctively knows that the kind of relationship described in one of Stevens' most beautiful poems will
never bind him to Azcan. This poem (the dedication of *Notes
toward a Supreme Fiction*) describes the escape from moral
isolation through the imagination:

And for what, except for you, do I feel love?
Do I press the extremest book of the wisest man
Close to me, hidden in me day and night?
In the uncertain light of single, certain truth,
Equal in living changingness to the light
In which I meet you, in which we sit and rest,
For a moment in the central of our being,
The vivid transparence that you bring is peace.

To achieve a very deep understanding of 'Bantams in Pine-Woods' it must be read with some such wide range of reference to the other poems as has been indicated here. I say 'some' because the references might easily have been to other poems than the ones actually selected in this paper. But this raises an extremely difficult problem of evaluation. By the time one has arrived at such a reading, it seems doubtful if one is really looking at the original poem any longer, or responding to it as it objectively exists. I said earlier that there is a sense in which a poet rewrites his collected works every time he writes a genuinely new poem, but there is also a sense in which both the poet and the interpreting critic can abuse the privileges implicit in this statement. I had chiefly in mind the increasing density of meaning in a vocabulary like Eliot's which has, as it were, passed with the inevitability of the natural world from a chilly spring to a ripening and abundant harvest. The progression in Stevens' poetry has been hardly less marked; but the vocabulary and images in his early poems are not saturated with the human experience that is the substance of Eliot's, and consequently an attempt to understand some of his poems is more like a project in archæological reconstruction than literary analysis. Admittedly the contemplation of pure craft (whatever that is), has its delight and value, but when the complex meaning of 'Bantams in Pine-Woods' is finally deciphered (if I *have* deciphered it here), its relations to its symbols and images seem largely arbitrary. On the one hand we have an arrestingly grotesque visual image, delineated with something like Swift's clean sense of deformity, and some fantastically exhilarating noises; on the other, a complex and humanly important meaning. But the hostility between Azcan and the inchling (the imagination and reality) may, I think, be taken as an adequate symbol of the ultimate failure of this poem (but I am not saying here that it does not have several remarkable *proximate successes*). If the poem means what I think it does, the meaning fails to be realized in the body of the verse. It is disowned by the very images that should proclaim it.

Before leaving, finally, this question of the interaction of images in Stevens' poetry, I should like to notice the presence of another of those 'interacting veins of life' in the group of poems already quoted here. From Stevens' work as a whole we know that one of the intrinsic elements of the imagination (as of life) is motion and change. The inchling identifies himself in the second line of 'Bantams in Pine-Woods' with his peremptory command to 'hult!' And the principal activity manifested by the inchling is that of bristling—the characteristic behaviour of animals brought to bay rather than of animals in flight. 'Single, certain truth' is in constant motion, is glimpsed and realized in moments of vital, vivid apprehension, and this act of apprehension itself may constitute ontologically a part, and perhaps a large part, of the truth. Turning back, now, to 'The Pastor Caballero', one discovers that the Capitan's flaring hat-brim, itself the symbol of imagination and spiritual poise, is described as 'grandiloquent gesture of a hand in rhapsody'. We have in an astonishingly literal sense here not 'language' but truth itself 'as gesture'. This theme of truth (or as Stevens prefers to call it, 'fiction') as motion, change, gesture, recurs repeatedly throughout his poetry in varying degrees of complexity. We get it in its simplest form in a lovely early poem, 'Infanta Marina' (*Harmonium*):

> She made of the motions of her wrist
> The grandiose gestures
> of her thought.
>
> .　　.　　.　　.　　.
>
> And thus she roamed
> In the roamings of her fan,

Partaking of the sea,
And of the evening,
As they flowed around
And uttered their subsiding sound.

The sea of which Marina partook is unmistakably the same
sea that taught Azcan and the Arabian their hoos, and the
evening throughout Stevens' verse has an even more suggestive connotation than the sea. One even feels a certain 'prophecy' in that word 'subsiding'. To confine oneself to the
quotations already given here, it surely carries a faint herald-
ing of 'the green flauntings of the hours of peace'. But the
important thing about 'Infanta Marina' is that a delicate,
trivial motion of the wrist is a means towards symbolizing
the major end of life, and this end is conceived in terms of
a motion that, from one point of view, is hardly separable
from the moving wrist by which it is symbolized.

(ii)

It was inevitable that in discussing Stevens' interaction of
imagery the meaning of his poetry should have been considered; and it will be equally inevitable now that in examining primarily his meaning, a good deal will have to be said
about the interaction of his images. Much has already been
written on Stevens' meaning, the best article being R. P.
Blackmur's; and if there has been radical disagreement
among critics, there has been a consensus on certain important points, which should be enough to start the reader
on his way. It is, of course, the early work that chiefly calls
for elucidation. The group of poems called *Notes toward a
Supreme Fiction*, which (counting Eliot in the English tradition) may easily be the most distinguished work written by
an American poet in this century, is not particularly difficult
to understand, nor, for that matter, is his recent poem, 'A
Primitive like an Orb'. If the meaning in Stevens' poetry is
again submitted to some scrutiny here, it is certainly not in
the belief that anything surprisingly new can be said; but
the substance of Stevens' poetry can be discussed in terms

that incorporate it more firmly in a traditional context, and I think that is important: for Stevens' poetry has been too much discussed in terms of relativism, misology, Hedonism— even Bergsonianism. If several of these terms can be justified —and of course they can—the result is nevertheless that of dislodging Stevens' poetry from the tradition in which it seems to me most richly assimilable.

There is one difficulty to be guarded against especially in any discussion of meaning in Stevens' verse. Such a discussion is likely to get as far away from any consideration of the poetry itself as a discussion of Milton's theology can carry on away from *Paradise Lost*. The present brief examination hardly affords an opportunity for detailed discussion of the poetry, but I wish to examine two early poems with a view to seeing (at least in the second example) how much of Stevens' meaning is actually realized in terms of the verse. Beyond that concrete realization of his meaning in the body of the poetry, the further rational perspectives that may be drawn from it ought not to interest the literary critic, at least *as* critic. They are not his province. It will be seen, I think, that the part of Stevens' meaning which is poetically significant declares him to be an exponent of Coleridge's theory of the imagination; and in terms of this tradition rather than in any 'modern' vocabulary one may be able to read his poetry with a new intimacy. I doubt if Stevens and Coleridge would have been much alike in any other way, but they seem to meet perfectly in, say, the final paragraphs of the chapter 'On the Imagination', in *Biographia Literaria*, or, perhaps especially, in the conclusion of the following chapter, 'Philosophic Definitions'. And the Coleridgean imagination has become the theme of Stevens' poetry as a whole in a way it never became the theme of Coleridge's poetry as a whole. His theme is the reconciliation of opposites by intuitive vision, the discovery of unity in diversity— and in that phrase we move back to the problem of the Many and the One, which was the great passion of the Meta-physicals: and perhaps no contemporary poet has more associations (however tenuous and qualified) with the earlier seventeenth century than Stevens. But a comparison would

184

hardly be fair to him, for it would tend to show how much better off they were than we, both in the concrete immediacy of their language and in the controlled precision of their abstractions.

'Poetry is the supreme fiction, Madame,' Stevens had written in the opening line of 'A High-Toned Old Christian Woman', that poem in *Harmonium* which had shocked Mr. Winters so much. And with that utterance, Stevens had proceeded to attempt a reconciliation of the conventionally irreconcilable. The poem is not much more than an effective piece of rhetoric, and the fusion fails to occur imaginatively, but the intention is clear. Stevens says that the High-Toned Old Christian Woman is aiming at very much the same sort of thing—perhaps less effectually—as the low-toned artists of whom she would hardly approve. Mr. Winters says of this: 'we learn that the "moral law" is not necessary as a framework of art, but that the "opposing law" will do just as well. . . .' Read this poem as I may, I cannot discover any more sinister meaning in it than that High-Toned (surely that adjective is suggestive of the sort of Brahminism Stevens had in mind) Old Christian Women do not hold a monopoly of spiritual experiences. Both the perspectives of the Old Christian Woman and the 'disaffected flagellants' open at last into similar palm-treed vistas, for 'fictive things wink as they will'. In other words, the shaping spirit of imagination is transcendent.

To hold oneself a little longer to the progress of Mr. Winters' analysis of Stevens—the critic proceeds from a consideration of 'A High-Toned Old Christian Woman' to one of the most rhythmically sensitive among Stevens' earlier poems, or for that matter, in the entire body of his work. The poem is somewhat inconsequently called, 'The Man Whose Pharynx Was Bad'. Mr. Winters quite rightly reprints the original version of the poem as it appeared in its periodical publication rather than the seriously mutilated version in *Harmonium,* in which its beauty is ruinously damaged. Of this poem Mr. Winters has to say:

The poet has progressed in this poem to the point at which

185 N

the intensity of emotion possible in actual human life has become insipid, and he conceives the possibility of ultimate satisfaction only in some impossible emotional finality of no matter what kind. In fact, the figurative opposites of summer and winter here offered suggest the opposites of the moral and the anti-moral which appear in 'A High-Toned Old Christian Woman'.

Here is the poem in its complete version as Mr. Winters reprints it:

> The time of year has grown indifferent.
> Mildew of summer and the deepening snow
> Are both alike in the routine I know:
> I am too dumbly in my spirit pent.
>
> The wind attendant on the solstices
> Blows on the shutters of the metropoles,
> Stirring no poet in his sleep, and tolls
> The grand ideas of the villages.
>
> The malady of the quotidian . . .
> Perhaps if summer ever came to rest
> And lengthened, deepened, comforted, caressed
> Through days like oceans in obsidian
>
> Horizons, full of night's midsummer blaze;
> Perhaps, if winter once could penetrate
> Through all its purples to the final slate,
> Persisting bleakly in an icy haze;
>
> One might in turn become less diffident,
> Out of such mildew plucking neater mould
> And spouting new orations of the cold.
> One might. One might. But time will not relent.

The ennui which is being described here is something more than the punishment meted out to Hedonists. The 'malady of the quotidian' which Stevens expresses with such deep poignancy is a characteristically human state that occurs at intervals in the best-regulated lives—and in spiritual writers its occurrence, or the occurrence of something very like it in a vastly aggravated form, is usually regarded as one of the more unpleasant symptoms of interior progress. But without wishing even to imply an analogy in that exalted direction, I would, at any rate, suggest that a comparison might profitably be made between this poem and Coleridge's 'Dejection Ode,' which it curiously, if modestly, resembles. Although the emotion of direct sensuous experience has ceased to move the poet, a new and deeper emotion arises from knowledge of his incapacity to respond in the old key. The kind of satisfaction that Stevens is looking for in the second half of the poem hardly seems as degraded as Mr. Winters thinks. The desire is to go behind the fragmentary and transitory in experience and grasp its essentiality, no longer perceived in a context in which the elements are vulgarized ('The grand ideas of the villages'), and constantly being lost again through the fitfulness of forms and faculties at the very moment of apprehension. The desire is for the 'vivid transparence' of peace—and if that peace would exclude some of the things that the High-Toned Old Christian Woman stood for, I do not believe that Stevens meant her as an adequate symbol for the best that has been said and thought in the Christian world. What the ultimate nature (in rigorous philosophical language) of the reality sought in such an absolute winter and perpetual summer would be is none of the critics' business. For the purposes of the poetry it plainly involves, like the earlier poem, a reconciliation of opposites towards comprehending the largest possible degree of reality, and in so doing it would conform to Coleridge's theory of the imagination—a creative willing together into a new and unified reality of hitherto separable quantities. It is the temporary cessation of this imaginative power that Stevens is talking about in his poem, just as Coleridge was lamenting its loss in his greatest poem—'The Dejection Ode'.

The imagery in this poem relates as closely to the later work as the poems previously considered here. But it is also perfectly self-contained, while its deeply personal rhythm offers a kind of satisfaction that cannot be derived from the

187

rhetorical cadences of, say, 'The Comedian as the Letter C'. Mr. Blackmur at one point in his treatment of Stevens' rhetoric invoked the name of Marlowe. Taking up his suggestive remark, I should say that this poem of Stevens compares to much of the remainder of *Harmonium* (particularly 'The Comedian as the Letter C') as the best passages in *Dr. Faustus* compare to *Tamburlaine*. But although 'The Man Whose Pharnyx Was Bad' is sufficient to itself, it is interesting to examine, in relation to it, these lines from the poem, 'That Which Cannot Be Fixed' (*Transport to Summer*):

> The human ocean beats against this rock
> Of earth, rises against it, tide by tide,
>
> Continually. And old John Zeller stands
> On his hill, watching the rising and falling, and sayoi
>
> Of what are these creatures, what element
> Or—yes: what elements, unreconciled
>
> Because there is no golden solvent here.

The ocean in this poem is a symbol of chaotic human experience, composed, as we learn in an unquoted part, not from one element, but from the traditional four that are unreconciled among themselves because there is no golden solvent—that is, no fire of the imagination. Now in 'The Man Whose Pharynx Was Bad' the ocean that is envisaged is really a human ocean in which the discords must also be reconciled—but instead of a 'golden solvent', a different image is used—'obsidian horizons'. Obsidian is volcanic glass, and therefore suggests the fiery fusing power of the imagination in the Coleridgean sense, and it looks forward to that lovely recurrent image of 'transparency' in the later verse. The field of the imagination is not confined within the palings of time, and therefore the reality which it creates would naturally move through timeless seasons—and we see the world and life and time itself caught and crystallized in the moment of imagination, just as the mid-ocean is completely and eternally surrounded and defined by the encircling radiance of the sky. 'The vivid transparence that you bring is peace'—that line provides an answer to the kind of dejection and longing in this poem on whose morals Mr. Winters has been so severe.

But if Mr. Winters and others have frequently thought of Stevens as an æsthete, and even a Hedonist—Stevens has not always been prudent about the poetry he has allowed to be published. Stevens used to be thought of as an unvoluminous writer, but in recent years, despite the excellence of *Transport to Summer* (undoubtedly his best volume), and what he has published since, he has allowed too many of his practice poems to appear. *Parts of a World* seems to me to number among its sixty-five titles very little of genuine distinction. For one thing, Stevens had progressed far enough in the expression of his meaning in his early volumes that a group of miscellaneous poems, all intent on saying, willy-nilly, pretty much the same thing in a wide (but related) variety of metaphors could add nothing to his achievement, and I frequently find the monotonous shadow of these poems falling over the real quality of his late work, and marring the purity of response. 'A Dish of Peaches in Russia', for example, seems regrettable to me:

> The peaches are large and round,

> Ah! and red; and they have peach fuzz, ah!
> They are full of juice and the skin is soft.

> They are full of the colours of my village
> And of fair weather, summer, dew, peace.

> .   .   .   .   .

> I did not know

> That such ferocities could tear
> One self from another, as these peaches do.

No doubt peaches can strike off imaginative feats in the proper observer, but that 'and they have peach fuzz, ah!'

leaves me uneasy. It doesn't seem to be leading up to the 'ferocities' in the last verse. But Stevens' subject-matter cannot be condemned because it happens, in this poem, to have failed disastrously. A good artist is entitled to his failures (if only he wouldn't publish them), and the failure here is not one of theory but one of practice. Imagination as subject-matter (implicit here, of course) is bound to look a little mauve and decadent if, in a given instance, it is unable to strain beyond Fancy.

I have made a point of this poem because it seems suggestive in several ways about Stevens' development as a poet. The enamelled images of *Harmonium* had carried certain limitations of expression with them, but they were sometimes of great beauty and peculiar subtlety. If in the late 'thirties Stevens did not actually, as some competent critics imagined, acquire a social consciousness, there does appear to have been a shift in his mode of experiencing— a gradual change in his verse rhythms. What was happening had nothing to do with taking up the social burden, but there was a withdrawal in Stevens' poetry from the predominance of the image, and Stevens (perhaps partly because of the shock of the war, although the change had begun earlier) began to feel increasingly in terms of an inquisitive and flexible line—a line capable of making deeper explorations and wider applications of his images to social reality than had been possible in many of his earlier saffron-starched verses. *Parts of a World* is unsuccessful (but this is said with a view only to explaining the success of his later work) because the conspicuous metaphor is still making a strong bid for controlling interest, but is steadily being supplanted by a new rhythmical interest which follows more closely the movements of the questioning and generous mind. And yet neither a balance nor an interesting tension is usually achieved in this volume between the two elements. They behave towards each other with the easy nonchalance of bar companions, and this is the more remarkable in that some of the poems treat of the nature of poetry itself with unusual insight. In *Transport to Summer* (although the dates of the composition of the poems in these two volumes must have overlapped) the balance is righted, and *Notes toward a Supreme Fiction*, reprinted in this book, will possibly be Stevens' greatest achievement, and it should be one of the great adornments of American literature—a set of thirty meditations on the nature of the imagination.

Finally, we have another of Stevens' best poems, 'A Primitive like an Orb'. In this poem the transition he has been making from an imagistically to a rhythmically controlled consciousness (this in itself implies something that might be mistaken for a social consciousness) is triumphantly completed; but not, it is interesting to note, without the assistance of Eliot's late poetry, which, without being derivative, it yet somehow resembles. It might be repetitious here to discuss this poem at any length, but I cannot drop the matter without commenting on the singular propriety of the title. We have seen how the adjective 'primitive', as a term of general application, signifies the triumph of the imagination in the world of Stevens' meaning. As a work of art, 'primitive' carries the same meaning, but focused more insistently on the imagination's goal of operation. In this sense its opposition to the academic and conventional is almost rhetorical. But since the 'Primitive' of the title aims at achieving an imaginative unity in diversity, at seeing the wholeness behind each fragment of experience, it is a primitive shaped like an orb. And the 'orb' is nothing less than the age-old circle of perfection which can be symbolized even in a little drop of dew, of which Marvell wrote:

> . . . the clear Region where 'twas born
> Round in itself encloses:
> And in its little Globes extent
> Frames as it can its native Element.

(iii)

Harmonium, good as it is, has been praised excessively at the expense of the late work, and the late work has a habit of being confused with 'transition' work; but in spite of all such confusions Stevens is almost certainly (with the exception of Eliot) the most considerable figure that American poetry has produced in this century. His meaning, insofar as it is operative within the fabric of his verse, has none of the immaturity that Winters accused it of, and it is large and coherent enough to form the basis of an important body of expression. Furthermore, its meaning is traditional, and it relates, in a way unusual in American art, to a European past. I do not mean that Stevens' poetry is a sycophant of Europe, but only that the tradition in which he thinks and feels and writes is not a provincial backwater. It is part of the main current, and one does not feel strange in speaking of him in relation to the great traditional non-American poets. He is validly related.

And he has a particular significance for our time. He has been immediately and painfully aware of the cultural disintegration that has closed in with such vehemence since the end of World War I. Perhaps in as intense a way as Yeats (the subject-matter of his poetry has been even more directly concerned) he has known that 'the centre does not hold', and his Princeton lecture contains one or two of the most anguished passages dealing with our cultural tragedy that come to mind. It is in relation to his sense of the catastrophic fragmentariness of the contemporary world that his belief in the unifying power of the imagination has achieved such rare distinction. It cannot, in the nature of the case, offer a solution theoretically as complete as Eliot's Christianity, but it does offer a reality that sometimes seems to be almost the unbaptized blood-brother of Eliot's reality—and it is a reality that finds frequent, but by no means invariable, realization in the poetry itself.

IV

Mencken
and the American Language[1]

THE recent publication in America of Mencken's *Supplement Two: The American Language* has been accompanied in the reviews and journals by the customary grateful acknowledgments any work of comparable size and arduousness that has already won conventional acceptance is sure to elicit. There is one kind of evaluation (in which the stress would be placed on the documentary value of the work—and here *The American Language* fully merits its status as a modern classic —and on the good offices of its humour in sustaining that enormous burden) that would justify a good deal of praise. But after reading a handful of such reviews one grows impatient at the absence of any other kind. Since there seems to be a general, if not very detailed, idea in America of Mencken's limitations, at least as a critic of literature, one is inclined to attribute the absence of a closer view to the faint but pleasant nostalgia for a remote national era that Mencken's name somehow evokes. Perhaps these critics consider the question closed, and now take Mencken for the pleasure one can have in reading him. And there is something in that. But returning to these reviews, one notes that they are, after all, accepting Mencken's attitude to American English at its face value; and that, if his limitations as a critic of poetry have vaguely been remarked on in the past, no one has so far thought it worthwhile to examine the possibility of these limitations having entered into the philological work. Some years ago Mencken estimated that perhaps a million

[1] *The American Language*, fourth edition, 1936, by H. L. Mencken (Alfred A. Knopf).

Supplement One: The American Language, 1945, by H. L. Mencken (Alfred A. Knopf).

Supplement Two: The American Language, 1948, by H. L. Mencken (Alfred A. Knopf).

words of criticism had been written about him. The small amount of this that has come under my own observation deals with questions that, to me at least, seem more or less gratuitous. As far as I know no one has examined with much interest the assumptions about language and literature that are implicit in Mencken's writings. I am not, certainly, referring to the most obvious assumption in Mencken's major work: that the American language has a life of its own and ought to live it. That Mencken was able to suggest this question was still undecided as late as the publication of the first edition of *The American Language* in 1919 is a substantial tribute to his control of dramatic effect. But there are other and somewhat less obvious assumptions present in that book (Mencken had, in fact, treated the validity of American English more as a thesis to be proved than as an assumption on which he wrote), but before analysing these assumptions it will be convenient to make an excursion into Mencken's notions on art as they appear scattered through his other writings produced through the 'twenties and earlier. If much of what will be said here seems too accessible to require extended comment, the fact remains that the transparent shallowness in Mencken's æsthetic writings controls the direction of movement in *The American Language*, which, as the recent reviews indicate, is far from sharing an equal degree of transparency.

(i)

I do not know if Edmund Wilson still holds the same opinion, but writing in *The New Republic* in 1921 he said: '... Mencken is the civilized consciousness of modern America, its learning, its intelligence and its taste, realizing the grossness of its manners and mind, and crying out in horror and chagrin'. To call a writer the 'civilized consciousness' of a nation is, if not the highest, then nearly the highest, praise he can merit; and as all major decorations presumably carry a meaning over and above mere honorary effulgence, so, I presume, does this one. For example, 'civilized consciousness' seems to imply a serious concern for standards, however defined, and a belief that they can operate effectively in at least some portion of society. This much is suggested by the barest etymology of the word 'civilized', which carries a public rather than a private significance, and points towards a classical acceptance of an ordered society rather than towards a romantic rejection. It suggests some system of appropriate subordinations, but its insistence would be on the organic unity of society rather than on its lines of internal division. I do not think this is forcing a meaning on the phrase, for if it does not mean this much then it is very loosely used. In applying this term to Mencken it is not important that Wilson may have over-estimated his subject's stature, but he seems to have miscalculated what the nature of Mencken's intentions has been all along. For Mencken has little faith in or affection for a civilized society in the sense in which that term is used here. He sometimes speaks of the necessity of a cultivated audience, or the desirability of being civilized (as in his essay on Huneker), but these formulations operate at a superficial level. One thinks of his long essay, *The National Letters*—the earliest modern attack on the Best-Seller I know of (and it is a good one)—and one hesitates. Undoubtedly Wilson had his reasons. But in the end such things as this are not enough and one is compelled to concur in Eliot's severity: the criticism of Mencken is merely destructive and facile. His recognitions are important in their way, and it is greatly to Mencken's credit to have made them; but they are useless unless followed up by practical judgments that can be depended on, or at least by some idea of the elements that would enter into a satisfactory practical judgment on the arts. But Mencken's conception of the function of art in society is wholly inadequate. However, these charges require substantiation, and I wish to show, as briefly as possible, that Mencken believes (1) an artist has no relationship with society other than withdrawal; (2) that his indiscriminate attacks on the word *moral* have destroyed the basis for any other kind of relationship; and that (3) these facts have coloured disastrously his judgments on literature, and hence on words themselves.

(1) To begin (with reference to Wilson's remark) on a stale

but still pertinent note: there is no 'horror' and no 'chagrin' present in any of Mencken's indictments of America—at least no chagrin of the kind that moves towards corrective action. (Naturally I do not mean corrective action in the sense that Mencken rightly deplores—corrective action based complacently on some official platform—but rather that urgency to correct and modify that is the inevitable consequence of relevant responses to an unsatisfactory cultural situation.) One even dares speak of responsibilities, but Mencken has rejected them repeatedly in some of his most vigorous language: 'What concerns me alone is myself, and the interest of a few close friends. For all I care, the rest of the world may go to hell at to-day's sunset.' If the dour institutions that perhaps pass off as a little too representative of America were to disappear, so far from considering this a victory Mencken would probably regret it since he has defined his literary personality largely through his hostility to them—and it is a kind of hostility that supports while it attacks. This is not a new observation, but it is conspicuously at variance with any idea of an artist's role as a 'civilized consciousness'; and if it seems vaguely unattached as stated here, it can be more easily focused on the particular when *The American Language* is considered.

It was certainly not shocking—at least not in the way intended—when Mencken wrote of the first war:

> On that day during the world war when the most critical battle was being fought, I sat in my still, sunlit, cozy library composing a chapter on æsthetics for a new book on the drama. And at five o'clock, my day's work done, I shook and drank half-a-dozen excellent apéritifs.

One need not dispute Mencken's view of the war to be disturbed by the tone of this passage (although it is damaged by being removed from its context). One is reminded of Ronald Firbank's boast that he would spend those same years eating breast of chicken and drinking champagne in the most expensive hotels. Apparently there is a point at which the values of the admirer of the *bête blonde* (Mencken's admiration for Nietzsche is always significant) and the æsthete intersect, and that point may be called moral indifference. It is not that one thinks a better occupation than serious criticism could have been found easily in those years; but starting from such indifference, and on the basis of such an exclusion, who could have trusted the criticism produced? (I'm aware that, in introducing this problem of the relation between the artist and society here in this particular way I may have left myself open to misinterpretation, but it is necessary to go on and trust that any ambiguity at this point will be cleared away later.) The question grows insistent: to what extent is Mencken, for all his aura of Baltimore and *The American Mercury*, an 'Art for art's sake' disciple? At its best his style sounds like Twain's, but how near are his intentions to a second-rate Pater's? The final answer will lie in Mencken's dealings with the word *moral* (to be considered shortly), and by the evidence offered in his theorizings and practical judgments on poetry. But something still remains to be said of the social position and attitudes of the civilized man (and artist) as Mencken sees him.

For the sake of brevity it will be convenient here to compress two terms into one, 'aristocrat' and 'creative artist', which Mencken usually employs separately. It will do Mencken no injustice since there is, indeed, a rather ominous tendency to separate practical action (he usually envisages the aristocrat in his specifically political function) and original thought. Still, Mencken's hypothetical aristocrat does represent everything positive that Mencken feels about the political world, and imperceptibly his figure merges into that of the creative artist. In describing this aristocracy Mencken sometimes seems to advance the theory of an élite upper class who are the dispensers of values: at least that is the impression one gets from such a superficially fine formulation of the disease of American life as 'the lack of a civilized aristocracy, secure in its position, animated by intelligent curiosity, skeptical of all facile generalizations, superior to the sentimentality of the mob, and delighting in the battle of ideas for its own sake'. But even here there are certain shades of tone that aren't quite right—for example, the rather vulgar contrast of 'superiority' with 'mob', itself implicitly a

197

facile generalization that turns its back too readily on the enormously complex questions involved in that juxtaposition; and the glib assumption that a battle of ideas for its own sake (a deeply American assumption), unrelated to practical considerations of value, is anything but a deadening exercise. But on the whole, it will be said, the formulation reads well. However, the last test of such an aristocracy as an effective civilizing agency would be in the kind of sensitivity with which Mencken would wish it to be endowed, and in what locality of interest he would encourage its sensibility to strike its most characteristic note. Beginning with the last question, one may quote a typical passage from Mencken describing what, one must suppose, would be the deepest belief that he would bequeath to these aristocrats—the conviction that 'human life is a seeking without a finding, that its purpose is impenetrable, that joy and sorrow are alike meaningless'. This

> you will see writ largely in the work of most great creative artists. It is obviously the final message, if any message is genuinely to be found there, of the nine symphonies of Beethoven. . . . Mark Twain was haunted by it, as Nietzsche was by the idea of eternal recurrence. . . . In Shakespeare . . . it amounts to a veritable obsession. And what else is there in Balzac, Goethe, Swift, Molière, Turgenev, Ibsen, Dostoyevsky, Romain Rolland, Anatole France?

The quotation continues to queue up Zola, Hauptmann, Hardy, Sudermann, Synge, Gorky, Frank Norris, Stephen Crane, Dreiser, and George Moore. This conception of art, which deploys the artists against eternity (personified, of course, in the implied Inscrutability), a conception that favours such phrases as: 'the unfathomable game', 'the elemental forces', 'the profound meaninglessness of life', 'the blind groping that we call aspiration', etc.—clearly this conception is as quasi-mystical as anything one could find. The above phrases are all quoted from an essay on Conrad in which Mencken attacks mysticism in literature, or for that matter, anywhere else—but in the face of the evidence the least one can say is that Mencken seems to be suffering from the self-imposed deprivation and doing his best to get around it. If the passage quoted makes anything clear it is that the locality of principal interest for his aristocrats is not a civilized society but the hinterland of the Unfathomable. This is merely an evasion of the most immediate and pressing problems of a culture, and the easiest way to escape the necessity of maintaining any standards at all. If one insists on retaining some shreds of the critical faculty, the nine symphonies of Beethoven are played, and one watches while the figures of Shakespeare and Frank Norris merge into one—a beautiful demonstration of what Mencken has called the fascination of 'the immense indifference of things'.

(2) Granting that this class, as conceived by Mencken, actually *were* interested in maintaining any standards in that society on which they seem to be constantly turning their backs to contemplate the profound meaninglessness of life, that vigilance would have to be exercised in a moral air capable of supporting a sense of mutual obligations. But Mencken's eagerness to escape into a realm of 'pure æsthetic judgment', free of the responsibilities and disciplines to which any less exalted artistic attitude would leave him exposed, has led him to simplify recklessly or to exclude entirely any real meaning from the word *moral*. Mencken uses it constantly in his criticism as a synonym for *puritan*, or sometimes for *ethical* (in order, perhaps, to discolour it with Y.M.C.A. associations). Consequently he destroys it for critical purposes altogether. Here are two representative examples of his usage:

> The American, try as he will, can never imagine any work of the imagination as wholly devoid of moral content.

> A novel or a play is judged among us, not by its dignity of conception, its artistic honesty, its perfection of workmanship, but almost entirely by its orthodoxy of doctrine, its platitudinousness, its usefulness as a moral tract.

These remarks have in view a particular and obnoxious situation that exists in America, and it is not unknown in England ('Fully nine-tenths of the reviews of Dreiser's *The*

Titan . . . were devoted chiefly to indignant denunciations of the morals of Frank Cowperwood . . .'), but when that situation is cleared away and Mencken is faced with the essential evaluation of a book, *moral* no longer exists for him except in a pejorative sense. He is forced to fall back on such substitutes as 'dignity of conception' and 'artistic honesty', and they aren't helpful since what meaning they may have had was itself dependent on at least some kind of significance attaching itself to the rejected term. In his hostility to the American scene Mencken has forgotten that a moral and a puritan judgment are not necessarily the same, and that the former is not essentially related to any specific body of doctrine at all; that it is, as it relates to a work of art, a concern for discovering and maintaining by incessant vigilance, the finest possible adjustments among the individual, the work of art, and the artist. It is the recognition that the greatest good of one of these terms must necessarily be the greatest good of all three. Such a moral concern will imply further that the term *individual* unfolds at once into the larger social term; but it will not vulgarly reduce society to an abstraction into which only the most 'pushing' critical distinctions and judgments may penetrate. Unfortunately, the 'pure æsthetic judgment' has no more use for *moral* in this sense than in any other. Perhaps it even dislikes this meaning more than most, for it is a reflection on its favourite doctrine of withdrawal as the best relation between an artist and society. By minimizing or excluding the social term (that term by virtue of which the individual shares part of his response to a work of art with the civilization of which he is a part) the 'pure æsthetic judgment' simplifies and intolerably reduces the range of possible complexity in an individual's response to a work of art, and in the ways in which it may address itself to him. The whole æsthetic attitude exists to deny the enormous difficulties of communication by ignoring a large part of the problem, and thereby it recommends third-rate art. The fact, then, that the hypothetical aristocrats who symbolize Mencken's ideal of the good society would probably be exponents of the 'pure æsthetic judgment' is no small matter.

(3) The question of how these conceptions affect Mencken's concrete response to poetry may be answered painfully by two quotations from his essays, from the sentiments of which Mencken seems never to have swerved:

In brief, poetry represents imagination's bold effort to escape from the cold and clammy facts that hedge us in—to soothe the wrinkled and fevered brow with beautiful balderdash.

Poetry, then, is capital medicine. First its sweet music lulls, and then its artful presentation of the beautifully improbable soothes and gives surcease. It is an escape from life, like religion, like enthusiasm, like glimpsing a pretty girl. And to the mere sensuous joy in it, to the mere low delight in getting away from the world for a bit, there is added, if the poetry be good, something vastly better, something reaching out into the realm of the intelligent, to wit, appreciation of good workmanship.

This will answer the question asked earlier as to how closely Mencken's intentions resemble a second-rate Pater's. Perhaps Mencken does not burn with a gemlike flame; but still, poetry is like religion to him also, and a means towards the longed-for escape from life.

Turning back now to Mencken's social criticism of America, one may understand a little better why, under the pleasure one took in reading it, there was an oppressive sense of emptiness. His social criticism does not relate to any adequate conception of civilized values. One is reminded of the epigrams of Wilde, and feels that the brilliance of invective, though so different in tone, has been nourished in both cases by that freedom to abuse that springs ultimately from irresponsibility and indifference. The insights of both men (and in Wilde they are frequently very impressive) often leave one dangling in mid-air from the end of some epigram one had hoped would lead back towards a practical urgency. And *The American Language* in a somewhat similar way leaves one dangling from the thread of its argument high up in an air which is now thoroughly small and dry.

(ii)

There are two assumptions in *The American Language* that should be analysed with some care: (1) the belief that the growth of language is anarchistic; that as long as language expands in a kind of wild growth it is alive, but that standards represent the cold hand of death—and by standards is meant not merely syntactical or pedagogical restraints, but any reference to a formal code or system of proprieties; the belief that words are noble savages and carry in themselves a thrill value that seems to rise in direct proportion to the eccentric vibrancy of the word. (2) The second assumption is that a great creative word-making period in a language may be indefinitely protracted, and maintained at a constant level of intensity. It would be possible, perhaps, to bring forward passages that might seem at variance with these assumptions as stated here. But the texture of Mencken's writing is loose, and one is sometimes confronted with statements that seem not easily reconciled, at least at any depth of probing to which it seems worthwhile carrying one's examination. But if these two propositions are occasionally out of sight, they are not often out of mind.

(1) Mencken wrote in 1923: 'I am against forbidding any-body to do anything, or say anything, or think anything so long as it is at all possible to imagine a habitable world in which he would be free to do, say, and think it.' The origin of this generous impulse has already been suggested: it arises from a distaste for those restraints that an ordered society is bound to impose on any attempt to relax the disciplines which hold it together in a solid front against the delusive profundity of the Unfathomable. But of course this is merely a way of putting it (derived from the unfortunate vocabulary that Mencken chose to use in a passage quoted earlier). What is really involved—and perhaps it is worth repeating—is the desire to escape the constant critical vigilance and the practical necessity of evaluating which such a society *should* impose. The doctrine of the Meaninglessness of Life conceals a good deal of solid physical comfort and intellectual leisure behind its heroic gesture. It is impatience with these deeper

restraints that lurks, deceptively, behind Mencken's opposition to academic rules of language and sacrosanct syntax.
These latter are straw men behind which the real attack on
standards is conducted. For example, when Mencken attacks
John Pickering for having written in 1816, '. . . we should
undoubtedly avoid all those words which are noticed by
English authors of reputation as expressions with which they
are unacquainted', he is only raising absurd old ghosts that
every reader will help him lay again. But when, later, he
quotes a long passage from James Fenimore Cooper's *The
American Democrat*, the purpose of which is, not to urge restrictions on American English from the outside, but to refer
American usage to some criterion that would neither arbi-
trarily impose British sanctions nor cater to American whimsicality, which would, in short, endeavour to find out a
decorous central norm by which the deviations of American
usage might be tested and the measure of their innate
propriety gauged, the response which the reader is invited
to give is not much different from that which (even without
Mencken's help) he would bring to Pickering's absurd suggestion. Cooper, Mencken says, 'was always a snob'. The
distinction between these two cases is sharp, and one is to be
condemned as wholly as the other is to be respectfully and
carefully considered. But Mencken blurs their edges, and
would end by folding them together into a single condemna-
tion. It is by such skilful strategy that he defends the absolute
freedom of the word.

Mencken prefers what he once called the 'clang-tint' of
words—a self-explanatory phrase. Delicate distinctions and
shades of meaning are so disagreeable that he has developed
a special talent for extinguishing them. He was once able to
grow enthusiastic over the sound of the speech beginning,
'Not poppy, nor mandragora', but he found it 'almost meaningless'; and 'two-thirds of the charm of reading Chaucer', he
remarked, 'comes out of the mere burble of words'. Sound
and fury, but above all, novelty, is desirable. 'Traditional',
Mencken has written, 'therefore irrational'.

Artistic freedom can be significant only in relation to some
order of established permanencies. Where, in Mencken's

world, could a writer find a moment of relative stability in the flux of words and phrases of sufficient duration to allow him to begin writing, or a language capable of offering a sufficient resistance to any creative intention to set up that internal organization of cross tensions and oppositions without which any piece of poetry or creative prose is lifeless? It may be objected that this excessive freedom is not in question, but it is difficult to find any principal of limitation or restraint intrinsic in the great disintegrative process that broods and threatens through these three volumes. Mencken has said that 'in nearly all first-rate novels the hero is defeated. In perhaps a majority he is completely destroyed.' Yet Mencken (and perhaps he has been intentionally sinister) has made the American language the hero of his philological treatise.

(2) The second assumption implicit in *The American Language* (that the word-making vitality of a language may be constant) is solidly entrenched in a set of quotations from scholars and critics who believe that modern American English is very near to Elizabethan English. These are made the basis of a deduction much larger than some of them (Virginia Woolf for instance) might have approved. But Charles E. Funk, who is more representative of the group, would hardly have registered his dissent from Mencken's final conclusions, for he writes:

> The art of neology is by no means dead or even decadent. It is distinctly alive and flourishing. Personally, I have no doubt that it is more robust than in the days of Shakespeare and Bacon, and that inventiveness of phrase is even more ingenious and delectable than in their day.

The conditions under which unusual creative vigour in a language originates are usually difficult to isolate, and admit of little generalization. Such a vitality seen from the viewpoint of the health of the whole history of the language would be manifested differently at different times. Occasionally its immediate goals would seem to shift into positions irreconcilable with ones previously sought. But its final aim would be a maturity of speech in which, at least today, the complex and coloured density of the Elizabethan words and rhythms would enter at last into combinations with the contributions of all the later periods, including the orderliness and urbanity that we have from the Augustans, and the elegance that still comes to us from the remoter Carolines. The great age of Elizabethan word-making lasted perhaps twenty years, or a little more: that is, if we assume a close and vital connection between word-making and literature. If we do not, what is the importance of irrelevant word-making? For the complex life of a time is contained, not in the simple pattern of sound and meaning which a single word can hold, but in the infinitely complicated pattern that can be created from many such single strands. But Mencken's tendency (though by no means his invariable practice) is to consider the word-making activity independently of the discipline and tests that literature imposes. This prejudice leads him towards such far-fetched conceptions as:

> That large facility for concocting new and picturesque words which characterized the English of the Seventeenth Century had begun to yield by the last half of the century following [Mencken apparently does not distinguish in this great span of time between the language of Donne and Cowley, or between the vitality of Dekker and Cibber] to the policing of the purists, and thereafter its prodigies were transferred to America. . . .[1]

Mencken ignores the fact that the Elizabethans had had strict word purists in such men as Spenser, Thomas Wilson,

---

[1] The above quotation is taken from *Supplement Two*, published in 1948. Ten years ago Mencken wrote in the fourth edition of *The American Language*: 'During the Seventeenth and Eighteenth Centuries England was wracked by a movement to standardize the language, alike in vocabulary, in pronunciation and spelling, and it went far enough to set up artificial standards that still survive.' This earlier remark, which is factually more nearly correct, seems to me in flat opposition to the more recent statement. But the more recent statement lies much nearer the spirit of Mencken's whole attitude. It is, no doubt, his desire to contemplate the anarchistic vitality of words that has caused this temporary lapse of memory. The discrepancy between these two quotations is not unusual, and points up the extremely shifting grounds of Mencken's writing.

George Puttenham, and Abraham Fraunce, and that towards the middle of his immense period the Royal Academy
began to exercise an influence over language in relation to
which the reservations of Dr. Johnson were mild, and the
restrictions of John Pickering and Henry Van Dyck on
American English merely casual. Even if one has been able
to overlook or deny the pressures of the exactingly refined
Stuart society on language, it is difficult to understand how
the presence of such sternly tangible disciplinarians of words
could be entirely dismissed from the period Mencken marks
out.

Transferring this liberal interpretation of the facts over to
America, Mencken would have it that the great American
period of word-making began before the American Revolution, and is stronger than ever today. But what an evapora-
tion of values has been occurring at a steadily accelerating
speed during even a short period in the time involved may
be guessed by reading a page of Mark Twain followed by a
page of Saroyan. And this is making the test at a pretty exalted level. American word-making has undeniably gathered
facility, and what may even pass as aggressiveness (but hardly
as courage). This is because the cellophane-wrapped propen-
sities of contemporary urban standards have seen to it that
the ride is downhill all the way. New words have no need
to be in touch with genuine values if they are in touch with
commercial values, or carry a snob appeal for New York
Café Society. Mencken is certainly aware of all this, but it is a
matter of little consequence to him. There is an occasional
warning (e.g. 'All this boldness of conceit, of course, makes
for vulgarity unrestrained by any critical sense') but these
warnings are too feeble and half-hearted (even if sincere) to
be heard above the clamour of his practical approval. It is
sheer quantity and clang-tint, and ultimately, the ability of
words to escape facts rather than face them, that counts.

We find him, for example, noting with evident approval
that by 1943, due to the presence of American troops,
'farmers' children deep in the heart of Ulster had learned to
say, "Aw, lay off"', and that 'Ili'ya, Babe' had become an
acceptable form of greeting. To Mencken this is, apparently,

vitality. At any rate, the relevant observation is neither made nor implied: that this does not represent a change in speech habits as importantly as it represents a deterioration in the quality of human relationships. In a similar fashion he praises the American vocabulary of denigration in preference to such English terms as *bounder, rotter, cad*. 'Such terms as *bonehead, pinhead*, and *boob*', he writes, 'have been invented to take the place of the English *ass*.' Or again, 'He [the Englishman] knows nothing of our common terms of disparagement, such as *kike, wop, yap*, and *rube*. His pet name for a tiller of the soil is not *Rube* or *Cy*, but *Hodge*.' What Mencken chooses to ignore is the implicit but invariable reference to some code of conduct (however faint) in the English terms. The American terms (the list is long and would include such additions as *dope, spook, goon, knot-head, fly-brain*, etc.) are contemptuous and insulting in an entirely different way, and it is open to question whether they are more degrading to the person who uses them or to the person to whom they are applied. Their intention is nothing less than degradation, for they have their origin in an ancient sense of inferiority (and perhaps guilt) seeking to escape from itself through brutality. A really useful and valuable treatise on American English would bring a scrutiny to the language that took full cognizance of elements such as this, but Mencken ignores the sociological and psychological background and tendency of words perhaps even more than he neglects their literary affiliations. He contends that the 'American *guy* meaning simply anybody' is a great improvement over the restricted English meaning of the word. But for anybody who has had the privilege of hearing *guy* in the American sense extensively used there can be little doubt that the tendency is to assume (however amiably or unconsciously) that literally *everybody* (including the user) is a *guy* in the English sense. Probably Mencken is aware of this, but he perversely seems to approve of it. In the first place, he hates the American bourgeois so thoroughly that it may be gratifying to one of his bellicose temperament to see the enemy committing suicide in his own language. In the second place, he mistakenly assumes that his aristocrats of language are so far above the general condition of men that they can dip into the language lottery and come off with a prize every time, no matter how great the odds against them are. 'Shakespeare and his fellow-dramatists . . . exercised a sound discretion; . . . the slang of the Bankside was full of words and phrases which they were never tempted to use.' This is an insidious simplification of the relation between an artist and his language, but Mencken may really believe that Shakespeare, living today, could produce comparable work in the idiom of contemporary America (though he might have a more difficult time in his ancient home since 'the finicky and always anti-American Samuel Johnson' left his 'bow-wow English' behind him). Shakespeare, in fact, would seem to be the only thing that American English is waiting for. As Mencken puts it: '—as yet American suffers from the lack of a poet bold enough to venture into it, as Chaucer ventured into the despised English of his day, and Dante into the Tuscan dialect . . .' It must be confessed that Mencken then proceeds, with almost frightening honesty, to make it clear what such a poet would be venturing into.

Supplement Two contains vast lists of words and phrases which the various occupations that make up any American city have contributed to the language. A large number of these words are professional or technical argot, and are not in wide popular use; but it is disheartening to observe (at least it is *my* impression from the lists given) that the occupation that seems to have impinged on the urban vocabulary most generally and successfully is the language of the beautician, with its bright euphemisms for embarrassing facts, its pseudo-scientific pretentiousness, and its heavy descents into professional jocosity, edged with an attempt at satirical overtones towards anyone who has intruded into that smug world insufficiently lubricated with loose coins and facile friendliness. And after the impact of the beautician on American English, the influence (but again this is only my personal impression) of the advertising agent seems to be next in line. Reading through these lists that Mencken has compiled (and for the lists themselves one must be very grateful) one is chiefly struck by how much further than one had supposed beyond the last likely hour for taking the imprint of a major poet American English has really gone. This is no fresh language, but a tired, thin-blooded language, deadlily sophisticated in a popular way, and afraid to stop moving lest it should not easily get into motion again.

In the very intelligent discussion of 'The English Language in America' which Harry Morgan Ayres contributed to *The Cambridge History of American Literature*, he remarked: 'The problem of American English resides, not in its difference from British English, nor yet in its own infinite variety . . . but in the attitude which it adopts towards itself.' It is impossible to find in Mencken's work the basis for any satisfactory attitude towards American English. The practical effect of such attitudes as run through *The American Language* would be to relinquish it into the hands of the commercial exploiters (where, to an alarming extent, it already finds itself). Edmund Wilson professed to find Mencken hopeful about the future of American English, but when one looks for signs of this hope one finds such passages as this:

> Given the poet, there may suddenly come a day when our *theirns* and *would'a hads* will take on the barbaric stateliness of the peasant locutions of old Maurya in 'Riders to the Sea'. They seem grotesque and absurd to-day because the folks who use them seem grotesque and absurd. In all human beings, if only understanding be brought to the business, dignity will be found, and that dignity cannot fail to reveal itself, soon or late, in the words and phrases with which they make known their high hopes and aspirations and cry out against the intolerable meaninglessness of life.[1]

If this is hope at all, it is very specious hope. It should be noted that our *theirns* and *would'a hads* is not the variety of Americanism about which Mencken has been most insistent (*rubberneck* is his own favourite American word); that Synge took over and charged with poetic overtones an idiom on the point of dissolution, and one to which he himself was an alien; that his plays were not written for the peasants them-

[1] This passage occurs in the first edition only, but it was the first edition that Mr. Wilson was writing of.

selves, but for a different audience altogether; and finally, I do not think that a language that winks at its own decay (and what else does Mencken suggest?) so that it can in some distant, blue, and twilight moment cry out against the intolerable meaninglessness of life is necessarily in a state of health. If this is the hope that Mr. Wilson once found in *The American Language*, I do not find it reassuring.

In discussing *The American Language* I have quoted both from the first edition and the fourth edition without necessarily distinguishing between them. This seems to me justified since I am interested only in discovering Mencken's basic attitudes to words, and not in his scholarly attainments; and, from this point of view, the first edition is sometimes more valuable since Mr. Mencken is more forthright there. The later editions represent a strategic and highly verbalized retreat from the areas of greatest exposure, but if Mr. Mencken has sometimes corrected and enlarged his erudition there is little evidence that he has ever deepened his sensibility.

V

Kenneth Burke as Literary Critic[1]

(i)

SINCE the publication of *A Grammar of Motives* in 1945
Kenneth Burke has become firmly lodged in the consciousness of an influential group of American writers as a
critic almost exquisitely rare, abounding with ideas and
enviably in control of the wide range of new knowledge that
characterizes the present century. If not widely read—if at
times even unreadable—he has had a genuine influence on
a few good critics, and, at a more general level, he has become
a paradigm of the *deliberately* serious, a state of affairs to
which his unreadability (such as it is) has no doubt contributed. 'Burke's ethical doctrine, the "neo-liberal ideal"',
writes a recent and enthusiastic appraiser, 'advanced pan-
realism definitely into the realm of the pragmatic'. So we
see that Burke is not being taken lightly. In fact how magni-
ficently turned out he seems to be, both in intellect and
sensibility, may be gauged by opening a new American book
by Stanley Edgar Hyman, *The Armed Vision*. In the final
paragraph of his essay on Burke, Mr. Hyman anticipates
Burke's future criticism as something 'almost unequalled for
power, lucidity, depth, and brilliance of perception'. He tells
us that 'we can be sure . . . that it will be a literary criticism
constituting a passionate avowal of the ultimate and transcendent importance of the creative act'. As a study in
relative values it is interesting then to turn to Mr. Hyman's
concluding estimate of T. S. Eliot whom he sees as a 'sick,
defeated, and suffering man'. 'Traditional criticism', he continues, 'can yet be, unlike Eliot's, turned with hope toward
the future, but it will want different things of literature and
it will have to choose a different tradition.' Ironic reflections

[1] *A Grammar of Motives.* Kenneth Burke (Dennis Dobson).

211

rise through the mind on placing these two estimates together, but one can only pause here to observe that if contemporary criticism is going to sail beyond the bath of western stars it is perhaps fitting that a 'neo-liberal pragmatist' should be at the helm. Before leaving this theme one might further remark that lodged somewhere in Mr. Hyman's book, between the essays on Eliot and Burke, there is an extended consideration of Christopher Caudwell, and it soon becomes evident that the critical vessel (as conceived by Mr. Hyman) is, by this time, well on its way to the salubrious airs of a Burkeian latitude. I say this with no more insidious intent than to indicate the temperament and prejudices which, if not necessary to, frequently accompany an enthusiasm for Burke.

It is obvious, then, that his criticism has the support and encouragement of a considerable group—and it is a group that has a good chance of growing in influence. This critical popularity is partly owing to the fact that although Burke has committed himself against the technological aspect of contemporary society he has evolved a 'methodology' of criticism that cannot help playing into the hands of those to whom technology may be much less present as a danger. In other words, though Burke's virtues are his own, he has certain qualities easily transmissible as vices at precisely that level he most thoroughly deplores. Another reason for a possible 'Burke boom' in America is that he has developed a vocabulary that insulates its user against the shock of the work of art itself—and it must be remembered that the American literary critic is naturally very sensitive about the distance that separates his own language and modes of feeling from the English literary tradition. To shift the Coleridgean phrase, he is uneasily aware that he must effect a willing suspension of nationality during the process of evaluation unless a distorted judgment is to result. To the unpleasantness of this situation Burke seems to have formulated an answer, or rather, a series of answers. 'Formulation' is, I think, the correct term here for there is little that is radically new in Burke. His originality consists chiefly in the creation of a vocabulary so well oiled and metallic that one would almost swear the machine is wholly a new thing. At any rate, it is a 'machine' in which those disciples who wish to put it to such uses will be able to speed away from any very exacting evaluation of a work of art without, in fact, displaying a noticeable cowardice during the process of escape. And finally, Burke's criticism represents an approach to literature sufficiently specialized to become the vested interest of a group. In this respect it is illuminating to revert again to Mr. Hyman. In his somewhat insulting essay on Edmund Wilson he quotes this passage from *Axel's Castle*:

> This discussion would, of course, lead us, if we pursued it, to the nature of language itself and hence to the mysteries of human psychology and what we mean when we talk about such things as 'reason', 'emotion', 'sensation' and 'imagination'. And this must be left to the philosophers. . . .

And then Mr. Hyman comments:

> These things are, oddly enough, the very things which the critic in our time *cannot* leave to the philosophers, but must concern himself with to the best of his ability. They constitute the cornerstone of any serious discussion of literature. The fact that Wilson has never permitted himself to go into them is merely another evidence that the attempt to interpret, 'translate', and promote major literature on no more solid a basis than that sharp reading and eclecticism cannot result in more than flashes of insight at its best. . . .

My own opinion of Mr. Hyman's view of the matter will, perhaps, become clear enough in the following pages, but here one might pause to note that, while few have ever doubted that all the arts and sciences at some higher level of unification become mutually assimilated in each other's being, this vision of inter-relatedness will hardly be discovered by mere promiscuity. The indiscreet introductions that so many psychologists in our time have effected between the various arts and sciences have so far resulted only in stillborn progeny, and one of the most notable things about Burke's criticism is that a radical indecision as to what constitutes the human personality weakens answers that he often gives the appearance of handing out pat. Burke is fond of referring to the 'unchanging structure of the neurological substance', but if this does anything it is simply to act as a fulcrum on which the material and spiritual interpretations of the soul can see-saw as occasion requires. For if Burke seems to favour the former he certainly maintains a kind of back-street relationship with the latter. Mr. Hyman accuses Wilson of being merely a translator, but there will be occasion to show that Burke has his own method of translating a poem into a symbolic act between which (*whatever* the intrinsic justification of such a procedure if discreetly used) and the verbal structure from which it is purportedly drawn, *he*, at least, demands only the roughest equivalence. It is in this farther, higher realm of act, this symbolic Heaven to which he sends good poems, that the fusion between literary criticism and the other sciences takes place in Burke's own criticism.

In the following remarks on Burke it will be necessary to say a good deal about the ideas he uses as a critical *procédé*, but I wish to say once and for all that it is not primarily towards a criticism of those ideas in themselves that I wish to direct this article. Like everything else that breeds too fast, ideas that come in flocks are likely to be something of a plague, but Burke's ideas taken separately are frequently stimulating, and are sometimes capable of providing genuine insights into a work of art. That such insights are so relatively few in his work is due, I think, to a misplaced emphasis— and it is an emphasis broad enough to include within its scope a wide range of particularizations. These must be the real subject of the following paper; but here, in a previsionary sort of way, and on the basis of the faint pencilling already sketched in, I would hazard the judgment that Burke's emphasis chiefly points to how little, at long last, he really cares for literature.

I wish, then, to look first at the tone of his criticism, to inspect his attitude to literature, an attitude that does not so much express itself in the specific ideas he advocates as it peeps *through* the eyes of these ideas as through a mask, and

214

changes the overall expression by a singularly fixed gaze. And secondly, I wish to examine with some particularity his conception of literature as Symbolic Action and Ritual: or, to be more precise, the ways in which he uses this conception, the end he seems to have in view, and the kind of satisfaction he appears to derive from it. This method may involve a degree of repetition; but perhaps this will be forgivable, for since Burke published his first critical work in 1931 his successive volumes have risen towards the prosperous precincts of *A Grammar of Motives* through a widening spiral which has in its steady repetitions, pushed upwards and outwards the original set of meanings discoverable in *Counter-Statement*. Nothing could be said legitimately against such a form of development, but it is noticeable that the later and more affluent generations of ideas demonstrate the attenuations of continued inbreeding, and one cannot help missing the greater forthrightness of the two first critical volumes (*Permanence and Change*, 1935, was the second). This is worth while noting because it suggests something of the difficulty one has in writing about his work. One can never be quite sure that Burke will not circle back on any given text in his books with a more elusive (but by no means contradictory) interpretation of his original meaning. However, in the end the strategy is likely to prove unfortunate since he has already given several indications that his meaning may someday entirely evanesce in a gust of his own dialectical subtlety.

(ii)

In writing of Burke as a literary critic one is up against a difficulty at the very outset. Many have doubted whether he is really a literary critic at all. In the book already named we find Mr. Hyman settling this problem with characteristic generosity:

> The reason reviewers and editors have had such trouble fastening on Burke's field is that he has no field, unless it be Burkology. In recent years it has become fashionable to say that he is not actually a literary critic, but a semanticist, social psychologist, or philosopher. A much more accurate statement

would be that he is not *only* a literary critic, but a literary critic plus those things and others.

I remember Burke's having expressed somewhere a certain dislike for Leonardo, and so he may have found the above passage disagreeable enough. However, whatever injustice is involved, it is *only* as a literary critic that I wish to consider him here, and his volumes as a whole give one reasonable grounds for supposing that he considers himself most fully defined in this term. Towards arriving at some sense of his critical tone I wish to review his criticism briefly here under three headings: (1) the central proposition of his critical theory and what it means; (2) his idea of the function of a critic; and (3) the principal ground of weakness in his criticism.

1. In the Foreword to his book, *The Philosophy of Literary Form*, 1941, Burke remarks that 'the reader who wants the specific criticism of books might be more disappointed [with *The Philosophy*] than the reader who wants a theory of the criticism of books'. Even though one may not like the kind of separation between theory and practice implicit in such a statement it is justifiable if there is a constant and intelligent communication between the two levels, neither level tyrannizing over the other, each increasing its effectiveness under disciplines suggested by the other. The passage indicates clearly enough the direction of Burke's bent away from the practical, and one feels that such a quick recognition of a natural predisposition *should* act as a safeguard against the abuses of theory; for the latter can be useful only as long as it works towards the elucidation of particular poems.

Burke's theory of criticism covers many points, but the heart of it may be summed up in this brief statement:

> To consider language as a mode of *action* is to consider it in terms of 'poetry'. For a poem is an act, the symbolic act of the poet who made it—an act of such a nature that, in surviving as a structure or object, it enables us as readers to re-enact it.

I have already said that with Burke's ideas in themselves one seldom quarrels, and here it is an agreeable task to point to the virtues of the theory itself. Poetry becomes, not a segregated experience, but an experience at one with all human action. Literature is, in such a view, brought into an arena of the widest significance, and theoretically its participation in life is complete—or rather, literature *is* life in an entirely realistic way. Poetry is therefore seen to be ethical, and of the deepest influence in shaping 'our structures of orientation'. Such a view, so far from being new, will be substantially familiar to everyone, but Burke does manage to give it a centrality and completeness of statement that is admirable. And at this point, in the face of the dark hints that have been made here about Burke's critical practices, and before offering substantiations, I should like to say that few critics have been more sensitively aware of the relationship between language and practical action than Burke has been, or have spoken with greater dramatic effectiveness of the problems of communication in contemporary society. *Permanence and Change* is filled with such pointed observations as: 'Speech takes its shape from the fact that it is used by people acting together. It is an adjunct of action—and thus naturally contains the elements of exhortation and threat which stimulate action and give it direction.' But at this time the theory of Symbolic Action was not fully evolved, and Burke was chiefly concerned with the operation of the word in it social context— a field in which he has considerable skill. But he has a proportionate lack of perception in literary matters, and when, in his next book, *Attitudes toward History*, 1937, he turned back to literary criticism again and developed his theory of Poetry as Symbolic Action with great explicitness it became clear that, whatever the virtues of such a view *could* be, Burke lacked the requisite critical tact and awareness to use it as anything other than an implement finally murderous. It was in this book that Burke began in real earnestness to shuttle back and forth from literature to sociology to economics to psychology to magic and religion [1] with a sometimes attrac-

---

[1] It is again necessary to repeat that I am speaking of Burke's critical practice, which is the only thing that matters, and not of his critical theory. As regards the latter, he seems to have, at least in his last book, *A Grammar of Motives*, a more exacting conscience about the integrity of separate sciences than previously. For example, he quotes as 'the prin-

tive but decidedly alarming air of irresponsibility as to which station he happened to be in at any given moment, and the situation became genuinely frightening when one gathered, from remarks dropped here and there along the way, that he was never quite certain that *any* station was *not* literary criticism, to which platform his mind *still* frequently reverts as 'home'. Even with such a slender definition of the theory as has been given above it must be obvious that only a very exacting literary critical control could prevent such a theory from sooner or later encountering catastrophe, could have the strength of will to turn down idle invitations often extended to rounds of dissipation during which the integrity of any poem would surely lose its health and die. But it may be that this extension of the influence of literary criticism over the adjacent sciences is partly due to Burke's Marxism. Burke is such a pastoral sort of Marxist (H. B. Parkes' excellent essay on Burke in *The Pragmatic Test* stresses certain political unorthodoxies in his Marxism), that one is likely to underestimate at first the influence of his political thought on his criticism, though Burke himself is terribly explicit about it in every volume. Mr. Hyman, however, suspiciously omits any reference whatever to Burke's politics.

2. But this theme moves the argument from Burke's theory to his idea of the function of the literary critic. In *Attitudes*

ciple of specification' the following remark from Kant: 'Rather than enlarging the sciences, we merely disfigure them when we lose sight of their respective limits'. Burke proceeds to comment: 'The principle of specification is particularly applicable . . . to terminologies of motives that attempt to treat of ethical issues in exclusively non-ethical terms, or of verbal action in terms of non-verbal motion, or of human motives generally in terms of non-human entities, such as the learning processes of lower animals, or the physiology of endocrine secretions, and the like. In brief, we violate the principle of specification when our terms for the examination of one field are got by simple importation from some other field.' However, I remember Burke's having, in an earlier book, discussed the various fields of research as an arbitrary parcelling out of lands at specific dates and in the dominant framework of a prevailing orientation, itself constituting a deflection from purity. In any case, he has always treated literary criticism with considerably more latitude, and his critical practice has never much taken cognizance of this 'principle'.

toward History we find a full definition of his conception of himself in this role:

> Our own program, as literary critic, is to integrate technical criticism with social criticism (propaganda and didactic) by taking the allegiance to the symbol of authority as our subject. We take this as our starting point, and 'radiate' from it. Since the symbols of authority are radically linked with property relationships, this point of departure automatically involves us in socio-economic criticism. Since works of art, as 'equipment for living', are formed with authoritative structures as their basis of reference, we also move automatically into the field of technical criticism (the 'tactics' of writers). And since the whole purpose of a 'revolutionary' critic is to contribute to a change in allegiance to the symbols of authority, we maintain our role as 'propagandist' by keeping this subject forever uppermost in our concerns. The approach, incidentally, gives one an 'organic' view of literature, sparing him the discomforts of discussing the 'social' and the 'technical' as though they were on two different levels. He spontaneously avoids a dualism of 'form' and 'content', 'beauty' and 'use', the 'practical' vs. the 'esthetic', etc. He gets a unitary approach to the matter of dialectical interaction.

Here one can see how easily, without an exacting critical conscience, Burke's theory moves through art to propaganda, how easily the literary merges into the revolutionary critic. It is not merely that one may not like what Burke is propagandizing ('Communism is a co-operative rationalization, or perspective, which fulfils the requirement suggested by the poetic metaphor,' he wrote in *Permanence and Change*); it is not that one wholly disagrees with the idea of art *as propaganda*, but the cold-blooded sacrifice of art *to* propaganda that is implicit here is repellent. (Burke always keeps his way out free, however, and anyone wishing to read his reservations on this position should look at *Attitudes toward History*, Volume 2, page 110, and there is also a relevant essay in *The Philosophy*.) And it might be noticed that even in what is commonly considered his best essay, *Symbolic Action in an Ode by Keats*, which will be analysed later, there is a good deal more of the Marxist critic than appears at first. The 'organic' view of literature recommended above involves an analysis of the work from the viewpoint of political purpose, and ironically enough, not the artist's but the critic's purpose. It also seems debatable whether the compression of motives that would result from interpreting a work towards such an end, so far from sparing the integrity of the work of art, would not result in a distortion far greater than the inevitable violations imposed by any given set of critical terms. And there would still be the 'dialectical inter-action' between two purposes—the poet's and the critic's—that would be resolved at last in an appropriately 'coached' estimate. But one feels how futile it is to discuss these things in Burke's writings at all. The reality he deals with comes increasingly to seem less the reality of the objective world (despite the 'pan-realism' attributed to him) than its image artfully mirrored in a great shiny vocabulary; and if that vocabulary follows the movements of the real world with some skill, it is independently capable of internal readjustments that, at a second's warning, can carry Burke by the grace of a shifting stress fairly off to dialectical safety.

The above passage, which is representative of his style, exhibits his technique at its usual level. Those words of which he hopes, sooner or later, to make special use, he appropriates for his strategies by enclosing in inverted commas. The various key-words in this passage mean in Burke pretty much what they mean anywhere else. Yet to anyone who reads this paragraph with Burke's writings as a whole in memory they will seem to have a great specialness about them. For Burke has endlessly discussed and defined them through his books. Thus: tactics, equipment for living, authoritative structures, basis of reference, symbols of authority, revolutionary, linkages, etc., have all been up for protracted analysis somewhere, and sometimes on a number of different occasions. Burke has seemed to attach quite new and precise meanings to such words, and he has frequently made striking and original comments on them; but in the end the performance exceeds the reality, and we are left very much as we were before. But if Burke has not significantly enlarged or narrowed the meanings of his words, he has in the meantime gained control of the reader's responses to them—he has given his reader great faith in them, and in those intervals when Burke himself is content not to be at grips with meaning, these highly trained words are capable of carrying on like so many theatrical wrestlers who know how to thrill an audience without much pain to themselves. But to return to the above passage more particularly: it is interesting to note his taste for the adverb 'automatically'. (Burke's criticism is especially American in a certain flair it has for the mechanical.) As one draws to the close of the paragraph, however, it is surprising to note that the third point at which he might have been expected to use 'automatically' he uses 'spontaneously' instead, an adverb characteristically applied to life rather than to mechanical processes. It is precisely Burke's tendency to think of literary criticism as, in the end, something automatic ; to speak of something living in mechanical terms, that would be a chief complaint against him. I realize, certainly, that when Burke says 'Poetry is Act' he is not referring to mechanical motion, and that he is as far from the merely automatic as he could get in such a phrase. But I am concerned here with the processes (still to be examined) by which Burke converts poetry into a supposedly equivalent act. I remarked in the beginning of this paper that although Burke hated technology and disliked science, at least insofar as it has provided a context for life, the critical 'methodology' he has evolved seems designed in tone to betray him into the hands of his enemies. And in a similar manner, he desires to emphasize the human act, to insist on the dramatistic aspect of literature (as opposed, for instance, to a behaviouristic criticism); but for that purpose he is willing to convert a poem into a graph (he analyses poems in terms of Chart, Prayer and Dream in *The Philosophy of Literary Form*), count image clusters to discover the neuroses of a poet, and interpret all art from the viewpoint of Symbols of Authority, which can mean little else in his case than to submit it to an evaluation ultimately Marxist. Or he likes to ring the changes on a rhetorical device by showing how it is at the heart of a variety of complex literary passages. Thus in *Counter-Statement* with great irrelevance he reduces scenes from Racine's

Iphigénie and Wilde's *Salome,* and verses from 'We are Seven', together with other specimens, to the trick of 'talking at cross-purposes'. And in his later work he has pointed to the ancient device of what he calls (under a new name in an intricately worked out schema) the 'Act-Scene ratio' as if its mere presence in a poem or play were enough to explain the range of the work's complexities. (The Act–Scene ratio is that tendency of an act and a scene in which it occurs to share a common imagery towards mutual enforcement of a common mood). And he has a tendency to consider later works of a writer as successive rewritings of some earlier work: thus, *Mario the Magician* is a rewriting of *Death in Venice.* Too much cannot be made of any one of these things, but together they provide Burke's criticism with an aspect I would call 'mechanical', for Burke uses these methods, not with any sensitive care for the life of the poem, but with the hope of getting beyond the poem entirely into a realm of loosely disciplined symbolism in which he can seek another kind of life and other kinds of satisfactions.

3. This glance at Burke's theory of Poetry as Act and at his conception of the critic's function does not go far in explaining that restlessness and energy that is characteristic of all his writing, and it leaves unnoticed one of the most insistent defects in his work: a monotonous absence of shade and highlight that reduces all of Burke's ideas to a monochrome significance. A book by Burke teems with local activity. Ideas scurry everywhere, and one watches them with something of the fascination with which one studies the combination of aimlessness and purpose that characterizes life in an ant hill. Just how exalted Burke's final purpose really is one realizes only gradually; but how he has laboured the means of reaching it is evident from the first. The greatest point of internal strain in Burke's ideological structure—and the strain is, after all, one of the chief results of all that labour—occurs in an area where two such passages as are quoted below, attempting to collaborate in a final vision of Burke's design, end up by mutually frustrating each other.

First, as illustrating the essential seriousness of his intentions, one could point to this passage from a recent essay:

But if one offered a synthesis of the fields covered by the various disciplines, which of the disciplines could possibly be competent to evaluate it? Where each specialty gets its worth precisely by moving towards diversity, how could any specialty possibly deal with a project that offered a *unification* among the diversities? Or, otherwise put: if one were to write on the inter-relatedness among ten specialties, one would be discussing something that lay outside the jurisdiction of them all.

It might be noted from the tone of this passage that theology would seem to be the only ground in which the desired unification might occur, although we know that such a unification for Burke would be achieved ultimately in a society 'in which the participant aspect of action attained its maximum expression', a society which he naturally visualizes as Marxist. The passage is further noteworthy as indicating the incapacity of his conception of literary criticism to act as a central discipline —but perhaps it is unfair to stress that point here since the passage ends on an inflection suggesting the desire is for an ontological reality different in nature from a mere evaluating discipline. The seriousness of tone is hardly short of religious. In another place, distressed by the confusion caused today by overlapping 'interpretative frames' in our society, Burke has asked 'What arises as a totality?' And he continues: 'The myriad orientations will be tragically wasted, the genius of one of the world's most vigorous centuries will be allowed to go unused, unless we can adapt its very welter of interpretations as sceptical grounding for our certainties.' The nervousness one feels in the fabric of Burke's writing, then, springs from his necessity of basing his certainties on uncertainties; and the fact that he is religiously solemn about the first, and lacks both the humour and the critical tact to dismiss the second with any assurance does not relieve the tension. But if Burke's readers suffer as a result, certainly Burke suffers more.

As contrasted with the first passage, the one below from *Permanence and Change* exhibits Burke bringing the uncertainties under control. Although it springs from the highly serious purpose just commented upon it demonstrates why so much of Burke's writing seems to end in frivolity, and to express a defective sensibility. The passage is an explanation of a phrase Burke frequently employs, 'perspective by incongruity'. Burke traces the phrase to Nietzsche, and he may also be indebted to Remy de Gourmont's dissociation of conceptual words which he discusses in *Counter-Statement*. 'Perspective by incongruity' is in itself a highly useful device. It operates in something of the manner of a metaphysical image that by collocating unexpected items is capable of providing new and unusual insights; or, by division on the same principle, may reveal unsuspected weaknesses in accepted formulations. Here is the passage:

> . . . we might say that planned incongruity should be deliberately cultivated for the purpose of experimentally wrenching apart all those molecular combinations of adjective and noun, substantive and verb, which still remain with us. It should subject language to the same 'cracking' process that chemists now use in their refining of oil. . . . An idea which commonly carries with it diminutive modifiers, for instance, should be treated by magnification, as were one to discuss the heinousness of an extra slice of beef, or the brain storm that rules when one has stumped one's toe. One should be prepared to chart the genesis, flourishing, and decay of a family witticism, precisely as though he were concerned with the broadest aspects of cultural change, basic patterns of psychology and history thus being conveniently brought within the scope of the laboratory. One should study one's dog for his Napoleonic qualities, or observe mosquitoes for signs of wisdom to which we are forever closed. One should discuss sneezing in terms heretofore reserved for the analysis of a brilliant invention, as if it were a creative act, a vast synthesis uniting in its simple self a multitude of prior factors. Conversely, when the accepted linkages have been of an imposing sort, one should establish perspective by looking through the reverse end of his glass, converting mastodons into microbes, or human beings into vermin upon the face of the earth. Or perhaps writing a history of medicine by a careful study of the quacks, one should, by the principle of the *lex continui*, extend his observations until they threw light upon the

processes of Pasteur. Or do a history of poetry by going among the odds and ends of Bohemia, asking oneself why some monkey jumper wore a flowing tie, and letting the answer serve as an explanation of Yeats or Valéry.

The kind of reversal being considered here only degrades the idea of 'perspective by incongruity'. The passage has a faded whimsicality that, so far from being original, has been exploited for many generations by middlebrow essayists who, in little after dinner gems of literature, have waxed solemn about their opera hats or frivolous about their great-aunts' funerals. So far from these distortions effecting new insights there is something about the tone in which Burke marshals them forward that rigidifies the sensibility in an old response at the very moment it should be most receptive to something new. But more important, the impersonal scientific metaphor with which the paragraph opens is unjustifiable. Any 'perspective by incongruity' would be a highly personal thing, since only *certain* terms would be chosen by any one person to be broken down in a *certain* way. The sensibility and wishes of the subject forming such a perspective would be an important factor, and inevitably his perspective would converge at some point previously proposed in some level of his consciousness. It is clear that such a method has great possibilities for a Marxist critic undertaking an interpretation of literature in relation to Symbols of Authority, and here one realizes with a start that the only shocking item in the above list—the last item—is the one by which Burke would be least shocked. The Bohemian's flowing tie as a romantic symbol of caste and function in a capitalist society would undoubtedly perform services similar to the ones Yeats' 'aristocratic' attitudes and imagery performed for him, and such services, we shall see, Burke considers one of the chief functions of literature. It is even a little odd that Burke should consider such an item as his last one a 'perspective by incongruity' at all.

By juxtaposing these two passages one sees Burke deeply concerned with certainties that he is both eager to realize himself and to propagate. One knows that the only tangible certainty he admits is a political one, but this, in all its rami-

225

fications, constitutes the 'good life'. He has a strong religious nostalgia, and it confers a solemn authority of tone on his ultimate goal. And as the religious sensibility is particularly sensitive to scepticism one sees him 'transcending' this weakness by behaving like a sceptic himself: and he toils away in the second passage among the contemporary uncertainties, using a neutral critical device, but in the somewhat weighted way that theologians sometimes make their appeals to secular subjects. In the end, his 'perspective by incongruity' converges on a Heavenly City that is not very new considering the circuitous approach he has chosen; and the deep earnestness of that final end, blunting a multitude of intermediary perceptions, is happy to tolerate frequent collapses of literary criticism into the lower regions of polemic. But I must apologize at this point for so largely presuming on the question of the religious inflection. I can only point ahead to a further stage when I shall attempt to isolate this tone more carefully.

(iii)

Against this general background it should now be possible to consider relevantly three central problems in Burke's criticism: (1) the manner in which he numerically individuates poems; (2) the practical way in which he translates a poem into Symbolic Action; and (3) the way he analyses Symbolic Action in terms of ritual.

1. By the problem of individuation is meant the manner in which a poem may claim to be itself. Does it exist by virtue of an ultimately inviolable identity, or does it possess its final and finest meaning *only* in terms of an organization of principles (however complex) that can be wholly explained away? Burke seems to wish to explain the poem entirely in terms of principles—at least the poem insofar as it exists as a verbal object. He can always, of course, step across the threshold into the Symbolic Act and confront such an accusation with the reply that he is actually stressing the dramatistic content, the human aspect of poetry; but I wish to suggest later that the transition is a questionable one as he effects it, and that meantime the verbal structure of the poem has been violated

226

by the assumption that it can be mechanically explained in its totality. He wishes to achieve this reduction by bringing principles to an ever-narrowing focus within the poem until any area of uniqueness is destroyed.

The problem is, of course, a metaphysical one, and Burke takes full advantage of this fact to so adjust the terms of controversy that he is able (with no justification) to call any critic using the term 'unique' a nominalist. Or, at any rate, his justification lies in unduly extending the grounds of the term 'unique' until it embraces literally everything in a poem. He blandly assumes that such critics inevitably confuse the terms 'unique' and 'intrinsic', which is no more true than that most critics who consider Byron's human personality unique would also add that his 'bleeding heart', considered merely as a physical organ, required any other kind of individuation than that conferred by quantitative extension. At this point, one is up against a definition of what the human personality is, and one feels more than ever how wrong Mr. Hyman was in the passage quoted earlier to attack the discreet Mr. Wilson for preferring *not* to consider these problems when he was trying to consider literature. But Burke forces metaphysical issues with a rashness that is all the greater when one considers how little he himself has settled the problem of personality. A puzzling ambiguity prevails in all his books. It is difficult to perceive at what level of final definition Burke employs the word 'identity', but it is not, in any eventuality, reassuring when he turns from a discussion of this subject to quote as an authority Mr. Harold Laski on social pluralism. And in the same volume he refuses *not* to believe in immortality lest he should be accused of fearing Hell. But the dilemma with which he is faced is perhaps most vividly summed up in the following paragraph from his essay, *The Problem of the Intrinsic*, which is his principal statement on the subject of individuating poems:

Indeed, the question as to what a thing is 'in itself' is not a scientific question at all (in the purely empiricist sense of the term), but a philosophical or metaphysical one. Recently, for instance, there appeared a very intelligent book by a contemporary psychiatrist, Dr. Andras Angyal, entitled *Foundations for a Science of Personality*. But opening it, one finds the entire first half of this project for a 'science' of personality constructed about the relationships between 'organism' and 'environment', two terms that in their very nature *dissolve* the concept of personality by reducing it to non-personal terms. Strictly speaking, the expression 'science of personality' is a contradiction in terms, a 'perspective by incongruity'. For 'personality' (derived from a word referring to a man's role) is a 'dramatist' concept, and as such involves philosophical or metaphysical notions of human identity. But a 'science' of personality would be evolved by translating matters of personality into terms wholly outside the personal as the biologistic terms 'organism' and 'environment' are outside the personal). I do not say there cannot be a 'science' of the personality, for Dr. Angyal's valuable book goes a long way towards showing that there can be. (Or at least it shows that there can be a 'scientific terminology' of the personality.) I am trying to suggest that such a science is totally 'extrinsic' in its approach, not aiming to consider the philosophic problem of what the personality is 'in itself', but perfectly at home in a vocabulary that simply dissolves the person into a non-person.

The most astonishing thing about this is the concluding line. It is impossible to think of a more deadly violation of the integrity of personality (once conceding it exists) than a scheme designed to dissolve the person into the non-person. I cannot think of any contributions a 'scientific terminology' of the personality might make towards refining life and knowledge if it were to be based on so fundamental a denial. But what I wish to point out here is that since a poem may be taken as an extension of the poet's personality, Dr. Angyal's 'science of personality' and Kenneth Burke's literary criticism both participate in an 'extrinsic' approach about which Burke, at least, is far from feeling easy. In apologizing for Dr. Angyal he is really apologizing for himself, and in doing so he reveals the weaknesses of his own criticism. For Burke abstracts the Act from the poem in a series of operations, or applications of a 'scientific terminology', that simply dissolves the verbal structure (the shell of the Act) into a series of principles. Remembering an earlier quotation given here from Burke, one might say that he would explain the final unity of the poem in terms of its diversities. (The diversities, in that event, would be the 'environment' of the final unity.) One recalls, from the same quotation, this further statement: 'if one were to write on the *interrelatedness* among ten specialties, one would be discussing something that lay outside the jurisdiction of them all'. To make an application of Burke's words that was not intended, one might say that it is this final unification among all the possible diversities in a poem—a unification that is finally explained *only* in terms of the poet's personality, and which is greater than any or all of its parts, and which gives meaning to all its parts—that most critics refer to when they say a poem is unique.

Whether, theoretically, the Symbolic Act of a poem, if educed and interpreted with great tact and discretion, yet always regarded as having significant existence for the literary critic *only* in the particular words themselves and nowhere else—whether or not such an Act would then be capable of bridging the gap in Burke's criticism between the deadening work of his principles operating within the verbal structure and the full vitality of the Symbolic Drama he conceives as overriding everything is a question that is answered by no practical examples in his volumes. The Symbolic Act so conceived *might* become a satisfactory way of approaching the uniqueness of a poem, but it would require a different kind of sensibility than Burke's to demonstrate the fact.

I am very conscious, however, that there are many passages in Burke that seem to attribute a complexity to a poem that might appear at variance with some of the criticisms I have been making. For example, he can write:

> Every act is a miracle, a synthesis that can be reduced to an infinity of components. For if it is by shrewd words that we dispel the mystery, and since every act fuses in a spontaneous instant to a complexity of factors that could not be verbally extricated in a lifetime, it follows that every act is a miracle.

There is no satisfactory indication here of what the nature

of the 'fusing' act would be, and Burke's scattered discussions of what he calls the Symbolic Merger are ultimately elusive. It is noticeable that the word 'miracle', and the magical image of dispelling mystery by shrewd words, are further emotive bridgings between Burke's sense of the part personality plays in literature and how little a 'scientific terminology' can in the end compass its effects. The kind of complexity that Burke here predicates of a poem has the sheer quantitative advantage that characterizes Richards' conception of a poem (at work in the sensibility) as an infinity of little swinging weights, capable of being added to indefinitely as new complexities arise. But in Burke's case as a whole the issues are complicated by the intrusion of what Richards would call the 'animistic' temptation. However, if Burke were content to let matters rest at the level of the passage just quoted there would be little cause to complain. But after such a general accolade to a poem's complexity as he gives here, Burke feels free to go ahead and 'extricate' whatever he likes in the time allowed him. Since he completely lacks the critical distinction of Richards, the results are usually unsatisfactory and sometimes ludicrous.

2. By saying that a poem is a constitutive act, a verbal object enduring in other temporal scenes than that in which it was first created, Burke probably means that the Act *is* fully contained in the words of the poem—it is difficult to be quite sure in view of his practice. But whether or not the literary quality, the verbal distinction of a poem, has anything at all to do with constituting the reality of the Act is a problem never touched on. The examination of the Symbolic Act which it will now be necessary to undertake will force the conclusion that the Act has nothing whatever to do with the literary distinction of the poem, and is useless in any attempt at practical evaluation. The most complete statement of Burke's theory of Symbolic Act is in *The Philosophy of Literary Form*. Burke submits it there to a long panoramic survey, but the only point there will be space to mention here is his gruesome substitution of the word 'statistical' for 'symbolic', an additional indication of his habit of thinking of vital processes in terms that submit them to a radical

reduction. By 'statistical' he means something similar to Caroline Spurgeon's indexing of images. By counting image clusters and psycho-analysing them he arrives at the psychological urgencies behind the composition, and these urgencies, since the neurological structure is unchanging, may be generalized into certain symbolic acts with individual modifications, according to the neuroses of the individual. Extensive biographical material must, naturally, be drawn on. Now tactfully employed such a procedure, which is by no means original with Burke, might occasionally prove enlightening in elucidating some novel or poem. To take a recent example, Lionel Trilling in his introduction to *The Princess Casamassima* has, in one passage, drawn to good purpose on James' relations with his brother and sister, and he has shown how, in a particular way, this led to an artistic identification between James and Hyacinth Robinson. But Mr. Trilling has used these observations with great diffidence, and solely as a literary critic. The result is that the structure of the novel gains an additional clarification, and we are drawn more fully into its intentions as a work of art, but never as a case history. How little Burke may be expected to exercise a similar tact is clear when he writes in *Attitudes toward History*: 'If a writer speaks of life on a mountain, for instance, we start with the impertinent question, "What is he talking about?" We automatically assume that he is *not* talking about life on a mountain. . . .' It is true that Burke adds in parentheses '(not talking *only* about that)', but I think the emphasis he wishes to make is quite clear.

But one had better, without further discussion, look at some samples of what Burke offers as Symbolic Action. One might take up, for example, the symbolic structure he finds in *Murder in the Cathedral*. An extended analysis occurs under this bumptious announcement of intentions: 'A work on Thomas the Saint, by Thomas the Poet, the Saint Louis boy who was too good for Saint Louis (why shouldn't he be!) Concerned with the royal road to God.' The central meaning of the Symbolic Act that Burke finds in the play is a sacrificial change of identity in Mr. Eliot, whose critical self slays his poetical self, and promises to do so every day with a daily resurrection of the poetic self 'towards nightfall'. This process is deeply involved in Burke's idea of how the Missouri boy finally managed to outwit the God of elegance by 'transcending' him, but there is no need to go into that story here. A much clearer illustration of the process of educting the Symbolic Act may be derived from his analysis of Nathan and Charles Reznikoff's *Early History of a Sewing Machine Operator*. This is the paragraph up for consideration:

> When I came into the house, she [my chum's mother] said, 'Come, sit near the stove and warm yourself.' Her husband looked at me sideways, out of his angry eyes, and went on chanting the psalms—not sorrowfully as my father and others did. When my chum's father came to the verse, 'I lift mine eyes to the hills whence comes my help,' he lifted his eyes, but saw the barrels of whisky he had for sale.

The only notable thing about this passage is its complete lack of any distinction. It is only a piece of flavourless reporting, but Burke makes quite a thing out of it. He paraphrases the first sentence in the passage in the following manner:

> I identified myself with my chum closely enough to think of entering his community. When I changed my identity by entering his community (the house) the mother-symbol of that community said to me, 'Come near me (in my associated form, the warm stove) and feel prosperous.'

The second sentence he symbolically translates as:

> The father-symbol that belonged to this new identity did not like the mother-symbol's offer that I should share her. This was symbolic incest. He meanwhile was proclaiming his identity, with respect to membership in a still wider community. But his words of affection were belied by his manner. He was a *bad* member of his community. He alienated me in my attempt at identification.

The third sentence Burke translates after this fashion:

> When the father-symbol of my new identity was proclaiming in turn his identity, and came to the verse, 'I look guiltily and

beseechingly at the mystery of *my* mother, whence comes my prosperity,' he looked not *beseechingly*, but with *brutal boldness*. And no wonder; for he had made of her a whore. Her belly is accordingly caricatured as a barrel—and he offers it for sale. It very properly contains a purely material kind of exaltation to be derived from *alcohol*. And in selling it, by a purely *quantitative* test of profit, he arrived at the monetary caricature of religion.

Perhaps no comment is necessary. At any rate, one clearly sees what R. P. Blackmur meant when he remarked in *The Double Agent* that it was impossible to make value distinctions with Burke's system. Burke replied in *The Philosophy of Literary Form* by saying: 'You can't properly put Marie Corelli and Shakespeare apart until you have first put them together. First genus, then differentia.' Apart from being a silly way in which to formulate a principle that, apparently, he holds very seriously, one might object that for a literary critic he has postponed the consideration of the differentiæ an uncommonly long time. He is supposed to follow up *A Grammar of Motives* with a *Rhetoric* [1] and a *Symbolic of Motives*, the latter being a critical consideration of the motives of the creative act. But if the differentiæ succeed in getting themselves evaluated there it will not be in terms of Burke's 'methodology' as it has so far been used by him.

The essay 'Symbolic Action in an Ode by Keats' is Burke's most successful analysis of a poem, and his most famous piece. It attempts to resolve the 'Beauty is truth, truth beauty' antagonism of an 'Ode on a Grecian Urn' within a highly interpretative framework, equating beauty with poetry and truth with science, and merging them together in an Act-Scene ratio in a final act of transcendence. 'Transcendence' was defined somewhere in Burke as an adoption of another point of view from which opposites cease to be opposites. Cleanth Brooks in *The Well Wrought Urn* arrived less brilliantly, but much more convincingly, at somewhat similar

---

[1] *A Rhetoric of Motives* has appeared since the first publication of this article, but it contains nothing that calls for separate treatment here.

conclusions about the Ode, and if a simpler interpretation of it continues to recommend itself to me, it is still not on the grounds of final disagreement with its conclusions that I wish to examine Burke's essay here. The important question is to what degree the Symbolic Act that Burke finds in the Ode is subtly suggested by gratuitous contributions of tone and cross associations. The essay contains several very good things, especially in the second half, but it is the larger critical strategy that must be considered here. Near the end of the essay Burke remarks that the 'Ode' 'begins with an ambiguous fever'. 'Fever', even at this late stage in his essay, is a heavily weighted word to describe what is occurring in the first stanza. This 'fever', which is the ground of the Symbolic Act in the poem as Burke interprets it, has been suggested by the closing lines of the first stanza, and by finding in the second stanza a double motivational level in the 'pipes and timbrel' theme. Here, in the region of the 'mystic oxymoron' (another highly charged phrase) where melodies are unheard and pipes play ditties of no tone, Burke suggests that Keats is reaching out towards the absolute. He is 'meditating upon absolute *sound*, the *essence* of sound, which would be soundless as the prime mover is motionless . . .' Burke then discusses the arrested 'pre-ecstacy' of the last four lines, and carries on into the third stanza where the so-called 'fever' divides into a 'transcendental fever, which is felicitous, divinely above "all human breathing passion"', and an 'earthly fever' that 'leaves a burning forehead and parching tongue'. 'From the bodily fever, which is a passion, and malign, there has split off a spiritual activity, a wholly benign aspect of the total agitation'. An extended analysis of the last two stanzas exhibits the final confirmation of this transcendence in the Scene-Act ratio.

Now this is an elaborate interpretation and would require, to justify itself, constant reference to the text. But in actual fact Burke makes hardly more pointed references to the poem as a word structure than has been made in the above brief paraphrase. In order to see clearly how little contact there is between the poem and Burke's analysis one should, by a kind of double entry criticism, place Burke's most persuasive arguments in one column and note the points where those arguments really touch the text in an opposite column. But that would be an extended essay in itself, and the most that can be done here is to remark that between the very inconclusive paragraphs in which Burke discusses the words themselves, the Symbolic Act slips most comfortably into the poem itself by means of certain tricky passages that Burke uses in the manner of forensic shoehorns. In interpreting the second stanza of the 'Ode' Burke appears in the following paragraph very much like a Greek bearing gifts of meaning to the original sense:

Add, now, our knowledge of the poem's place as an enactment in a particular cultural scene, and we likewise note in this second stanza a variant of the identification between death and sexual love that was so typical of nineteenth-century romanticism and was to attain its musical monument in the Wagnerian *Liebestod*. On a purely dialectical basis, to die in love would be to be born in love (the lovers dying as individual identities that they might be transformed into a common identity). Adding historical factors, one can note the part that capitalist individualism plays in sharpening this consummation (since a property structure that heightens the sense of individual identity would thus make it more imperiously a 'death' for the individual to take on the new identity made by the union of two). We can thus see why the love-death equation would be particularly representative of a romanticism that was the reflex of business.

The 'fever', which is the *sine qua non* of this Symbolic Act, was more or less assumed in the first stanza, and here it begins to be incarnated in an emotional image of romantic love-death drawn out of a Marxist interpretation of the economic environment in which the poem was composed. It is worth noting that the Wagnerian music acts very persuasively in making the transition from the economic background to the particular symbology of the Act. And here, incidentally, one might stop to wonder if Burke really likes the Ode at all. He might be expected to dislike it as an expression of capitalism, for commenting on capitalist 'snobbism' in *Attitudes toward*

History Burke remarked: 'The body was "vile" and the mind was "pure" and eventually vile body would attain the spirituality of pure mind'. According to Burke's interpretation of the Ode the transcendence it achieves is precisely of this kind. But to return more particularly to the essay: having deposited the central motive or 'fever' of the Symbolic Act in a deceptively concrete image of romantic love-death, Burke clinches the relation between love-death and private property by an appeal to the 'unimpeachable authority' of Shakespeare's 'The Phoenix and the Turtle'. Whatever else this does (a point that is vague to me), it provides him with its 'pun on sexual burning' to add to the original relationship, and so endow the final transcendence with a highly emotive passion. This 'sexual burning' naturally leads into the question of Keats' tubercular fever and his love for Fanny Brawne. An appropriate passage is quoted from one of Keats' letters to his mistress, stressing the connection in his mind between fever and love, and there follows a discussion of the poet's illness. 'Whatever transformations of mind and body he experienced, his illness was there as a kind of constitutional substrate . . .' Additional letters are quoted to show that Keats used his sickness to write poetry 'somewhat as Hart Crane could write poetry only by modes of living that . . . led to his dissolution'. Burke then sums up what he has been saying in this part of his argument with another shoehorn passage:

> Speaking of agents, patients, and action here, we might pause to glance back over the centuries thus: in the Aristotelian grammar of motives, action has its reciprocal in passion, hence *passion* is the property of a *patient*. But by the Christian paradox (which made the martyr's action identical with his passion, as the accounts of the martyrs were called both Acts and Passionals), patience is the property of a moral *agent*. And this Christian view, as secularized in the philosophy of romanticism, with its stress upon creativeness, leads us to the possibility of a bodily suffering redeemed by a poetic act.

Thus Burke concludes the first stage in his construction of the Ode's Symbolic Act—the establishment of a kind of

'fever' or motive composed of intellectual or spiritual action
and bodily passion capable of being separated in a particular
way. The above paragraph ends this part of the argument
on the very note that Burke, for his purposes, had to make as
explicit as possible, and yet we have arrived at it, not in
terms of the first two stanzas, but in terms of certain generalizations about romantic love-death in the nineteenth century,
and further generalizations about private property; we have
been given two stanzas of a poem by Shelley, and two stanzas
from 'The Phoenix and the Turtle'; we have seen the Symbolic Act take shape under pressure of Hart Crane's death,
and in terms of a discussion of Keats' illness, with quotations
from his letters, and in terms of his love affair, with additional
quotations from the letters. Finally we came to the first pause
in the argument with the paragraph just quoted, out of the
quicker-than-eye manœuvring of which 'a bodily suffering
redeemed by a poetic act' is lifted as a rabbit from a hat—
and we cannot press back the conviction that it is presented
to us on behalf of a progression of inevitable critical discoveries within the poem itself. And we have in the middle of
it all Burke's customary statement of the purity of his critical
intentions:

> . . . linguistic analysis has opened up new possibilities in the
> correlating of producer and product—and these concerns have
> such important bearing upon matters of culture and conduct in
> general that no sheer conventions or ideals of criticism should
> be allowed to interfere with their development,

a statement with which, at certain levels, one might agree
strongly enough to neglect an investigation of what Burke
means by the 'sheer conventions or ideals of criticism'. It is
significant that out of the three and a half pages devoted to
the first two stanzas, only a page and a half is concerned with
the actual text, and this includes the space taken up (a full
third) by reprinting the two stanzas. The remainder is devoted
to the information that has been outlined here. This takes
the essay through only a third of its length, but there is no
space for a more extended comment on it, and perhaps my
point has already been too much laboured.

237

3. It will have become clear by this time how Symbolic Action is interpreted as ritual. Burke has frequent and extended discussions on the nature of ritualism in his books, and anyone interested in this aspect of his criticism should turn to the chapters, 'Ritual Drama as the Hub', in *The Philosophy of Literary Form*, and 'The General Nature of Ritual', in *Attitudes toward History*. The idea of literature as ritual is probably based on the ritualistic function of Greek drama. American writers have become very fond of quoting from the books of the classical anthropologists at Cambridge. However, I cannot throw off the suspicion that Burke's own sense of ritual is merely an extension, in terms of modern anthropology, of the old religiose-æsthetic tradition of nineteenth century England. I have already quoted, in relation to Burke, Richards' somewhat disinfected phrase. Richards, it will be recalled, was much aware (in others) of those 'temptations to revert to animism from which psychologists, and especially literary psychologists, suffer'. Burke's prolonged dickering with this problem has resulted in a tone already familiar to most readers. In *Counter-Statement* he has an enthusiastic essay on Pater, and anyone who takes the trouble to reread *Marius the Epicurean* after finishing with Burke's volumes will be surprised at the resemblance which, if very spotty, is sometimes deep. Here, for example, is a passage from *Marius*:

There were days when he could suspect, though it was a suspicion he was careful at first to put from him, that that early, much cherished religion of the villa might come to count with him as but one form of poetic beauty, or of the ideal, in things; as but one voice, in a world where there were many voices it would be a moral weakness not to listen to. And yet this voice, through its forcible preoccupation of his childish conscience, still seemed to make a claim of a quite exclusive character, defining itself as one of but two possible leaders of his spirit, the other proposing to him unlimited self-expansion in a world of various sunshine. The contrast was so pronounced as to make the easy, light-hearted, unsuspecting exercise of himself among the temptations of the new phase of life which had now

238

begun, seem nothing less than a rival *religion*, a rival *religious* service.

And here is a passage from Burke:

> Might the great plethora of symbolizations lead, through the science of symbolism itself, back to a concern with 'the Way', the old notion of Tao, the conviction that there is one fundamental course of human satisfaction, forever being glimpsed and lost again, and forever being restated in the changing terms of reference that correspond with the changes of historic texture. All that earlier thinkers said of the *universe* might at least be taken as applying to the nature of man. One may doubt that such places as heaven, hell, and purgatory await us after death—but one may well suspect that the psychological patterns which they symbolize lie at the roots of our conduct here and now.

Such similarity as exists between these passages is based on a somewhat scheming scepticism of temperament endeavouring to overreach its secular plainness by clothing itself in the emotive garb of a mystagogic vocabulary safely disengaged from any real theological substance; and any rigorous conclusions about the nature of personality are avoided by comforting generalizations that might be classified as examples of eating one's cake and having it too. But Burke, due to the advances in psychology and anthropology that have taken place since Pater's death, is able to make poetry into 'a rival *religion*, a rival *religious* service', with a completeness that might even have shocked the elder man. I do not wish to go into a detailed discussion of Burke's ritualistic literary practices here, but they are more or less summed up by his assertion:

> Our basic principle is that all symbolism can be treated as the ritualistic naming and changing of identity (whereby a man fits himself for a role in accordance with established co-ordinates or for a change of role in accordance with new co-ordinates which necessity has forced upon him.

He proceeds to show that 'these rituals of change or "purification" centre about three kinds of imagery: purification by ice, by fire, or by decay. "Ice" tends to emphasize castration and frigidity . . . Purification by fire . . . probably suggests "incest awe" ', and so on. Great faith in this sort of thing leads Burke to such irrelevant groupings as *The Waste Land* with Dos Passos' *The Big Money* on the basis of their imagery of desiccation.

I should not, however, wish to offer a criticism here of the kinds of activity Burke sees as going on within a poem. That is a subject too large to come, properly, within the scope of any essay on Burke. The most one can do is to criticize the vocabulary with which he endeavours to compass these operations, and to note the kind of deflection implicit in it. The changes of identity, the scapegoat, etc., would all seem to be somewhat pretentious extensions of catharsis fancied up by an occult overlay. Since a good part of Burke's vocabulary is based on primitive ritual there may be some risk in using the word 'occult' here. Classical anthropology exercises powerful prerogatives in contemporary criticism, whose exponents frequently seem to think that its myths and symbols can be lugged over from their original context to the present time with all their magic intact—a state of mind that suggests not only a collapse of the historical sense but an incredible simplification of the nature of man. In introducing Pater I have already implied what I mean in saying that Burke's vocabulary deflects his fundamental meanings towards the occult, but it is a statement that requires rounding out in these closing paragraphs. In *Counter-Statement* he accused those critics who believe in a unique correspondence between meaning and rhythm and rhythm and imagery in a poem of being quasi-mystics; but quasi-mystical is exactly what I should be inclined to call a paragraph such as the following which describes the artist's symbolic suicide and emergence in the poem as a new self carrying on in a new role:

> Since the symbolic transformation involves a sloughing off, you may expect to find some variant of killing in the work. (I treat indictment, vituperation, vindictiveness against a 'villain', etc., as attenuated aspects of this same function). So we get to

the 'scapegoat', the 'representative' or 'vessel' of certain un-
wanted evils, the sacrificial animal upon whose back the burden
of these evils is ritualistically loaded. He becomes 'charismatic'
(if we may incongruously extend this word beyond the purely
'benign' category into the 'malign' category). We are now
brought into the area of tragedy, the 'goat-song'—and may
profitably recall that, whereas in primitive societies, the purifying function could be ritualistically delegated to an animal, as
societies grew in social complexity and sophistication, the tendency was to endow the sacrificial animal with social co-ordin-
ates, so that the goat became replaced by the 'sacrificial
King'.

In order to give special point to this quotation one should
have the space to follow it up with several examples of the
'transformations' that Burke sees going on in literature, but
only one must serve. Joyce, for whom Burke has an especial
esteem, has been able, Burke believes, to become during the
course of his writing (and as a result of his writing) a genuine
physical scapegoat in a way denied to men of lesser genius.
Speaking of Joyce's blindness, Burke observes:

> Modern medicine sufficiently recognizes a correspondence
> between our attitudes and our physical disabilities for one to
> feel justified in relating Joyce's misfortunes, as well as his attain-
> ments, to his intense skill at heretically disintegrating his child-
> hood meanings. . . . This conflict between his earliest pieties
> and the reclassifications that went with his later perspective
> could, in a man whose responses are so thorough, result in a
> mental concern with a disintegration which would have
> physical counterparts.

If one is able to get by this (the chief difficulty with such
observations in Burke is the indiscriminate and facile ease
with which he hands them out), the irritation one feels
becomes sharper a moment later when he begins to talk about
'The self-imposed blindness of Œdipus who had outraged the
most awesome pieties of his tribe.' The occult closes in and
leaves one with a superstitious and religiose sense of what a
strange thing literature is, and what a fine Established

Church it could become if taken over by the right kind of social organization.

Basing his observation on the fact that it had already returned to Santa Claus, Burke expressed his belief in the 'thirties in Russia's imminent return to God. One might think that his consistent choice of theological metaphors (it has been convenient to stress his classical-ritualistic metaphors here, but a Christian terminology is also abundantly present) was at least equally suggestive of some such orientation on his part. But we have seen that in Burke all things tend towards a Marxist end. In that technological 'frame of acceptance' into which Burke sees our society plunging, salvation may be achieved by a 'corrective philosophy' that ordinarily would be a religious one. But

> . . . in a world which has lost its faith in transcendental revela tion, the poetic metaphor enables us to start from a point of reference wherein the 'revelation' is of a secular nature: the biologic assertion itself. Projecting the metaphor by analogical extension, we find that the entire universe again takes life, as a mighty drama still in progress. And even if we are led to fear that this drama is essentially tragic, the poetic metaphor reminds us that in a perfect tragedy there is a 'catharsis', hence we may be heartened to inquire what form this catharsis may take.

The 'catharsis', of course, takes form in the 'participant aspect of action' achieved through the poetic metaphor in a Communist society. Hence, in conformity with this picture literature will be distorted to scale, and a religiose approach to it will decidedly help. But this religiose aspect of literature will not be confined to an emotive colouring of vocabulary. It is seen as performing the functions reserved in more polite societies for the Sacrament of Penance (the sloughing off of the old identity), the Sacrament of Baptism (the taking on of a new name), and communion with the faithful in the Mystical Body (socialization of impulses in the ultimately Communist state). I hardly know whether to think of Burke as a literary critic or as the High Priest of a new critical liturgicism.

These remarks have been sufficiently extended to make an elaborate conclusion unnecessary. Under whatever other aspects than that of a literary critic he may be considered, his chief importance in this favoured role lies in his representative quality, and in his influence among the 'New Critics' in America. He might easily become the archetypal pattern for an unfortunate trend in American criticism, a trend that would place literature against a background of sciences rather than in a traditional social (as opposed to socialist) context, that would expunge words from literature at the very moment it seemed to be giving them detailed attention, that would consider literature as a bag of vicarious satisfactions at the very moment it called it 'equipment for living', and arranging the discoveries of literary criticism from the viewpoint of purpose (Burke calls this 'teleological criticism') would have the purpose carefully selected before the criticism was undertaken. There may be nothing wrong with Burke's ideas beyond the way he uses them. But any critical vocabulary so highly organized, no matter how desperately it may reach out towards flexibility, has misunderstood the nature of literature and rigidified the sensibility of the critic in certain set responses. Burke has condemned traditional critical vocabularies in terms similar to these, but surely his own is at least as guilty, if in slightly different ways. 'Poetry as Act' purports to emphasize the ethical aspects of literature, and to set poetry in the mid-arena of life. As Burke practises the theory the poem itself is too often the flunkey of the Act to whom it administers in a servile capacity, and life ends up by being where Burke would like it to be—in short, Poetry and Life collide at the enchanted turn-stile of Marxism.

Index

245